About the Author

Nick Vause studied English at York University in the 1970s and then trained as an actor at the Bristol Old Vic Theatre School. He went on to work as a drama teacher at schools in North London, directing and writing plays for his students. He is also an active member of his local amateur theatre community. A keen and voracious reader, *That Covid Year* is his first book.

That Covid Year

Nick Vause

That Covid Year

Olympia Publishers
London

www.olympiapublishers.com
OLYMPIA PAPERBACK EDITION

Copyright © Nick Vause 2024

The right of Nick Vause to be identified as author of
this work has been asserted in accordance with sections 77 and 78 of
the Copyright, Designs and Patents Act 1988.

All Rights Reserved

No reproduction, copy or transmission of this publication
may be made without written permission.
No paragraph of this publication may be reproduced,
copied or transmitted save with the written permission of the publisher,
or in accordance with the provisions
of the Copyright Act 1956 (as amended).

Any person who commits any unauthorised act in relation to
this publication may be liable to criminal
prosecution and civil claims for damage.

A CIP catalogue record for this title is
available from the British Library.

ISBN: 978-1-80074-981-8

First Published in 2024

**Olympia Publishers
Tallis House
2 Tallis Street
London
EC4Y 0AB**

Printed in Great Britain

The Months Before: January

The world outside sounded as if it had died. No traffic sounds or bird song. Pulling back the duvet cover, I lifted the curtain and looked out at the grey, empty sky. Blank, nothing.

God, what a start to the New Year. What it would be like to wake up on January 1st and not have a stinking hangover, I wondered. As always, when I had consumed a large amount of booze, I had hardly slept. My heart was racing and I was feeling agitated and nervy. I kind of wanted to be up and about but I was staying over at my friend's place after an extremely indulgent New Year's Eve night of drinking and over-eating. I felt duty bound to wait for him to surface before I could comfortably slope off and get the tube back to my home in North London. My friend's place was in Greenwich.

I tried to listen out for sounds of activity from the room next door. From past experience, I knew that my mate didn't usually get up much before ten and it was now only just gone 8. It would be another couple of hours at least before I could get up and get dressed and start to make the long trek home. We'd need to do breakfast, first: commiserating with each other on the severity of our hangovers and the poor quality of our sleep. Consoling ourselves with the fact that we had had a good evening the night before: we'd slagged off the newly elected Tory government; gossiped about all of our mutual friends; bemoaned the dreadful offerings of the Christmas broadcasting companies; got excited about the forthcoming new plays, movies and novels which 2020 promised to deliver; shared our dread of the havoc which Brexit set to wreak on all of our lives and generally set the world to rights. It had been a good evening. A night of free-wheeling chatter and shared confidences, with much laughter and unburdening of souls. The sort of night you can only have with an old friend from way back. In fact, so involved and engaged had we been in our conversation, that neither of us noticed the chimes of midnight, which came and went without pause. It was only when one of us glanced over at the clock and saw that it was already one in the morning that we realised that the New Year festivities had passed us by.

The next morning, however, and by now sober and raw from too much alcohol the night before, the conversation was inevitably more halting and occasionally even strained. We'd said most of what we had wanted to say to each other the previous evening and now it was just a matter of sharing pleasantries and then releasing each other to go and get on with the first day of the new year. I could feel a palpable depression of the spirits. The morning of January 1st was always a grisly one. That daunting sense of the whole year stretching ahead, like a great uphill struggle: with Christmas passed a week before and now even New Year's Eve over, it felt like the time for celebration, fun and misrule was over. It was back to dull routines and what Auden called "Minding your Ps and Qs".

My friend Jonathan and I had spent every New Year's Eve together for the last twenty years or so. It was a ritual that we set aside to share with each other every year. Sometimes other friends were invited: other members of our friendship circle or new acquaintances that Jonathan wanted to get to know better – but more often than not it was just the two of us. We'd never spent a Christmas or Easter together and hardly ever accompanied each other on holiday but New Year's Eve was a night we always arranged to spend in each other's company. It felt like a safe and reassuring ritual, and it was amazing how quickly it seemed to come around each year.

This year, though, was made slightly different by the fact that I was now on the brink of a major change in my life. I had decided that after thirty-six years in the teaching profession, 2020 was the year in which at the age of sixty-three, I was going to retire. Having spent so many previous New Year's Eves ushering in a year that would end up being pretty much like every other, this year it seemed that things were set to change. Inexorably, I imagined. And I found that prospect both terrifying and exhilarating in equal measure. The immediate question, though, was would I have the courage to do it? If I was going to retire, then I would have to give in my notice within the first few weeks of the new term, which started in a few days' time. And once that was handed in, there would be no going back.

I had a dilemma because, for the most part, I enjoyed my work. I was a drama teacher at a very good school and I had managed to establish for myself a commendable track record, largely based on a string of impressive and highly lauded drama productions over the years. I had a very comfortable niche at the school and was surrounded by much-loved colleagues and talented, amenable students. There was much to enjoy. I liked the rhythm of the school year: the sense of everything gearing up in September, the long haul through the autumn term in which most of the serious work got done. The huge end of term school play, with its various plaudits and then the challenges of the spring term when all the exam classes were being prepared for their final assessments and then the more leisurely pace of the summer term, when most of the older students had left and it was time to turn attention to the demands of the non-exam classes. After all those years, these patterns were ingrained and the thought of a life without that structure and rhythm was alarming in the extreme. Did I really want to retire?

On the other hand, I could not ignore the fact that I was getting on. In 2020, I would turn sixty-three and that would make me the oldest member of staff at the school. Certainly, when I first entered the teaching profession it was more or less the norm for teachers to retire in their early or mid-fifties and very few staff continued to work full time after their sixtieth birthdays. Part of the problem for me, though, was that I didn't feel particularly old. I did not feel like a guy in his sixties. I still had energy and what I thought was a reasonably youthful outlook. I went to the gym every morning for an hour before work; I had a busy and very active social life. I loved living in London and took full advantage of everything it had to offer, always packing the weekend with the latest plays, art exhibitions, films, bars and trendy restaurants. At the same time, I could not continue to delude myself that at nearly fifty years older than some of the children I taught, I could no longer claim to be truly in touch with their world. I found technology baffling and had little time for social media or for the music, games and fashions which characterise contemporary youth culture. I was lucky enough to work in a school which prized individuality, even eccentricity, as well as academic learning so I had been able to survive there quite happily for over thirty years. I doubt that I would have had as easy a ride in a more conventional school, though. I had never had much 'street cred' and my devotion to the great Musical Theatre hits of the 1950s might have been much appreciated and indulged at the school in which I had spent most of my working life but I am not sure that it would have gone down as well elsewhere. Apart from that, wasn't it time to be a bit brave? To cast off and to see what else life had to offer? People spoke of the endless opportunities that would be open to me if and when I eventually retired: the exotic and unusual places I could visit; the new skills I could learn; the interesting courses I could do; the fascinating new people I might meet; the amazingly rich creative opportunities that might be open to me. I could finally write that Booker prize winning novel or take that camper van round the Outback or do that round the world tour or buy that little bolt-hole in a Cornish fishing village or sell up and get myself a 'pied a terre' overlooking the Thames or buy a house with a garden or even get a dog. I could learn to become a better cook or run the London Marathon or start learning Italian or take up the piano again. The world was my oyster. Did I really want to hang on in my job doing the same old thing for another three years or so or did I have the guts to say, "enough is enough"? Let's move on. Let's quit while I'm winning. Let's go and sample all that life has still to offer.

So, this was my big preoccupation on that late morning of January 1st 2020, as I made my way back across London from my friend Jonathan's place back to my flat in Enfield. As I sat in the tube train coming back from North Greenwich and getting ready to change on to the Northern Line at London Bridge with my eyes half-closed and my head lolling against the window of the carriage, I looked at the jaded faces of my fellow passengers. Every one of us looked like we were still in yesterday's clothes, most of us still half-asleep from a late night the evening before. Any plans for the day were unlikely to happen. All I wanted to do was get back home, run myself a bath and then collapse on the sofa and indulge in a few hours of trash TV and a good bout of comfort eating (as if I hadn't already scoffed enough that Christmas and New Year). I just wanted to give myself over to the fact that today was another day of holiday and there was no requirement to do anything at all except recover and brace myself for the return to work in a few days' time.

I emerged from the tube at Wood Green and waited for the bus to take me up Green Lanes, in the direction of Enfield Town. I'd done this journey countless times before, usually late at night after an evening out in the West End, either going to watch a play or drinking in a Soho bar. It felt so different doing it in the middle of the day rather than at night-time. Most of the other people in the bus queue were shoppers, laden with carrier bags from the nearby Morrisons. Only a few looked like they were New Year revellers returning from a boozy evening the night before. I got on to the lower deck of the bus and squeezed into my seat, getting out my phone to check for New Year greetings – some of which seemed to have been sent before midnight but were only just starting to come through now. Some of the messages were optimistic and forward-looking; others had the grim gallows humour of the "here we go again" variety. Scrolling through them and pinging off suitable replies helped to pass the time as the bus slowly snaked its way up to the North Circular and chugged through the semi-deserted streets of Palmers Green and Winchmore Hill.

I got off the bus and walked the short distance to my flat. It was almost a relief to be back and to know that the weeks of December revelry were now officially over. For a few weeks there would be no more dinner parties or drinks dos or staff outings or family gatherings to attend. It was now "eyes down" and concentrate on work and on staying sober and eating sensibly.

I chucked off my clothes and got into the shower, relishing the feel of the hot water on my skin and scrubbing away furiously with the shampoo and shower gel, as if to rid myself of all the various excesses of the last few weeks. The enormous gin cocktails we'd consumed the night before really were starting to take their toll and, as always on the morning after, I was baffled at how on earth we had managed to sink quite so many drinks in the course of a single evening. So enjoyable at the time but, God, I was paying for it now!

I thought about walking up to my gym for a swim. That might help make me feel a bit more refreshed. I also needed to throw off that drink-induced depression and anxiety that I could feel was about to cloud over the rest of the day. Thirty brisk lengths in the pool and ten minutes languishing in the jacuzzi after would surely improve things: a good spike of exercise induced endorphins and some rejuvenating hot steam in the gym spa suddenly seemed like a very enticing prospect. Also, being New Year's Day, the place would probably be less crowded than normal. I couldn't imagine that there would be many others there at that time.

It seemed to have worked, I acknowledged, as I sat floating in the jacuzzi, allowing the bubbles and the swirling water to work their magic. I had the gym spa almost to myself and gave myself up to a delicious feeling of indolence and recovery. It was lovely: the knowledge that I didn't have to be anywhere or do anything for the rest of the day. I just stretched my arms out on the tiles surrounding the spa bath and enjoyed the sensation of the warm water lapping around my limbs. It felt very healing.

Returning to my flat, I made myself a ham sandwich and settled down for the rest of the afternoon with some catch-up TV, looking at some of the programmes I hadn't been able to watch over the festive season because I'd either been out with friends or holed up with relatives and had had to accept their viewing choices. Having been forced to watch "Call the Midwife", "Vicar of Dibley" "Downton" "Mrs Brown" "Strictly" and the usual repeats of Victoria Wood and Morecambe and Wise, it was a relief to now be able to work my way through some of the things I wanted to watch. At about six p.m., I just switched over to the news. It was the usual stuff about Brexit and also this story from China that they had kept pushing all over Christmas: a virus in Wuhan that seemed to be having fatal consequences. Wuhan was a place I'd never heard of before and it seemed so far away. Why on earth did they keep going on about it?

There were only a few days left of the school holiday before the return to work for the start of the spring term. I wanted to make the most of them so I booked some tickets for an all-day performance at the National Theatre: a trilogy of plays based on the Neapolitan novels of Elena Ferrante "My Brilliant Friend". A day spent at the National watching these plays in the Olivier auditorium seemed like a worthy use of the time and I had booked to go there with my friend Tony on the 3rd of January. It felt good to be doing something cultural with the day and Tony, like me, was an avid theatre-goer. I knew that he would appreciate the experience and would be a good, congenial companion with whom to share the day's performance, which would start at two p.m. in the afternoon and end around 10 o'clock in the evening.

There was only one snag. For the past few days, I had not

been feeling terribly well. This was not just the effects of over-indulgence during the festive period. It was more like a muscular aching all down my arms and legs and was really quite agonizing until I was able to make the pain go away with either Ibuprofen or paracetamol. It seemed to have come on shortly after Christmas and had affected me for several days. If I took some pain killers, it would recede for a few hours but I did not seem to be able to get rid of it. Sitting still for any length of time was particularly difficult and it was at those times that the pain in my legs would become almost unbearable. The thought of sitting in the theatre and watching six hours' worth of drama was not an enticing prospect in the circumstances.

Suitably armed with a new pack of paracetamol and a bottle of water, I arrived at the National Theatre on the morning of the performance, having arranged to meet my friend Tony for lunch beforehand. Ever reliable, sure enough there was my mate sitting at a table in the cafeteria downstairs near to the bookstall. He seemed ebullient and full of life and gossip and laughter, as always. We got ourselves some coffees and sandwiches and proceeded to dissect Christmas with our different families and to congratulate ourselves on the fact that we weren't yet back at work and had a few more days left to go of the winter holiday. We talked about how we had both spent Christmas Day and the state of our respective ageing parents. My Dad was approaching ninety (my mum having passed away in 2012) and Tony's parents are both in their mid-eighties but generally sounded as if they were doing pretty well. Tony talked about his brother and his nephew and I chatted about my sister and the nieces. We swapped opinions on the different TV shows we'd been watching during the holiday and the other friends we had seen. Soon it was time to go into the theatre for the first play of the afternoon and it was with that usual sense of anticipation and delight and that we made our way to our seats in the middle of the stalls of the Olivier auditorium. It was a Thursday afternoon and there was an expectant buzz among the rows of seats. The theatre was almost full. Clearly, many others had also been drawn by the allure of a whole day of live theatre, thinking that it would be a good antidote to all those hours slumped on the sofa in front of the telly in overheated living rooms. The audience was very chatty and clearly keen to be entertained and enthralled. It was a younger audience than the usual mid-week matinee crowd: clearly educated, articulate, confident, liberal; most of them probably still in full time work and all in their winter clothes of parkas, scarves, woolly hats, puffer jackets and assorted rainwear.

The lights went down on the enormous Olivier stage. The set revolved round to reveal an impressive structure of balconies, staircases, walkways and a plethora of different entrances and exits. Washing lines were strewn between the various tall buildings represented, transporting us all to the backstreets of Naples, where most of the action would be set. The costumes and hairstyles clearly identified the time period of the play as the 1950s and there were a large number of characters. I found myself having to work quite hard to keep up with who was supposed to be who – not that easy as many of the characters were similar types and from our seats near the back of the auditorium, it wasn't always easy to distinguish the features of the different actors. Much of that hardly seemed to matter, though. It was great just to be out for the day and I basked in the pleasure of simply being there: in a seat at the

National and watching some of our finest actors tell a story I did not know.

Sure enough, though, it was not long before the aching sensation from which I had been suffering for at least a couple of days returned and that made the play a rather uncomfortable watch. I was glad when the interval came and then, at the end of the play, when we were able to get out of the theatre and go and find a restaurant nearby for a meal between the two plays. I swallowed a couple more Ibuprofen and began to feel a bit better. We found a pizza place underneath the arches near Waterloo station and sat there happily, continuing our conversation from earlier on.

When we returned to the theatre for the second part of the production, we were able to take the same seats and seemed to be surrounded by most of the same crowd. It seemed that everybody else had wanted to devote the whole day to the production, which seemed to be hoping to garner the reputation won by some of those other legendary all day theatrical epics of previous years like "Nicholas Nickleby" or "The Orestaeia". Not sure that this had quite the same grip as those masterpieces or that it would ever attain that sort of status and renown but there were many fine and dramatic moments and it certainly seemed like a worthwhile use of the day.

The show must have ended at about 10.30 p.m., after which it was time to go and get the tube home. Normally, we might have made for a bar in Soho and a continuation of the evening but it had been a long day and at that hour we were both just keen to get back to our own homes.

The last few remaining days of the school holiday were spent with preparations for the return to work and an attempt to throw off the persistent aching feeling in my muscles which was now starting to feel quite debilitating. I wondered whether I should pay the doctor a visit. I certainly didn't want to be going back to work not feeling on top form. The start of the spring term and battling through the grim, dark days of January was always hard enough, without feeling physically below par as well. I booked an appointment.

I had also noticed a new facility which had opened at the little parade of shops just down the road from me, on the corner of Green Lanes. It was actually a Massage Parlour, but they had been putting leaflets and flyers through the door for the last few weeks and were clearly legitimate and respectable. (As a teacher in a local school, I certainly could not possibly risk being seen going in and out of anywhere dodgy!) Studying their leaflet, they seemed to offer a range of different types of massage but my aching body certainly craved the pummelling and kneading which I imagined would be involved. After studying the leaflet (which was also at pains to make it clear that this was a legitimate service and that any sexual activity would be immediately referred to the police), I logged on to their website and booked myself an appointment. I booked it for a Sunday morning, at 12.30 p.m. and was surprised when I turned up that there were various forms to fill in with my contact details, medical history, next of kin etc to complete. The man behind the desk who welcomed me to the facility was certainly very formal and professional, allaying any fears I might have had that his business was in any way dubious. I had to admit that I wasn't quite sure which type of massage I wanted but somehow the idea of "deep tissue" was the one that appealed to me the most. That was what I thought I wanted. I wanted someone to get right down into the sinews and fibres of my muscles and to give them a really strong but restorative pounding.

After discussing my requirements with the gentleman on the desk, he disappeared for a few moments to negotiate with his team of masseuses. On his return, I was ushered into a small, windowless room, decorated in neutral colours, with a massage table in the middle of the room, a chair and a small bedside cabinet. Piped music, vaguely Oriental and New-Age came through a sound system and a couple of fairly low voltage lights cast a calming, orange light over the room. A friendly young Asian lady in shorts and t-shirt came smiling into the room and asked me to undress and to wrap a thick, white towel around my middle. I assumed that I was permitted to retain my underwear, so did as she said while she slipped out of the room momentarily to allow me some privacy. I removed my clothes and sat in the chair with the towel wrapped round while I waited for her to return. When she did so, she invited me to lie face down on the massage table and she then proceeded to trickle oil down my back and began to rub this gently into my skin. Although quite a slight person, her hands felt strong and forceful. I am afraid to admit that I was slightly nervous of the whole process and so she had to keep asking me to relax. I could feel the tension in my shoulders and neck and could not help but flinch at her touch and this made her giggle at my obvious timidity. Nevertheless, she worked away at my limbs, stroking and then stretching and pulling and squeezing and punching. I started to feel that she was working her way into my skin and getting deep down into the sinews of my muscles. I also marvelled at her stamina, that she was able to keep it up for so long, the relentless up and down motion as she worked her way into the deepest fibres of my body.

The session was supposed to last for forty-five minutes but after about half an hour of it, I was beginning to feel that I had had enough. I had been warned by the man on the desk that part of the process would involve the masseuse walking on my back and he asked if I would be OK with that. I'd said that this would be fine but I must admit to becoming slightly alarmed as I sensed her feet starting to promenade up and down on my back, turning me into the human equivalent of a treadmill at the gym. When she then started to bounce up and down on me, I couldn't help but get seriously worried and waited for some part of me to snap or crack underneath her weight. In spite of the fact that she was only a very slight person, I wasn't sure that I could really cope with her fully body weight trampolining up and down on me in the way that she was now starting to do. Somewhat feebly, I couldn't help but grimace and make visible my discomfort.

"You okay?" she cooed. "Just relaaaax..." she giggled. "You so tense..."

I mumbled apologetically and tried to brace myself for further pummelling, by now having had more than enough and wanting to get to the end of my forty-five-minute session. Eventually I could tell we were on the last stretch as the pounding and more vigorous movements gave way to a much gentler stroking and a light running of her fingers up and down the backs of my arms and legs. Knowing that we were almost at the end, I did finally manage to give myself up to the experience and started to appreciate the touch of another human hand on my skin. It felt warming, comforting, calming.

At the end of the session, I sat up and the lady and I smiled at each other. I thanked her effusively and gave her a five-pound tip. She seemed to me to have worked really hard for the last forty-five minutes: tough, physical work with almost no let up. She deserved every penny of the modest £35 fee I had been charged.

I am not sure that the mysterious aching sensation in my muscles necessarily disappeared after the massage but having them worked over so thoroughly certainly improved things. That afternoon, I went back to my gym spa and sat again in the jacuzzi in the hope that I would be back to normal before the return to work.

The doctor, when I got to see him, was non-committal and wasn't really able to help. He advised me to have a break from the gym for a week or so and to get plenty of rest and to drink plenty of fluids. He warned me to stay off the painkillers and assured me that it was probably a virus and that it would pass with time. I just had to take it easy!

Having spent the last couple of weeks of the Christmas holiday mainly slumped on the sofa watching television or lying around in bed and trying to catch up on sleep, I was not sure that I had been doing anything else recently apart from "taking it easy". Admittedly, I had been socializing quite hard: out most evenings drinking and eating with friends, desperate to cram as much activity as I could into the two-week holiday before the shutters came down again in January. Perhaps I had overdone it and a few days of sobriety, early nights and no strenuous exertion at the gym were what I needed. Not having offered me any medication, it seemed that I had little alternative but to take the doctor's advice and go into an abstemious New Year in the hope that the debilitating condition from which I had suffered would eventually subside.

It wasn't great to be going back to work feeling like that

but I knew that I would just have to buckle down and get on with it. If it was a virus from which I was suffering, and it was certainly making me feel physically weak and generally washed out, I was still just about able to function and therefore did not think I could justify taking any time off work.

That first day of the January term in school is always pretty grim. All teachers will tell you that however many years they have been doing it, most of them never manage to sleep the night before a new term. We lie awake, mourning the end of the holiday and, with it, the freedom to do just as we like. You start going through all those uncompleted tasks which you promised yourself you would do in readiness for the new term. When it came to it, though, you just really couldn't be bothered to even think about them: the new Set Text for your A-level class; the practical assessments which needed to be planned for your GCSE students; the policy documents to be updated and revised in preparation for a short notice visit by Ofsted inspectors; the substantial pile of marking, untouched and still lying unopened in your brief case in the hall. You had all this time. Two weeks. What on earth had you done with it? Why give yourself all the added stress? It was hideous to be going back to work so underprepared.

On the other hand, the holiday took over and rightly so, you tell yourself. It was Christmas. I needed that time to get to the shops, to buy presents, to write cards. I needed to catch up with friends and relatives I had not seen for months. Surely it was OK to have a few boozy lunches and to write off the rest of the day, on at least a couple of the holiday afternoons? And then there were those films I wanted to sit down and watch; the novel I wanted to read; those great long walks that took up another couple of afternoons. So important to get out and get some fresh air. Then there was my Dad who needed ferrying around. There were also church services to attend. After all, it was Christmas and it wouldn't be the same without some carol singing and a bit of homage to Jesus. There were the sales to visit and the Panto to go and watch. In fact, amazing that you were able to pack so much in to fourteen days. No wonder work hadn't had a look in.

Therefore, as you reach for the alarm on that first Monday morning in January, having allowed yourself to languish in bed until at least half-past eight for the previous two weeks, you can't help but feel hard-done-by and aggrieved. It's six thirty a.m. Feels like the middle of the night. Outside it is still pitch dark. Feeling like a zombie, you stumble towards the bathroom, shave and brush your teeth and then pull on your shirt, tie and sensible trousers in the hope that this uniform might transform you into something resembling a functioning professional person.

Like an automaton, you switch on Radio 4 and the kettle. You pour out some muesli and, still barely conscious, consume your modest breakfast. You shove a few things into the washing up bowl, visit the loo and pull on your coat and a pair of scuffed brogues. You descend the stairs and make for the car park. You'd normally stop off for a quick half hour workout at the gym but that is now against doctor's orders, so you brave the early morning traffic and sit in a queue to cross the Great Cambridge Road and eventually arrive at work.

The weather is frosty and there is a nasty biting cold in the air. It is still barely daylight and as you emerge from your car in the school car park, you keep your head down, keen to avoid any form of social inter-action until you feel a bit more ready.

You get into your part of the school building and shove open the door of your office. Your cleaner Lesley is there and you exchange the first of many similar greetings:

"Happy New Year! How was your holiday? Did you get away anywhere? Isn't it awful to be back?"

You walk down the corridor of the main building, nodding and exchanging similar greetings with other staff and with the occasional student. Nobody seems pleased to be back. Most people looked exhausted and cross.

It still seems too early in the day. It is only just gone eight o'clock in the morning. For the last couple of weeks at this time, most of you would still have been in bed or having your first cup of tea or walking the dog or watching the tv breakfast shows. Not bustling about at work, trying to get yourself organised and attempting to assemble the materials for a successful day of learning: grappling with the photocopier or trying to get your printer to work or trawling through a fortnight's worth of unanswered emails.

Scrambling to get myself ready before the first bell for registration, I staggered along to the Year 11 corridor where my form group were waiting to start the new term. They all looked suitably weary and despondent as I marched through the door. In an attempt to jolly them all along, I put on my best "game show host" persona and bellowed "Happy New Year, everyone!" as I skipped into the room, knowing full well that this would elicit little or no response, apart from some rather peeved scowls.

"All raring to go before your last full term at school?" Being Year 11 students, they were due to take their GCSE exams starting in May and by the end of June would have left school – at least four weeks or so before the other non-exam students.

Most of them were staring blankly into space, clearly still stunned by the earliness of the hour and unable to process the fact that they were up and about and conscious at the ungodly time of 8.35 a.m. Some even had their heads buried in their hands on their desks and scowled over grumpily at my unwelcome (but totally assumed) cheeriness.

I started to call out the names on the register; that time honoured ritual with which all school mornings had begun since time immemorial. I had known this group for nearly five years, having welcomed them to the school as tiny Year 7 students several Septembers ago. I had been with them ever since, as their form teacher. Registering them in the morning, handing out their timetables and locker keys at the start of each school year; checking that their uniforms were in order every day; handing out letters home; reading out notices about clubs and societies and room changes and directives from the Deputy Head about use of mobile phones and how to behave at the bus stop on the way home; collecting in money for Charity events; passing on detention slips for homework not handed in or uniform worn incorrectly or for poor behaviour in a lesson. These had been the daily currency of our interactions together, filling that fifteen- minute slot between my taking the register and them stirring themselves to lurch off to their first lessons of the day. Occasionally, I would have cause to talk to one of them individually. Perhaps there had been an incident of bad behaviour reported by a colleague or the child kept arriving late to school or there had been a sudden decline in standards of work or there was some issue at home that was causing concern: a parent in hospital or a family bereavement, for example. And sometimes, when I had the energy, I would just call them up to come and speak to me because I wanted to know how they were getting on. We were in a highly academic school, with a competitive and demanding ethos. The environment was pressurised and could be tough on any student who was struggling either academically or socially. After many years in the job, I was well aware that some students could go for days without having any individual conversations with their teachers and Form Time was sometimes a good opportunity to rectify this. Besides which, it was a pleasant way in which to pass the time. I liked hearing the students' thoughts and observations. They always seemed so much nicer when they were chatting to me on a one-to-one basis than they appeared to be when they were en masse. Together, as a group of thirty-one fifteen-year-olds, they could sometimes come across as surly or apathetic. Individually, they could all be chatty and funny and full of insights and each with their own sharp brand of teenage wisdom and experience.

As I stood at the exit to the form room, chivvying them to get along to their first lessons of the morning, it struck me how far they had come since they had first arrived at the school four and a half years ago. For a start, the boys were all now fully grown and most of them now towered above me, as they went out of the door. They had all seemed so small and puny when they had joined the school as little Year 7s. The girls, also, were now confident and assertive young women, all the timidity and shyness of their eleven-year-old selves long since left behind. Some of the boys now thought it fit to adopt a kind of "matey" tone with me as I stood by the door nodding encouragingly and

telling them all to "have a good day".
"See you later, sir!"
"Have a good one!"

Leaving the form room, I made my way back to the drama department for my first proper lesson of the morning. It was a Year 8 drama class. Hardly my favourite and I really wasn't in the mood for anything too energetic – as, I imagined, neither were they. I'm afraid I took the drama teacher's easy way out and grabbed a set of play-scripts for them to read out loud. That way, I could keep everyone tightly under control as we sat on chairs in a circle and read through the play. I certainly wasn't in the mood for any noisy group work and didn't want to allow any opportunity for poor behaviour. I'd do something more creative with them later in the term. I'd help them to make plays in small groups based on some weird and wacky American Urban Legends, which always seemed to go down well with that age group. But not today.

The class entered the room in almost as subdued a manner as my form group, who were three years older. They too looked tired and rather put-out at having to be in school at all. For all of us, it seemed, the holiday had not been long enough.

I doled out the copies of the script we were going to read. It was the dramatic equivalent of one of those "Young Adult" novels that were all the rage. A slightly angst-ridden family drama, full of issues around parent/ child relationships and with a worthy moral message about how to negotiate the dangers of the contemporary world. Gangs, drugs, shop-lifting, mental health, family break-up were all touched on at some point. To me, it was hardly up there with the likes of Ibsen, Brecht or Tennessee Williams but the students seemed to enjoy it. There was the odd bit of swearing and the opportunity for some sub-EastEnders style acting which the more histrionically inclined could throw themselves into and leave the lesson feeling like they had done a bit of "proper acting".

We managed to read most of the script in the hour and twenty minutes that the lesson took to run. It did feel like a bit of a long haul and I knew that just sitting round reading a play was hardly "teaching" as such but, honestly, on that first day back after a school holiday it really was just a question of trying to get through it. Teaching and instruction would follow later in the rest of the term's lessons but for now it was enough just to keep the students occupied.

Relieved that I had at least got through the first part of the morning, I made my way over to the staff room for the mid-morning break. This would be a chance to catch up with colleagues and to have a bit of a laugh and a gossip and to commiserate with each other at the sheer awfulness of being back to the daily grind. As I walked into the staff room, there was the usual queue by the coffee urn as people filled their mugs and walked over to sit down on the ancient staff-room chairs next to their friends. There was a bit of a buzz in the room as people swapped stories about their Christmases: the usual moans about aging parents and obnoxious in-laws and disappointing presents and uninspiring tv schedules. Some had encountered uncharacteristically bad weather or had had long and difficult journeys to far flung places or had fallen ill with dodgy tummies or heavy colds. Nobody could believe how quickly the two weeks had gone or how long it had taken them to recover from the exhaustion of the previous term. All dreaded the next six weeks, which would be cold and dark, with not much to look forward to. However, as always, there was a kind of camaraderie and sense of community that was almost infectious. There was laughter and smiles and little whoops of astonishment and admiration and empathy and even though most people would probably have preferred to be back at home with their families or partners or just doing their own thing, it felt heart-warming to be back in that school community, surrounded by familiar faces and voices.

After only fifteen minutes to catch up with people not seen for over a fortnight, the bell sounded for the next lesson. Reluctantly pulling away from conversations to be resumed later on, we all went off to our separate lessons, slightly more energised after this little burst of social contact with each other. The day started to fall into place and I taught my following classes with as much energy and enthusiasm as could be expected on a chilly day in early January.

My main task as a teacher of drama at this point in the year was to prepare my A-level students for their practical assessment. As part of their A-level course in Theatre Studies, they had to create a piece of Devised Drama which would be performed in front of a visiting examiner and which would contribute to thirty per cent of their total marks. We'd been working on this since November: trying to find a suitable theme on which to base the piece and then trying to shape the material in order to make an engaging piece of "original" theatre. As had always been the way with this part of the course, there had been several false starts while we tried out different ideas. In previous years, students had generally based their ideas on a book or short story that one of them had read. It was always a long and tortuous process, effectively trying to write a play in a group and not just make the script but then rehearse it and eventually perform it with costumes, a setting, lighting and sound. Each member of the group needed a moment to show what they could do so whatever stimulus was chosen needed to contain a good range of characters so that each student would get an opportunity to "wow" the audience and to get that elusive top A* grade, which they were all expected to achieve.

This year's A-level Theatre Studies class was tiny. There were only four students and this was the smallest group I had ever had. In some years, I had managed to get the group numbers up to as many as fifteen. That was a very respectable number of students all wanting to study Drama at A-level but, for a variety of reasons, the group sizes had started to decline. This was partly to do with parental pressure. Parents did not believe that an A-level in Drama was going to be worth very much in the future, either in the world of work or on a university application form. Therefore, they discouraged their children from taking the subject as one of their A-level choices. They would rather that they studied Maths or a Science subject, perceiving these options as much more academically respectable and more likely to be of value in later life. Of course, I had to fight against this. At parents' evenings, I tried to promote the worth of an A-level in a subject not only steeped in thousands of years of cultural heritage (Greek Tragedy, Shakespearean Comedy, the Nineteenth Century Naturalism of Ibsen and Chekhov, the Twentieth Century innovations of Beckett, Pinter and Arthur Miller etc etc). I also talked about the ways in which it developed creativity and the imagination; the ways in which it fostered group collaboration, teamwork and social cohesion; and, also, the need for students to study something they actually enjoyed and that the study of theatre would provide them with the foundation for a life-time's pleasure, both as makers of theatre and as informed members of an audience.

It appeared that none of this washed with the parents or, it would seem, even with the students themselves. Those who wanted a more "solid" A-level choice opted for English or History and those who were keen to express their more creative urges chose Art or Music. Many were also drawn to Media Studies, which offered more opportunities to explore contemporary culture, with many more possibilities for the creative use of technology in a way that I had never embraced as a teacher of drama.

Sadly, therefore, my numbers had dwindled over the years, to the point where the subject was scarcely viable any more. I was extremely grateful to the Senior Management of the school that it was still permitted to run. I could see that using a teacher of my experience to teach four students for the equivalent of fourteen lessons a week was hardly an economic use of my time. I could probably have been more usefully employed teaching a GCSE English set or taking thirty-one Key Stage Three pupils. It was always hard to get teachers to do Year 8 English, for example, with all the attendant marking and record keeping. Could I not have been more gainfully employed elsewhere in the school?

Luckily, this was a conversation I was not asked to have and my small A-level Drama classes were permitted to continue but I was aware of the fact that their days were numbered...

Nevertheless, this did not affect my current class and I was very grateful for the opportunity to continue teaching them. There were four students in the group: three girls and one boy. They were a delightful bunch: hard-working, talented, funny, bright and all with very individual and quirky personalities. Every so often, it happens in teaching - especially with smaller groups of older students – that you manage to get a particular class in which it barely feels like you are teaching at all. The lessons are more like a meeting between a like-minded group of equals, coming together to share their fondness for the subject. In groups such as these there is plenty of "banter" and laughter but there's also a lot of serious work done as well but it feels easy, unforced. You get to a point where you feel as if you can say anything to the students; there's an atmosphere of complete spontaneity and in every lesson, there is a real meeting of minds.

This group had chosen to adapt a short story by the American writer Flannery 0'Connor, "A Good Man is Hard to Find" and my task during those first weeks of this spring term was to help them to turn the material into an arresting piece of theatre. This was for their module in Devised Drama, so every lesson for the last month or so of the previous term had been spent "workshopping" the story, trying to come up with interesting and creative ideas for scenes inspired by the text. This meant lifting bits of dialogue from the story and using some of its imagery to make striking stage pictures. It was an exhausting process.

As always with A-level Drama groups, I had to insist that the students worked outside the lesson at lunchtimes and after school in order to make the finished piece. Lesson time on its own was not enough. Devising was a slow and time-consuming business, involving endless experimentation and discarding of ideas. Therefore, for the first three weeks of January, they would stay behind in order to polish and refine their play. It never ceased to amaze me that they were willing to do this. Long after all of the other students had gone home, they would be there in the Drama Studio until nearly six o'clock working on their play. Sometimes it was agonizing: the need to constantly invent, to continually evaluate, to be energised and committed without mentally wandering off was draining and demanding of even the most talented and creative students. This lot were doing well and I appreciated their stamina and the constant good humour with which they approached the task. It took some doing to be willing to work away in a cold Drama studio at 5.45 p.m. on a dark winter afternoon in January and not let it curb your enthusiasm.

Personally, I wasn't that keen on the material they had chosen. The short story they were working on didn't excite me and it seemed wilfully obscure in places. It also had some awkwardly religious overtones that barely made sense to a group of non-believers such as we all were. Nevertheless, they had insisted from the outset that this was the story they wanted to do and I could tell that the macabre and even violent aspects of the material held some appeal to a group brought up on Tarantino and an assortment of lurid computer games. As their teacher, I had to respect their intentions. After all, it was not my piece – it was theirs. This was what they wanted to do and I had to find ways of enabling them to do it but also to get good grades in the process.

As a drama teacher in a school, you get used to working long hours because of the huge amount of time you have to put in to rehearsing; rehearsing the big prestigious school productions but also rehearsing the work prepared for public examinations. There was hardly a time in the year when I wasn't working after hours rehearsing something: the school play in the autumn term; the GCSE and A-level performances in the spring term and then the junior production in the summer. As a rule, my car would almost always be the last one to leave the school car park. Most of the year, I didn't mind. This was the nature of the job and almost the best times of the school day were those hours when I was rehearsing a play with a talented group of students. The lines and moves had been learnt and the students were starting to grow into their roles, bringing the play to life as we began to run the scenes with a real sense of performance. That process was always a joy to behold and it never mattered that I was getting into my car to go home at nearly six o'clock when the rest of the school had been heading for the door at 3.45 p.m.

Working on the Devised piece with a smaller group of students had less of a buzz about it, I had to admit. Not having a published and tried-and-tested script to work from made the process doubly onerous and there was always that sense of bashing away at it, trying to wrest the material into a live and engaging piece of theatre. It felt like a slog and all the more so given the fact that we were doing it on a cold, dark January afternoon, with the excitement and joy of Christmas and New Year long since faded from memory.

There was also a new twist on the proceedings this year. Normally, we would have been working towards showing the final piece to a visiting examiner from AQA, in front of an invited audience of parents, friends and interested colleagues. This was always quite a big deal. While it never had the razzamatazz of the big school show, performed in the main school hall with a "cast of thousands", an orchestra, an army of stage hands and watched by an audience of several hundred, there was still that sense of working towards a final performance in front of a live audience. However, this year, apparently, that "live audience" was not to be. In the last weeks of January, there were already rumblings about this strange new

Corona virus thing and how schools were being discouraged from having large groups of people assembled in one place. This obviously was going to have an impact on subjects like Drama, in which the students depended to a large extent on having an audience to perform to. Moreover, exam boards were starting to send out communications to school in which they were saying that examiners would no longer be visiting schools (and presumably in order to avoid risking them spreading the virus around the different schools they were visiting). Therefore, it transpired, that teachers were now being asked to film and mark the work themselves and would then be expected to send their marks off to the exam boards, without the students' live performances ever having been seen by an examiner (apart from through the unreliable medium of a video recording).

To some extent this seemed as if it was going to take the pressure off a bit. Although we'd still do an evening showing of the work for parents, there just wouldn't be an examiner in the audience this year. At that stage, I have to say, this all seemed like an over-cautious response from the exam boards and it was difficult to take seriously. The performance would go ahead, as usual, and I would just mark it myself – and I'd need to make sure that the video recorder was working!

This was just the first instance of the virus beginning to make its mark in schools. Gradually, word came through that there would no longer be any externally examined performances for GCSE Drama... or Music or Art or PE. Various other departments started to cancel trips and exchange visits: no French and German exchange partners would be coming over this year; no Geography field trips to Dorset or the Highlands; no History department expeditions to the Normandy beaches or the Western Front; no A-level English trips to Stratford on

Avon; no Outdoor Pursuits trips for Year 9 to Wales. Parents' Evenings were starting to be moved online or postponed until later in the school year. Slowly we were starting to become aware that this phenomenon was going to make a major impact on the normal routines of our lives.

At the same time as this was all going on, I was trying to deal with my own personal dilemma: did I want to continue in the job I had been doing for the last thirty-six years or was it time to let go and to dare to start some sort of new life?

Certainly, the cold and grey January days did not help and the encroaching sense of the world outside starting to change must also have been a factor. However, at that stage it still seemed almost impossible to take the threat of the virus seriously. The fact that it had led to the cancellation of some school events and to a stepping back of the exam boards just seemed, to be honest, like the Health and Safety brigade gone mad. Surely this was something that was happening on the other side of the world, in a city in China that nobody had ever heard of? They did things differently there. Yes, the authorities were wandering around in space suits and masks and bundling people into police vans if they thought they had been in contact with the virus but that was never going to happen here, was it?

As the grim news started to come through, towards the end of the month, that the virus had finally landed here and that some individuals were now infected and then when the first couple of people actually died, even then there was a sense that people were over-reacting. OK, some unfortunate individuals had been unlucky enough to fall victim to infection but they were now in hospital and they were being treated. Didn't that mean that it was being contained and dealt with? Our NHS was surely capable of containing this thing. No need to panic, was there? It seemed as if the media was just whipping us all up into a state of fear and paranoia.

While much of January seemed like something just to be endured and got through, there were nevertheless a couple of treats on the horizon to lighten the load. The first of these was the annual trip to the Palladium Pantomime. For several years now I had booked tickets for this mid-winter camp-fest to go to one of the Saturday afternoon performances in early January with my work-colleague and fellow pantomime-devotee, Anna. This wonderful extravaganza was always looked on by us as an oasis of fun and laughter which would help us to get through the bleakest month of the year.

This year, it was "Goldilocks and the Three Bears" and on that second Saturday afternoon in January, we climbed our way up to the Balcony of the London Palladium in order to give ourselves what always proved to be a life-enhancing experience. There was something so joyous about these shows: the sheer lavishness of the costumes and the scenery and the utter daftness of the script full of laugh-out-loud moments, especially from the utterly outrageous Julian Clarey (who just left you gob-smacked that he was able to get away with some of his "filth" in front of an, at times, bewildered family audience). Although it was the Palladium, the show still had all the ingredients of the traditional pantomime: the audience participation, the communal singing, the cross-dressing, the patter songs, the slapstick, the ad-libbing and the magic tricks. Particularly memorable this year was the daredevil act of motorcyclists who performed a death-defying sequence in a vast spherical metal cage which gradually filled with more and more guys on motorbikes who appeared to hurtle round at top speed in the most "heart in your mouth" manner. And it really didn't matter that none of this had any relevance at all to the Goldilocks story. In fact, the entire plot seemed to have gone out of the window after the first ten minutes or so. The whole thing was just an excuse for laughter, fun and spectacle – and we certainly weren't disappointed!

Afterwards we went off to John Lewis on Oxford Street to the cafe on the second floor there for tea and a slice of cake and to bask in the joyous feeling that the pantomime had infused in us. We both had a positive glow from it and chuckled as we relived some of the show's most hilarious moments. As I made my way back home on the tube, still feeling buoyed up by the afternoon's splendid entertainment, I had one of those moments when I just had to remind myself how lucky I was: to have world-class entertainment such as we'd just experienced on the doorstep; to have a lovely friend to share it with; to be able to enjoy a delicious lunch beforehand, an ice cream in the interval and a scrumptious slice of cake afterwards. Life felt good!

The other "beacon" during those weeks was my father's birthday on 31st of January. He was going to be 90 this year and so my sister and I had planned something special for it. He lived down in Teddington, not far from the Thames, so we decided to treat ourselves to a good lunch at a local riverside restaurant, The Wharf. My brother, who for several years had lived down in Devon, was also coming up for this with his partner and so it was going to be a real family occasion. Not often did we all sit down to a meal together as a whole family but this year it was going to be me, my sister and her husband and two children, plus my brother and his fiancée with my Dad as guest of honour, of course! The table was booked for 1pm and we all did the short walk from his house, setting off at about 12.30.

Because none of us ever had much money, it was quite unusual for us to go to what my Dad would have called a "fancy" restaurant. The Wharf certainly seemed more lavish and sophisticated than the usual Pizza or fast-food places we generally ended up in as a family. This had crisp white table cloths and some very well-drilled and immaculate, highly attentive staff. We were not used to being served so graciously and with such courtesy and as the extremely solicitous maitre d' ushered us to our table and then started to take our orders, we knew were going to be in for a treat.

"And can I get you any drinks?" was the waiter's first question. We looked at each other. Most of our family events were usually dry and it felt rather decadent to be ordering alcohol in the middle of the day. But as we kept telling ourselves, it was a "special occasion" and so two bottles of house white were duly ordered. Why not? Some wine would help to make things go with a bit more of a swing.

For some reason, I was given the task of tasting the wine when it arrived. Hmmm. After four weeks of "dry January" it tasted particularly good and I nodded to the waiter to fill everyone's glasses. Starters were ordered (again, an uncharacteristic extravagance for our family group but it was "a special occasion") and then there were the main courses to decide upon. My Dad, brother and I all ordered the steak and chips; sister and her husband the fish pie; and the others various options from either the kids' menu or the vegetarian choices. With the wine poured, the conversation started to flow: we talked about our jobs; our holiday plans; the stuff we'd been watching on the telly recently; our friends and their foibles; our neighbours and plans for moving house. I broached the subject of my intention to retire from my job and that caused a flurry of interest and my father, suddenly more voluble as we ordered a third and fourth bottles of wine, started to hold forth in a way that he hadn't seemed to do for years, reminiscing about his two years of National Service in the 1950s and rehearsing familiar anecdotes from his working life as a Civil Servant. The afternoon passed in a convivial and light-hearted way and it felt good that we were all able to come together to mark this momentous occasion.

Added to which, we had all successfully got through January. The days were starting to become just a touch lighter, the weather was a tad warmer and for those of us still either working in or attending school, it was only two weeks to go until the half-term holiday. Again, life really wasn't that bad.

The Months Before: February

Literally, light at the end of the tunnel: not just slightly longer days but brighter skies as well. There was a sense that the spring was approaching: daffodils were starting to be sold in the shops and Easter eggs were already on the shelves in the supermarkets.

At school, we had been busy with mock exam marking and report writing. The GCSE classes had returned to normal lessons after a couple of weeks of Study Leave, during which they had been sitting their mock exams in the big main hall. Although the Head consistently denied that the school was an "exam factory", exams were nevertheless taken extremely seriously there and the mock exams were given almost as much prestige, reverence and solemnity as the real thing. For two weeks, none of us were able to go near the exam hall. All surrounding corridors were out of bounds and a tomb-like silence surrounded the massive chamber in which the exam students were put through their paces. The papers would be scrupulously marked and the results all sent home to parents, who would have the opportunity to discuss these grades with teachers in a Parents' Consultation Evening immediately following. Except that this year, the consultation evening was postponed because of concerns about Coronavirus. We were told that this would now be later in the term and that any immediate worries should be sent home by email.

In the meantime, I had the job of preparing my GCSE class

for their practical exam. In their case, this involved them performing two scenes from a play – two extracts of about fifteen minutes each – in which they would be marked on the quality of their Acting skills. The performance would be at the end of term and I would do my best to make it as big a deal as possible. I'd invite parents and other teachers to come along and be an audience and we'd hire in a professional Technician for the day to do the lighting and sound so that the students' work could be as well-presented as possible. I always enjoyed working with the students on these performances. To me, this was the culmination of two years' worth of work. The play extracts were their chance to show what they could do as actors and often the results were extremely impressive. It was wonderful to watch some of them really take off and fly in the extracts chosen. This was their chance to show that they could really act and I very much looked forward to the prospect of directing and coaching them in their final pieces in order to achieve the best possible outcome.

I had spent several weeks selecting the plays that they were going to perform. Nearly every day over the Christmas holiday, I had been reading through plays, trying to select scenes which I thought would best suit the students in my class. I had been doing this for years and never liked to repeat the same extracts, so every year I would look for something different to do with each Year 11 class I taught. This was what kept the job interesting and fresh for me. I'd always like to find pieces that would suit the talents and personalities of the particular individuals in that class. That was why I didn't like repeating stuff. An extract from "Look Back in Anger" might have worked very well, for example, the year before with a particular student who had the right angst-ridden personality for Jimmy

Porter but there was no guarantee that it would work as well the second time around, with a completely different set of students. This meant that the extracts chosen were all tailor made to fit the group. Added to which, the extracts needed to be the right length and have enough material in them for each student to shine. Also, because it needed to be two extracts from the same play, each bit needed to offer opportunities for each individual. No good picking a play in which one person had loads to do in the first extract and not much at all in the second. Especially as they would be awarded a separate mark for each performance. Therefore, finding a set of play extracts which were not only interesting and appealing to the students but also fitted the exam board criteria and which we had never done before was no mean task. Not surprising that it took me most of the Christmas holiday and several weeks afterwards to find what was needed.

Finding the right play extracts felt like a major task accomplished. I wanted the students to know the time and trouble I had taken to find their examination pieces. Therefore, I really built them up, telling them that each play had been really carefully selected and that the parts I had chosen for them would enable them to show the full range of their talents and were guaranteed to get them that coveted top grade 9.

I remember the afternoon on which I distributed the scripts. There was a palpable buzz in the air, as I walked into the lesson clutching the sets of photocopied play-extracts. I organised the students into their acting groups and then distributed copies of the scripts. As I handed them out, I could see the students leafing through the pieces I had given them, desperately totting up the numbers of lines they would have to learn and glancing through the stage directions which described the characters they would be playing. Odd lines leapt off the page, particularly lines with any 'inappropriate' or overly colourful language. There were shrieks of disbelief ("Oh my God, I can't believe I've got to say this!" "Can you see what it says here about my character...?" "Aaaaaaah! It says 'They kiss passionately for several seconds' Ugh – you've gotta be joking!").

As happened every single year, there were some students who seemed excited, intrigued and hugely enthusiastic when they read through the scenes they were going to be working on and some who just could not visualise their plays in performance at all. The term "lead balloon" came to mind. There was one group who had been given what I thought was a lovely comedy about a group of young city slickers suddenly marooned on a desert island by a plane crash but they just did not appear to be able to see the potential of the piece at all. To me it had seemed like a delicious piece of comic writing, chock full of funny one-liners and brilliantly acerbic put-downs. But sitting and listening to the group reading it, in downbeat and lacklustre voices with no sense of timing or energy was not encouraging. One member of the group had the temerity to turn round to a friend in another group and shout across the room "We've got the worst piece!" My hackles rose at this. It was going to be an uphill task getting them to bring this piece to life. I could see that now – in a way that I could not have envisaged when I had been sat at home during the holiday reading the script and believing that it was clearly comedy gold.

I was so annoyed at the lack of enthusiasm from that particular young lady that I half-thought about asking her to stay behind afterwards to justify her antipathy to the material I had so thoughtfully selected for her. However, it was the last lesson of the day and the students had only recently returned from Exam leave. The weather was still cold and dispiriting and morale was generally low. There didn't seem much point in trying to convince the girl that eventually, after she had worked on it with me and I'd had the chance to direct her in it and to bring out the scene's comic potential, that she would then begin to enjoy the scene and to relish the opportunities which it would give her. I wanted to say "This is a perfect role for you. It will get you a very good mark. Stick with it!" ...Instead, I let it go and watched her walk sulkily out of the door, bracing myself for the parental email that would surely follow: "Concerned that my daughter is not happy with the role she has been given in her GCSE Drama piece. Is there any possibility that the play you have given them can be changed? Drama used to be her favourite subject but last night she came home in tears saying that she wished she had never chosen it..."

Strange how an issue like this can play havoc with a teacher's mental state. You take it home and it circles around in your head all evening. You try and talk to other colleagues about it and they kind of understand. We all just want our students to be happy and for them to feel that we have chosen material with their best interests at heart. It won't let go, though. It's at the back of your mind all through the drive home and then while you're cooking and eating dinner, then later on when you're watching TV and again when you're trying to get to sleep. It's then there again first thing in the morning. The preoccupations of being a teacher.

And all through this time, the issue of whether or not to retire at the end of that academic year, was also constantly at the back of my mind. At weekends, it was the dominant topic of my social conversations with friends and of my phone calls to family members and at the start of February, I decided to do something about it.

I asked the Head's secretary if I could make an appointment to see her and at the end of one Thursday afternoon, I went into her office and tried to express my intentions:

"I am going to be sixty-three next birthday and I think it is probably time to go."

"Really? I am surprised. You don't seem to me like someone who wants to retire. Are you absolutely sure that this is what you want to do?"

I weakened.

"Well... yes, I think so. I want to leave while I can still do the job and while I have still got the energy to go off and do other things."

"What are the other things you want to do?"

I faltered.

"Well... I ugh... want to travel... I want to write a bit... I want to do more productions with my amateur theatre group... I've got my Dad to look after... I want to be able to see more plays, films... go to more art galleries..."

I petered out unconvincingly.

She looked at me shrewdly, a slight smile playing on her lips.

"I don't think you are sure...If you have doubts, you shouldn't go. I've been a Head in four different schools now and in each of those I've always been able to tell the staff who were ready to retire; the ones who seemed worn out or no longer able to do the job...but you don't seem to me to be like that yet. I'm sure there might come a time when you are. We all get to that in the end but you are not. And if you are not ready, you shouldn't go."

I hummed, and hawed and mumbled some more before I

started to feel and sound rather foolish. I was floundering and, of course, the fact was that I wasn't absolutely sure. How could I be? This was a major life decision. Deciding to leave work after thirty-three years in the same school, when the routine of it was burnt into my very being. The school was in my DNA. In some ways, the prospect of leaving it all behind was terrifying.

"Tell you what" she said before we finished. "Let me ask you to think about something. If you really do feel that you want to retire, why don't we both think about some sort of half-way house?"

"What would that be?"

"What if I was to pay you to come in and do the part of the job that you enjoy most: the productions? Let's say, I pay you to produce the big show in the autumn, the drama competition in the spring and the junior production in the summer?"

I started to become excited.

"How would that work?"

"Not sure exactly yet, but at my last school, we employed somebody to come in just to do the school shows. They did a pantomime at Christmas and a musical in the summer. I'm sure we could do something similar here… Why don't you have a think about it and let me know?"

A few minutes later, I left the Head's office with her proposal going through my mind. It was certainly something to think about. The best parts of the job: the excitement of the big shows but with no marking, no lesson preparation, no exams to prepare for. Just the fun part, the bit of the job I had always adored and, though I say it myself, had always done brilliantly well. Some serious thought to be given, I reckoned.

Never one to rush into anything and certainly not prepared to change my life of over thirty years on a whim, I went off and discussed this offer with various friends and relatives. Some were all for it. I remember my brother and his fiancée telling me that I should "bite her hand off" in response to an offer like this from the Head. This was the dream deal: able to stop full time work but still keep my hand in by doing the part of the job I really loved. My school shows had acquired a reputation over the years. "Better than the West End" was the universal response. "Best school shows in the country" was the comment of one parent (who was actually a celebrity parent and a well-known television actor, so he certainly knew his onions!). "The best week of the school year" was how some colleagues were kind enough to describe the school show week, although this was not just empty flattery. I was always aware of it myself. In the weeks of the school show (the big autumn production and the summer show) there was most definitely always a palpable buzz about the place. The whole school got excited about it and people talked about it for days beforehand and afterwards. It was a focal point for the whole school community and I had always loved being at the centre of this. This was one of the reasons why I had been so reluctant to retire. The thought of giving up that wonderfully energizing and focusing project was something I could barely contemplate. Also, on a personal level, it just allowed me to indulge my dreams of working in the theatre. For a few weeks leading up to the show and most definitely on the nights of the performances, I could play at being Trevor Nunn or Nick Hytner or Peter Hall as the audiences gathered to watch my productions of "Oklahoma" or "Guys and Dolls" or "Twelfth Night" or "A Midsummer Night's Dream". Those production weeks were utterly magical to me and the thought of renouncing those forever was very painful. And yet, here I was being offered a chance to hold on to the most creative and exciting parts of my job – and still get paid for it.

"Perfect solution!" my friend Jonathan exclaimed, as we met for a night out in King's Cross in early February. "If she's offering you all that, you'd be mad not to say 'Yes'. It gives you everything you want. Go for it!"

He carried on, convincing me that this was the perfect solution to my life quandary of whether or not to retire. "Gives you the day free to do what you like. Go to the gym, read, potter about and then at four o'clock, off you go into work for a couple of hours to rehearse a show and then back home in time to enjoy the rest of your evening...I know you were worried about how you are going to fill your time when you retire but this way you've got a focus, you're not cutting yourself off completely from the job and the other people you've worked with and we have both always said that you are the sort of person who is going to find it very difficult to just STOP... this way, you don't have to. She's offering you a solution..."

It was generous of him to be so solicitous and concerned and, in fact, I thought that he was talking a lot of sense. I was especially appreciative of the fact that I had more or less dragged him out to King's Cross that evening for our meet-up. I'd needed a place I could get to relatively easily after a late finish at work – just a twenty-five-minute journey on the overland train from my local station. I knew that it wasn't an area that especially appealed to him for a night out. It was, though, somewhere I had enjoyed visiting on evenings out with my teacher friends and we had had some good times there, knocking back expensive cocktails and being served by hipster barmen. However, on that night, the bars were all massively overcrowded with young suited folks, all braying and shouting at each other as they tried to make themselves heard over the sound systems that blared music out in every bar we attempted to enter. As luck would have it, nowhere seemed to have a table available for a quiet drink. Each place was guarded by a doorman who asked if we'd booked or reserved a space and, of course, we hadn't. Many of the bars had outside space, generally overlooking the waters of the Regent's Canal but even these tables had been commandeered by boisterous groups of office workers, who all looked and behaved as if they had just stepped off the set of "The Apprentice". Even though it was a chilly February evening, these open-air seating areas were all heaving and seemed incredibly popular. The chances of our finding a quiet corner for a cosy chat about my future seemed more and more remote.

Every place we stepped into seemed over run or deafening or looked like it would be impossible to get served and I could tell that he was starting to get annoyed. We must have traipsed around for at least half an hour. All I wanted was a drink and somewhere to sit down. It really didn't bother me at all if the bar looked "naff" or "too full of awful people" – I just wanted a bloody drink!

Eventually we found somewhere. It wasn't much better than anywhere else but at least there was a bench on which to sit down and there seemed be enough people serving behind the bar to make it look as if we might eventually get served.

We settled down with a couple of pints of strong lager and I began to relax. I went through the deal that the Head had put to me and then rehearsed the counter arguments which had been put to me by other friends:

"Isn't it going to be a dreadful tie? Aren't there going to be other things that you want to do with your day? Aren't you just going to be having one eye on the clock all day, waiting to go into work at four o'clock?"

"Don't you just want a clean break? It's great that she thinks so highly of you and wants to keep you on but haven't you got other things that you want to do? Don't you want to travel? Do some more studying? Write a novel? Walk the Great North Way? Paint and spruce up your flat?"

"And what about the other staff? Aren't they going to be almightily pissed off? There they are – they've just done a full teaching day and been there since eight o'clock in the morning and you pitch up at four p.m., work for a couple of hours and get paid for it, while they are all there just doing it out of the goodness of their hearts?"

These and other such arguments were all put forward and my friend listened patiently but still kept coming back to the fact that I was going to be paid to do something that I loved and it seemed like a wonderful way of easing myself gently into retirement.

We finished our pints of lager and ordered two more. By now, we were both well into the swing of the evening. The disgruntlement of the trudging around trying to find a congenial bar had vanished and we were now enjoying each other's company whole-heartedly and I felt that I was being wisely counselled as I discussed the possible options for my future.

Leaving the bar, we went off in search of the "cheap and cheerful" pizza place Jonathan had booked for us on York Way. There we ordered a bottle of house red and continued putting the world to rights and sorting out my future options.

The pizzas when they arrived were enormous and, as always happened when we went out to eat together, we had massively over-ordered and by the time we had worked our way through a huge selection of starters, neither of us had much room left for the main event. However, we both had the capacity for more booze and so a second bottle of wine was ordered and we swiftly managed to guzzle our way through that as well.

As we finally staggered out at about 10.30 p.m., it was with the sense of a good evening having been had and I felt well supported in my decision to leave work but to continue in a part-time, almost "Consultant" capacity.

Meanwhile, we were marching towards half-term. The mood at work had not improved vastly from that first day back in January. The days were still grey, cold and cheerless and work felt, for the most part, like drudgery with all of my exam classes needing to be coached for their practical exams and dragged kicking and screaming through the accompanying written documentation which the exam boards now required. This meant an endless programme of rehearsals every lunchtime and after school with one group or another. I would work out the physical shape of their scenes, the set on which they needed to perform represented by an array of chairs and tables. After that we would map out the moves, trying to make the action as clear as possible. Then I would help the students to develop their characters, constantly questioning them about who they were. What job do you do? How old are you? Where are you living? What are your relationships? What time of year is it? What else was going on in the world at the time when this play was set? Who was the Prime Minister or President at the time? What movies were playing at time when this play is set? Who were the icons and personalities that might have influenced your character's personal style?

Then there would be all those questions about the dialogue

between the characters. Why are you saying that? What do you feel when he/she says that? What are you NOT saying here? Why do you use that word? Why does the playwright want a pause there?

It was exhausting – for both me and I would imagine for the students as well. Most of the time they had barely thought about their characters. In fact, for the majority of the time, their attention was confined to trying to remember the words and getting them in the right order. And most of my time was actually taken up with prompting them and trying to help them remember what they needed to say. Therefore, most of those early rehearsals with the students were not especially rewarding. It really did feel like coaching. Also, I had to resist a bad habit of mine, which was telling the student how to say the line, demonstrating it and then expecting them to parrot it back to me, copying exactly my delivery and intonation. Unfortunately, I could not help but do this. I was an actor "manque" and this was my opportunity to perform. The students had to like it or lump it, I'm afraid – but it did not fit in at all with modern teaching methods in which the students were expected to work everything out for themselves.

And so the weeks went by, every afternoon after school a rehearsal for an hour and a half with a different exam group and then dull start-of-the-year evenings: not going out, not having any alcohol, trying to cut down on carbs and sweets and cheese; trying not to watch more than an hour or so of TV a night; trying not to fritter away time surfing the internet. It was still the beginning of the year – that time of self-denial and restraint, of "no fun" "no treats". And it was tough. January and February are always grim months in school. There doesn't seem to be much to look forward to. You are not working towards the communal jollity inspired by the run up to Christmas. Nor is the weather good enough to allow lessons outside or, at least, a sandwich outside while the sun is shining. There is none of that promise of the long summer holiday stretching ahead which you begin to feel in, say late April or early May. No. It just feels like "eyes down" and get on with preparing for exams. This is the time when the serious coursework needs to be tackled and I would spend most weekends wading through drafts of Student Portfolios, constantly correcting and adding suggestions and comments for more depth, more evidence of research, more examples, more quotes from sources, more clarity, better expression and more intellectual rigour. At the same time, we seemed to be stuck in the middle of the school year with little end in sight. The novelty of September and that rejuvenating sense of a "new leaf" and a fresh start had vanished months before. All that seemed to stretch ahead were months of marking and setting deadlines and chasing up work not done and handing back work which needed re-writing and constantly checking the exam board specification to see that key areas had been covered and trying to reassure myself that the students had been adequately prepared.

Once again, the thought of leaving all this behind forever by retiring from it was starting to seem like an ever-enticing prospect. I was still coming to terms with the fact that this was my choice and that in itself seemed remarkable. It really was up to me. I could decide to go. I was entitled to go. In fact, at nearly sixty-three years old, I was considerably older than most teachers when they decided to retire. I had known many to leave at fifty-five and certainly most had gone by sixty. Why was I still hanging on? Wasn't it partly through fear? Fear that without the job as my great crutch and support, I would wither away and just curl up and die?

The job had become an essential part of my life: it gave me my identity; it gave me structure; it gave me my sense of purpose. How would these things be replaced if I walked away from it? What would I do instead?

Friends would cheerfully suggest all the things that I would be free to go and do but I cannot say that any of them excited me that much: choirs I could join; painting classes I could go to; musical appreciation and walking groups; courses I could sign up for; The University of the Third Age. But frankly, most of these just gave me the willies. They sounded universally drab and just time wasting. It seemed irredeemably sad to me to retire after all those years of work and then be scrabbling around trying to think of dull but worthy ways in which to then pass the days.

On the other hand, as I gathered up my lesson materials to go and teach another bored but extremely obstreperous Year 8 class, dreading the prospect of having to spend the next hour and twenty minutes in their company and knowing how annoyed and furious I would have got with them by the end of the lesson, I had to ask myself the question: "Did I really still want to be doing this a year from now?" Was this really the best that life had to offer?

Who knew how much longer I had left? I was sixty-three. If I was lucky, I might have another seven years of reasonable health, when I still felt fit enough to go jogging in the park and to swim thirty lengths at the pool. When I could still go out for a few drinks in the West End with friends and just about get myself back on the night bus without incident; when I was happy to take myself off to a European city and wander round it for a few days, absorbing the atmosphere and behaving like a teenager, eating in fast food places, sunbathing in the park, getting pissed in the bars. Did I really want to spend what remained of these years stuck on the treadmill of work – partly because I was too frightened to let go? Weren't there other things I would rather be doing? As I sat in that lesson, trying to feign interest in some ghastly improvised plays that I had tried to get the Year 8 students to put together in what had been a very effortful lesson involving much cajoling, arguing, shouting, flattering, demanding and constantly refraining from screaming my head off while battling with my own exhaustion, jadedness, weariness and general sense that I had just been doing it all for too long. Did I really still want to be doing this in a year's time? Wouldn't that all feel like I was just hanging on? Like I had lost the battle? That I had been too scared to take the opportunity of jumping ship when it was offered and that I was now here for the duration?

One of the best things about February was the week's half-term holiday, which was in the middle of it. I decided to celebrate of the first day of this week off by meeting my friend Robin for lunch. This was always a typical half-term treat. Robin was not a school teacher but, for some reason, our meetings always had to fit into the school holidays. This was one of those follow-ups from the Christmas holiday when we'd exchanged cards and promised that we "must get together". But the Christmas holiday always seemed to vanish so quickly and got so filled with family obligations and other immovable social events, that our meeting got shunted into the next available slot: the first weekend of the February half-term. We were going to meet in Soho: we'd begin with a couple of pints in one of our favourite bars and then we would go off and find somewhere to eat. On this particular afternoon, we opted for a Chinese restaurant right in the middle of Chinatown and ordered the Set Menu. The restaurant and, in fact, all of the streets of Soho seemed strangely deserted for a Saturday afternoon. When we got inside, the waiters were all wearing face masks. Never one to hold back, Robin collared one of them:

"Do you think people are put off coming to you because of all this stuff about the Virus?"

The waiter replied in a fairly non-committal way, explaining that business had been a bit down but that he expected it to pick up again soon. Like most of us, he seemed to give the impression that the 'health scares' were a temporary phenomenon, even an over-reaction, and that we'd all be done with it in a few weeks' time.

"Well…" Robin stated assertively. "Doesn't put me off, I must say. Load of fuss and nonsense, if you ask me! What shall we have to drink?"

We ordered a bottle white wine and congratulated ourselves on our defiance and "bravery" at venturing into the "unsafe" territory of a Chinese restaurant during this fearful time. I always found it intensely enjoyable, drinking in the middle of the day and it felt great to be out and on holiday from work. Normally on Saturdays, I spent almost the whole day at my desk marking (essays, drafts of coursework, student portfolios to accompany their performances) and it was usually a full working day. Today was a day off, though, and it was great just to be able to chat and drink and forget about anything much else except having fun. After the restaurant, we went off to a pub for more drinks (gin and tonics by this time) and I was more than a little tipsy by the time I got on the tube at about five p.m. It felt like a glorious luxury, just to be able to write the whole day off like that. I must have got home about 6.30 and spent the rest of the evening slumped on the sofa immersed in the drivel of Saturday night television and thankful that I had more than one day off before I had to go back to work again.

The rest of the half-term holiday passed pleasantly enough. I went down to see my Dad in Teddington on the following day. As usual on Sunday, the trains were all disrupted by engineering work and I had to keep changing trains and then getting buses before I finally arrived at my destination. This didn't put me in a very good mood but we were able to get out and find a pub for lunch (no alcohol for me this time, just a J2O) and for the rest of the afternoon, I was able to sit quietly on the sofa reading the Sunday paper while my Dad nodded off in his chair. So not too many demands there.

On the Monday, I thought I might try and get to the Barbican Cinema to see 'Parasite' which was the film tipped to win the Oscars that year. As always, I didn't book and was somewhat disgruntled to be told that the afternoon showing was "fully booked". How on earth could it be? Who else was going to the movies on a dull Monday afternoon in February? Well, enough people for that showing to be sold out apparently. I wasn't sure what do after that, so wandered over to the Barbican Centre in search of a coffee and one of those lovely, comfortable sofas which litter their foyer where I imagined I'd be able to sit down and read for a bit before catching the train home. I had a copy of the new Tom Stoppard play in my bag that I was currently working my way through. I had tickets for the production at the start of the following month but wanted to read the script because I knew how complicated and involved some of his texts could be. Best to be prepared.

And it was a good job that I was. This play

("Leopoldstadt") seemed incredibly complex: a huge number of characters: middle class members of a large Viennese Jewish family from before the Second World War but so many of them! It was almost impossible to keep up with who was related to who – whose aunt, cousin, nephew, grand-daughter was whose. All of the characters seemed to come on for a brief appearance and deliver a short piece of dialogue and then disappear again. There didn't seem to be time for anything to develop – or time for the audience to really get to know the characters. But I suppose that was part of the point, one could argue, if being charitable. The scenes were like snapshots, like photos in an album; little glimpses of a whole clan, each of them vivid and alive with their ideas and concerns but all about to be obliterated by the impending forces of fascism. A big concept but I got the sense that the concept was more important than the individual personal dramas of the characters. I guess it would take the production itself and the actors and the costumes and settings in order to fill the roles out and to breathe life and substance into the words I was reading on the page, I hoped.

As I sat there in the Barbican foyer, reading my Stoppard play and sipping my coffee, I could sort of pretend to myself that I was some well-healed Barbican flat-dweller and that I lived in one of the swanky apartments that surrounded the arts complex, overlooking the fountains and piazzas of the Barbican Centre. What a pleasant place to live that would be. So different from suburban Enfield.

The afternoon started to drag a little, as it always did during the first few days of a holiday from work. Funny how you would spend weeks longing for some time off and then when it finally came you would feel aimless and disorientated. It was also lonely, sitting around in the foyer for the afternoon rather than being at work and interacting with dozens of different people all day long. Maybe it wasn't such a good idea to retire from work after all?

Having imagined that I could settle down for the afternoon on one of those big comfy Barbican foyer chairs, I now felt restless and distracted. Distracted by all the different comings and goings: the Arts lovers beginning to arrive for the concert or play that would be performed there that evening; the gallery-goers, the city types, the day-trippers, maybe even the Barbican residents themselves who must occasionally hang out down there when they wanted to escape from the confines of their posh flats, in need of a coffee or a slice of cake or just to drink in the muted bustle of the atmosphere. I tried to read the play-script I had brought with me, determined to finish it by the end of the afternoon so that I could allow myself to go on to something more gripping for my next read. I can't say that I was gripped by the play. Yes, it had a strong and important central idea about history and families but the characters seemed only very thinly sketched in and there were very few sustained passages of dialogue to engage the reader. Of course, there were the odd witty one-liners and there was some clever word-play, as one would expect from a Stoppard but I couldn't exactly call it a page turner.

Feeling that I had had enough, I wondered whether I should try for the next showing of the film, having successfully killed a couple of hours waiting around, I started to gather my belongings when there was a ping on my phone. It was a text message from my colleague Hayley asking me whether I wanted to see the film at the cinema in Crouch End later on in the week. Instantly, that was a much more appealing prospect than watching it now, alone. Therefore, I texted her back to say

"Yes" and within a few minutes she texted back to say that she had booked the tickets and we had arranged a time and place to meet later that week.

This seemed like a cue to abandon the Barbican and head home. Being February, it was still cold even though the late afternoons were now a little lighter. It was a relief to get back and to settle down to a Monday evening of television and some food. As soon as I got in, I made myself a mug of tea and a couple of slices of toast. I turned on the six o'clock news. Rather frightening stories starting to come out of Italy about the new virus that seemed to be spreading out of China now. Several towns in northern Italy were beginning to record deaths in quite high numbers and there was some distressing news footage of elderly Italian ladies grieving for husbands who had recently passed away from the disease. Over here, there were also news stories about people being hospitalised and now deaths, too, were being reported. Surely it couldn't get a hold here? Not in the way that it seemed to be doing in Italy? There was more footage of the authorities in Wuhan manhandling people who would not quarantine at home or who were suspected of carrying the illness. Futuristic images of groups of police in what looked like space suits, covered from head to toe, and dragging their writhing victims into police vans started to dominate the news. Nobody would ever behave like that here, though, would they? Surely this was just because they were an authoritarian country and effectively a police state? Also, presumably they didn't have anything like our extremely advanced health service and therefore did not have the wherewithal to fight the virus, as we would do, were it ever to take hold here?

The rest of the half-term week passed uneventfully enough.

I spent another day at my Dad's going out with him for a walk in the early spring sunshine and making him his tea. My sister came over for a bit and we chatted as we got on with a few chores around his house: taking out his rubbish, giving his kitchen a bit of a clean and tidying up the piles of old newspapers. The other days, I was at home but getting up a bit later than normal, going off to the gym at the more civilised time of 10 am or so and then shopping, trying out some new recipes, reading, chatting to friends on the phone or catching up on tv programmes that I wanted to watch. Nothing that exciting but easy and undemanding and suitably restful.

I had arranged to meet Hayley for the movie "Parasite" later on that week at the trendy art-cinema in Crouch End. I'd not been there before and liked the Bohemian atmosphere of the place. It felt like a very "cool" venue in which to watch a film, with its subdued lighting and the old movie posters which lined the walls of the staircase leading up to the auditorium. It could not have been more different from the Enfield multiplex in which I normally watched the latest films, with its Pick n Mix and buckets of Popcorn and frenetic youth-oriented atmosphere. This place was calming, sophisticated and civilised. We had a coffee beforehand and both expressed our relief at being off work for the week. Neither of us had done anything particularly momentous but we both agreed that it had been lovely to be free and to be able to set our own timetables for the day.

When the film started, we both got swept up into its strange and quirky world. It was a Taiwanese thriller and provided a fascinating insight into a completely different culture. The star of the movie was the house in which most of the action was set: an extraordinary "palace" of contemporary architecture, full of amazing gadgets and the very last word in stylish design. It was in extreme contrast to the urban poverty from which the protagonist of the film had come. He had managed to trick his way into this affluent household by taking on the role of personal tutor to one of the children of the rich family. Gradually, the poorer character and his relatives took over in a bizarre reversal of status. The film was gripping and incredibly original but also shocking in places. It was certainly quite unlike anything either of us had ever seen before and was well deserving of its Oscar win.

As I had been walking from the station to meet Hayley at the cinema, I had noticed an attractive looking pizza place and suggested that we go there for a bite to eat afterwards. She was happy to do this and so we plonked ourselves down at a table for two and ordered a bottle of house red, while we decided which pizzas to order. We chatted about the film and then moved on to work, both off-loading our different gripes about the stresses, strains and responsibilities of teaching. Hayley was a sympathetic and supportive listener and it felt good to be able to offload. As always with my friends at this time, I wanted to get her feedback on my plans to retire at the end of that school year and she listened attentively to my ideas. She was kind enough to say how much she would miss me but also said that if she was old enough to retire then she would do. She seemed to be able to see no drawbacks or any downside to my decision and I felt validated and supported in my intention.

We were enjoying chatting to each other so much that I think we ordered a second bottle of wine. Probably a mistake but neither of us wanted to curtail the evening and it felt good to be able to lose oneself in a conversation with a close colleague and friend. When we finally emerged from the restaurant a couple of hours later, I walked back up to the station feeling that we had had a good, companionable evening and that there had been a real connection between us.

The following afternoon, I was due to attend a performance by my amateur theatre group of a play that, on this occasion, I had had very little to do with but knew that it was my duty to go and support. The play was a Three Act affair and was to be performed in a new Studio theatre space converted out of an old rehearsal room in the building which housed the municipal theatre in which the group normally performed. This was to be a kind of "Fringe theatre" event. The Studio space held an audience of around a hundred, seated in three rows arranged in a horseshoe shape around the simple stage setting of a desk and a few chairs. The plays were adaptations of short radio plays and were each about half an hour long, with a pair of actors in each one.

If I'm completely honest, I have to say that it felt like a bit of a chore to have to go along and support this venture. But there were a couple of friends of mine in it, who I knew would appreciate my support and I reckoned that it was important to turn up and be one of the "bums on seats" these events needed in order to thrive. As it transpired, when I got there, I was greeted warmly by my acquaintances at the theatre and, even though I was on my own, there were plenty of people there to chat to, all of whom were friendly and welcoming when we spoke. That made me feel good, as if I was part of something.

The plays were slickly produced and well- performed. The acting was confident and assured and each of the three plays were entertaining and had a good story to tell. At the same time, I was very glad not to be in the production myself and pleased that all I had to do was turn up and support and I was thankful that, at the end of the performance, I could just slip away. After the first play, there was a short interval for the audience to get up and stretch their legs, go to the toilet, get an ice cream and chat to each other. As we sat down to take our seats for the second play, the man next to me (to whom I had been chatting away quite easily during the interval) remarked on the proximity of a Chinese gentleman in the seat in front. This person coughed slightly as the play was about to start and my acquaintance turned and grimaced theatrically in my direction, whispering something extremely politically incorrect which I had to try and pretend I hadn't heard.

Of course, as a school teacher, I couldn't condone such flippancy and so pulled a disapproving face. I knew that in school recently, there had been some comments from the Asian children about how they had been on the receiving end of derogatory or threatening remarks and that people had been accusing them of spreading the deadly virus and how appalled we all were at these displays of uncharacteristic bigotry and prejudice. On this occasion, it was clear that the remark had been intended as satirical and not to be taken seriously. Even so...

The half-term holiday slipped by as quickly as these things always do and by the last week of February, we were back at school with the usual "start of term" blues. That lovely week off in the middle of the month was always such a bonus at this time of the year: the chance to get up a bit later in the morning and being able to linger over tea, toast and Radio Four and not having to battle through the "school run" traffic. That alone made the week pleasurable, not to mention the opportunities to catch up with pals and the just not having to work. School, on the other hand, was starting to feel relentless. The exams were looming; the final assessed practical performances with all their hours of extra rehearsal and the accompanying written coursework were all entering their crucial final stages. The next six weeks would be full on and extremely intense and, among all the staff, there was that usual feeling around this time of year, that work would dominate now until the next school holiday. Weekends would be taken over with marking; lessons would need to be more carefully planned than ever. The weeks ahead would be nothing but hard graft. I guess it was this prospect that made for the slightly dazed atmosphere of those first few days after half-term: everyone knowing that the stakes were high now; these were the last weeks before the all-important exams and that we would all be held accountable for whatever results our students achieved.

More and more for me, however, was that sense of "here we go again". The patterns of the school year were so ingrained and so much a part of my life blood, it was as if the different rhythms of it were now a part of my DNA. What would it be like, I kept wondering; what would it be like, not to have this?

Did I really want to be going through all this again in a year's time? And then, again, the year after that and the year after that? Was this the best way I could imagine of living the rest of my life? Was there really no alternative?

The harsh reality was that unless I made a definite decision and then acted on it and put it into operation, I would sleepwalk into another year. The only person who could change things was me. I needed to take responsibility.

I was starting to torment myself. When do I do it? When do I set these wheels in motion? Do I wait another week? Another month? What is the right day? Do I do it on a Monday morning or wait until Friday afternoon? Or go for the middle of the week? Do I need to be feeling in the right mood? Or is that just an excuse? What would the right mood be? Combative, confident, adventurous, calm?

Almost every night now, I would lie awake thinking "Tomorrow should be the day….but maybe not. Maybe wait just a little bit longer. Don't burn your boats…After all, once you have done it, there's no going back".

That weekend, I was meeting my close friend Deborah to go to a play at the National Theatre. We met at the cafe a couple of hours beforehand, planning to have something to eat and a soft drink before going in to watch "The Ocean at the End of the Lane". This was the National's Christmas show for that year and we were both hoping that it would be another "Warhorse" or "Coram Boy". One of those lovely, big National Theatre spectaculars that would use all of the resources of this terrific theatre to create a hugely engrossing and magical theatrical experience. As it turned out, this production didn't seem to either of us to be quite in that league. For a start, it wasn't performed on the massive arena stage of the Olivier. This was much more of a chamber piece and was being staged at the Dorfman, with a small cast and with much more modest staging. I'm afraid the production disappointed us both. The characters were unappealing and the storyline unengaging. There was also too much of that annoying whimsy that characterises so much theatre aimed at younger audiences that we just found cloying and twee.

Nevertheless, in spite of the disappointments of the production, it was still nice to be out and to be watching a show at one of the best theatres in the world on a Saturday night. It was great to be there in all the buzz and chatter of the National Theatre foyer; to be sat together at a table in their cafe people-watching and enjoying their food and gossiping together, offloading about our week and bemoaning the frustrations and challenges of our working lives. Inevitably, I had to get the subject back to my future and what I was going to do. I apologised for the fact that this just went round and round with no resolution on my part and that, as one of my closest friends, Deborah had to be constantly on the receiving end of "What do I do? When do I tell them? Shall I wait another year?"

She was quite clear: "Look – just do it! You will feel so much better when you do. Just make up your mind this weekend that on Monday you are going to go into the Head and say that this is what I want to do".

She was voicing what I was feeling, of course. I needed to stop dithering; stop tormenting myself. I just needed to do it, to take action, to be decisive. There was no point in simply allowing the situation to drag on. I had made the decision in my mind and now I just needed to take the action required in order to bring it about. Of course, it was terrifying: the prospect of my way of life for so many years now changing forever. And I could not get out of my head, this image of myself as cast adrift, lost, floundering…without work and, therefore, my whole life then without purpose or meaning. Of course, I realised, that it would be up to me to create a new sense of purpose: to construct plans, ambitions, projects. That was daunting, of course, because I could not imagine for a moment that any of these things would just fall into my lap. I would have to make plans, set goals and, in many ways, be as focused and driven in my new life as I had been for all the years that I had been working. This was going to be essential if I wasn't to allow myself to just drift. I did fear for that, though. I did fear for my ability to steer and manage my life when for so much of it I had been part of a big institution with every minute of every day timetabled and organised for me. To some extent, all I had ever had to do was to turn up and then play my part as the cog in that massive machine. I had hardly had to make any decisions myself much more demanding than choosing a holiday destination to go to in August. The rest of the year had always been managed for me.

On the Sunday night, at the end of the weekend, I hardly slept. I had told myself that the following day would be the day. I had a free lesson just before break and I would make an appointment to see the Head then and make my move. That would have to be it. There was to be no more dithering and indecision. The time had come, the hour was here.

After my first couple of lessons of the morning, I emailed the Head's secretary and asked for an appointment. She emailed me back to say that the Head happened to be free at that moment and did I want to come over now? I rang her and said that I was on my way.

I felt nervous and sweaty and could hear that my voice sounded strained and breathy. I was ushered into the Head's office. I told her that I had thought carefully about her very generous offer of a part-time post and that I was very chuffed that she had even considered paying me to come back and do the school shows but that I thought that, attractive as this prospect was, I needed a clean break and that I had decided to retire at the end of the school year and would not be coming back in any capacity. Unlike the previous occasion on which I had attempted to resign, she could see now that my mind was made up and that I meant it. The decision was final.

"I'm sad." she said. "Sad to lose you and to be losing your friendship, as well" (which very nearly choked me up) "But I can see that you've thought it all through and that this is what you want to do…So you now need to put it in writing. I can't accept your resignation until you have done that. It's probably better to let me have that sooner rather than later."

We exchanged a few pleasantries about how it had been a hard decision to make and how it was good for me to have finally made up my mind before I scurried back out, past the secretaries and the others who worked in the school reception area. For a few moments, I felt a strange kind of euphoria that after months and months of vacillation, I had finally taken action and was now in charge of my own destiny. "I've done it!" I wanted to holler down the corridor. "I've bloody done it!" There was a strange kind of lightness and an almost joyful feeling that something so momentous as the ending of a thirty-six year career could be achieved in a few minutes. At last, I was unshackled and free and incredibly excited at the thought that I had just opened the door to the next phase of my life. How wonderful was that?

Convinced that I needed to seize the moment, I dashed off an official letter of resignation, outlining my intention to resign my post as Head of Drama, as from the last day of August and thanking the Head for all her support over the five years that we had known each other. It was a couple of sentences: straightforward, clear, professional. No need to elaborate on any of my reasons for leaving. After all, I was sixty-three and considerably older than any of my other colleagues in the staff room. That alone was more than enough reason to finish and I had certainly notched up a more than respectable number of years of service.

I printed off the letter and put it in an envelope and took it back over to the office. Within minutes, I had received a formal reply thanking me for my contribution and wishing me every happiness for my retirement. By the end of the morning, the whole process was officially ratified and completed. It had felt like a momentous morning's work.

When I got home that night, I pinged off a few texts to interested friends and got messages of congratulation back, all of them wishing me well and applauding me for having finally "done it". Nobody made me feel that I had been rash or impulsive and all seemed pleased that I had finally done something that I had been talking about for years.

As I lay in bed that night, I did not experience the "my God, what on earth have I been and gone and done" feeling that I had imagined I might feel. On the contrary, it was more of a feeling of relief. The constant to-ing and fro-ing of recent months was over. For the first time in years, an exciting future stretched ahead. I found myself able to look forward in a way that I had not been able to do for many years. Suddenly the future was alive with adventure and possibility. I could now write that novel or go on that road trip round America or buy that house in the country or go and do that Creative Writing course I'd been meaning to sign up to for years or learn to paint or move to a different part of London or start ballroom dancing lessons or learn how to become a pastry chef or begin speaking Italian. The possibilities were endless! I thought of all the new movies I was going to be able to see the week that they came out and all the classical music concerts I was going to be able to go to at the Barbican or Festival Hall. All the mid-week matinees of plays I was going to be sitting through and all the exciting and hitherto unknown Fringe theatre spaces I was going to be exploring. The days and weeks and months teemed with possibility!

Over the next few days at school, I started to let a few of my closer friends on the staff know that I had finally handed in my resignation – after so many months of vacillation and infuriating indecision. Rather flatteringly, they all claimed to be devastated but were also understanding of my position and each seemed to think that, on balance, I had made the right choice. They all said that they would be very sad to see me go and I also found it hard to imagine my life without them; without those little daily interactions; the quips, the running gags; the gossip; the in-jokes; that wonderful sense of having found another person on the same wave-length; an ally; a staunch supporter and port in any storm. Every so often, I would allow myself a little moment of panic: how on earth would I survive without the daily currency of our shared laughter and tittle-tattle? If I permitted it, a sad vision of myself sat silent and alone in my armchair at home, dressed in cardigan and slippers and descending slowly into a lonely dotage while school colleagues continued to roll along, merrily joshing each other in the photocopying room and roaring with laughter over stories shared at mid-morning break. However bleak these occasional imagined glimpses of the future, the fact that I was free and had taken charge of my own fate, continued to outweigh any momentary misgivings. Already, an exhilarating holiday feeling was taking over. Suddenly, there was a future. Drudgery and repetition and that dismal sense of declining interest and motivation was giving way to an exciting and more optimistic mood as I began to contemplate the future.

One important person I had not told was my sister. For some reason, this news seemed too momentous to tell during a phone call, so I saved it up for the end of the week when I went over to see my Dad. I got to my father's house before she had arrived and quickly told him that I had finally resigned from my job. I am not sure that he was quite able to take it in and he kept asking me questions:

"So you're going to retire, are you?"
"What sort of pension will you get?"
"Will you be able to live off that?"
"What will you do with yourself if you're not going to work?"

I offered my usual rather vague and non-committal replies. It was in the nature of his condition for him to keep asking me questions and he asked the same four or five questions again and again and I gave more or less the same reply each time. I think he was taking some of it in but every time we met over the course of the next few weeks, we repeated exactly the same conversation. I wondered if he was able to think about the impact my decision might make on him and on our relationship? It would certainly mean that I would have more time to visit and to take him out although (extremely selfishly) I didn't want him to feel that I was now going to slip into the role of unpaid "carer". The fact that I wasn't going to be working any more certainly didn't mean that I was now going to be permanently available to trek over to the other side of London to visit on a more than weekly basis at the most.

Slightly more difficult was broaching the subject with my sister. When she finally arrived at the house, later on that Sunday afternoon, it suddenly struck me as furtive and odd that I had not broken the news before now. Why had I felt it necessary to keep it a secret for four days? Was it something to do with the fact that I suspected she might not be fully supportive of my decision and that I did not want her to 'rain on my parade'? She'd been badgering me to retire for months…

years, even. She kept telling me that it was "all too much" and that I shouldn't care so much and should step aside and let other younger and more resilient types take over the baton. She'd been concerned for my health, fully aware of the stresses of the job and its impact on my mental health, my blood pressure, my well-being, my ability to sleep and to relax, switch off. On the other hand, she'd always been a bit of a "doom and gloom" merchant, warning me that retirement wouldn't be "just like being on holiday, you know". She was only too keen to tell me how difficult it was to "just be at home all day"; how much self-discipline it required to organise one's own schedule, to not fritter away the time; to stay positive and motivated.

Therefore, I had no idea how she would react. I needed her to validate and approve my decision. I needed her to share my new found sense of optimism and my certainty that I had set myself on the right course.

As it was, I waited until we were alone together and washing up my father's lunch things in his kitchen, while he dozed off in front of the afternoon television shows.

"I've got something really important to tell you." I announced dramatically.

I could see a look of alarm flash across her face. What was she imagining? A terrible illness; financial ruin; a criminal act?

I needed to put her out of her misery quickly.

"I've handed in my resignation…"

Her response was careful and measured. Sensible.

I was slightly disappointed. Did I want her to be congratulatory? Over-joyed? I could certainly have done with her being a bit more over-the-top in her reaction.

We talked more and gradually she came round. "Yes, you are right. I think that's good. It's the right time. You'd had enough. You had to do it at some time."

We continued washing up and made a pot of tea to take into my dad. She was beginning to seem more voluble and positive in her support. I guess it was just a bit of a shock for her. By the time, we emerged from the kitchen, I could tell that she was used to the idea. It must have taken some getting used to, I could see that, after so many months and even years of me threatening to leave my job but then never actually doing anything about it, now I had finally done it and that must have been quite hard to comprehend.

I felt a strange closeness to her that afternoon. It wasn't very often that I really let down my guard but now I was doing. I told her about my feelings of trepidation and my worries about how I was going to fill the time and make the most of my newfound freedom. She was sympathetic and I felt heard and supported. It was refreshing to be so frank with each other. Most importantly, I felt that I needed her blessing and by the end of our conversation, I felt that I had been given that.

We went back into the living room and sat with my father, while he nodded off in front of the tv. After a while, we put on our coats and went for a short stroll in the late afternoon sunshine. It was the last weekend in February and there was still a sharp and biting cold in the air but the afternoons were certainly getting longer and the sunshine was almost spring-like.

After the walk, we came back and made some sandwiches and ate some chocolate cake from the Co-Op at the end of the road. We turned on the news. The death toll from the virus in China had been escalating steadily over the last few weeks and now it seemed to have taken a stronger hold than ever in Northern Italy. There were more distressing scenes of what looked like field hospitals, makeshift camp beds, set up in halls because the actual hospitals had become overwhelmed. There was one particularly upsetting piece of footage, which showed an elderly Italian lady weeping because she was not able to be at her husband's side during his last moments. She herself had a terrible hacking cough and was holding a handkerchief over her mouth, while two younger relatives helplessly attempted to comfort her. The scene looked so hopeless and grim. It was all the more alarming because it was taking place at a location most people thought of as affluent and sophisticated: Lombardy with its capital Milan, that hub of banking and fashion. Milan. How could such awfulness be taking place there?

March

The first days of March arrived but they were accompanied by a heavy sense of foreboding. If the virus was starting to rampage through Italy, which by all accounts had a highly sophisticated health service, surely it was going to make its way over to us soon? Wasn't it only a matter of time?

There was much talk on the news of foreign travel and the ways in which that was responsible for spreading this deadly virus. Again, Northern Italy seemed to be the focus here. A popular location for ski trips, it was a favourite destination for half-term travellers in February. Many a school trip had taken place there and stories started to circulate of school students and their teachers returning from ski trips and then being laid low with the virus shortly afterwards. This seemed very concerning because it meant that the virus was effectively being imported from holiday resorts and then airports on an almost daily basis. Pundits on the six o'clock news made grim predictions that the rapid rise in infections and deaths seen in Italy then was about to be replicated here and that this was certain to happen within a few weeks. In Italy, they had started to close the schools and then the bars, restaurants and shops. It looked as though people were being marooned in their own homes. Laws had now come in preventing people from leaving their apartments, except to buy essential foods and for medical supplies.

I started to panic. How would I cope if they had to bring in something similar here? For me, my apartment (a small modern flat in Enfield) had only ever been a base from which to go out and see my friends and explore everything that our wonderful capital city has to offer. What with work and socializing and going to visit my dad and gym visits, I was hardly ever there. At weekends, I did little more than sleep there and during holiday times, I spent as much time away from it as I could, loving the adventure of foreign travel and trips away. The thought of being incarcerated in my flat for weeks on end was horrifying to me.

At the same time, life was continuing to go on. Yes, there was a somewhat po-faced public broadcast by the Health Secretary warning the nation of a 'serious threat' but minutes later these dire warnings appeared to be undermined by the Prime Minister, who bluffly asserted that he was continuing to shake hands with people in hospitals and who kept underplaying the seriousness of the disease. He told us that for most people, it wouldn't be more than a 'flu type' illness and would be unlikely to cause more than mild discomfort. Just remember to "wash your hands for as long as it takes you to sing Happy Birthday," he chortled, appearing to hardly take the threat of the deadly virus seriously at all. Yes, there had been horrifying and apocalyptic scenes coming out of China and more recently Italy but now, with ominous echoes of Brexit, there was the sense that this was all an over-reaction by "Jonny Foreigner" and that once the thing took hold over here, we would see it off with our characteristic British pluck – not dissimilar to Winston Churchill sending Adolf Hitler packing!

And I guess that was what most of us wanted to believe. Nobody here would ever countenance their lives being inconvenienced in the way that things seemed to be in those other countries where the coronavirus had taken hold. We had our lives to be getting on with. I had my retirement to work towards and to plan. I certainly didn't want my life to be disrupted by these inconvenient outside forces. Unfortunately, though, it was starting to look as if none of us were going to have any choice in the matter.

That weekend, I had theatre tickets for the new Stoppard play I had been reading over half-term, "Leopoldstadt". There were rumours starting to circulate that the theatres might have to close. If this virus was passed on by social contact then a theatre auditorium containing several hundred people all sitting in close proximity, was likely to be one of the first casualties of this epidemic. For the time being, though, the theatres had stayed open.

I was due to meet my friend Stephanie for the performance and we had arranged to have a meal beforehand at "Mon Plaisir" in Covent Garden. She was travelling in to the West End from Hertfordshire and said that she was going to get a taxi from Kings Cross to the restaurant at which we had agreed to meet. I wondered why she had decided to do this and it became apparent when we met that she was feeling fearful of taking the tube in the current climate and had thought that a taxi might be a safer option.

When I arrived at the restaurant to meet her, I made as if to give her a hug (which was how we would usually greet each other) but she pulled back and laughingly reminded me that we had been told (by our betters) to maintain a physical distance, so we bumped elbows instead. We laughed and made light of the ridiculousness of this new form of greeting, both gamely performing the new ritual that we had been instructed to participate in. At the restaurant table, we sat diagonally opposite each other, rather than directly facing – again, observing the new rules. It felt like a strange 'phoney' war in which we were now engaged, barely taking it seriously and almost slightly enjoying the new modes of behaviour which we were being forced to adopt. Not that this made much of an impact on the rest of our evening, which went on pretty much as it would have done before. We ate our meal and were served in the normal way. We sat next to each other at the theatre in the middle of a row of people, squeezed into the cheaper seats with dozens of others in front and behind. The theatre was absolutely packed. This was a hot ticket – the premiere of a new play by our foremost living author and there was a large crowd there to see it. The audience was a vocal and self-confident lot: the "chattering classes" out in full force and all making their presence heard and felt, with loud guffaws during the performance and their braying chatter around the bars and foyers during the intervals. It seemed a world away from the doleful tales of people holed up in their apartments in Italy. How could two countries which were so close geographically be behaving so differently?

The following day, I went to my local Sainsbury's to stock up for the week. There were tales of people starting to panic buy items like toilet rolls and pasta and soap but I wasn't sure how seriously to take these. Just as a precaution, I'd nipped into the little general store next door to my school one morning before work to stock up but there didn't seem to be any shortages there. I emerged with a pack of four toilet rolls, some kitchen towels and cleaning products – no problem at all and not even a queue. What were people talking about?

Sainsbury's on that Sunday morning was a different matter altogether. As soon as I drove into the car park, I could see that something was seriously amiss. It was only about half past ten on a Sunday morning – normally a quiet time, with just a few customers there for a Sunday paper and a loaf of bread or a pint of milk. However, today there were hordes of people streaming in. There were almost no spaces available in the car park and it seemed that all of the trolleys had been taken. More than that, there was a frantic, desperate atmosphere there. Rather than sauntering in half-asleep, as normal, the customers today were stony-faced and grimly determined, elbowing each other to get to the limited number of items on offer. The news the previous day had depicted empty supermarket shelves and, sure enough, that seemed to be the case now. In aisle after aisle, there was almost nothing there. There was certainly no toilet paper and no cleaning products in evidence: no bleach, no sprays, no jay-cloths, no wipes. I grabbed what I could: some rice, some tins of tuna, a packet of sad-looking chicken breasts and took what was available. There was some bread and still some cheese and cans of soup. Would that be enough to hole up for weeks if we were told to stay inside like our Italian friends? Taking as much as I could, I marched my trolley towards the checkout. Where was the queue? There didn't seem to be one, just a scrum of agitated people, all jostling and pushing and being generally aggressive and behaving in the most awful, selfish ways. Some people had piled their trolleys so high; they could barely contain the mountains of toilet paper and multiple packets of pasta that they seemed to be intent on hording. I tried to join a queue but each time got told that "this is not the end of the queue, mate. It's down the end of that aisle," pointing me in the direction of the other end of the store. There must have been about a hundred people in each queue. Crazy. I realised that I was going to be in here for the rest of the morning, at least. I half thought about abandoning my trolley and just going home but then if I did that, I'd have no food for the week. No alternative but to join the back of the endless line and to wait my turn. The queues seemed to be barely moving. This was mainly because every single person had piled so many items into their trolleys that they were taking an age to get through each checkout. The woman I stood behind kept leaving her trolley to go and grab more items, as we slowly pushed forward, all at a snail's pace. She was piling so much stuff in that items kept falling out and on to the floor. She had to steady the ever-expanding pile with her hand, as if performing some elaborate balancing act.

All I could feel was an overwhelming sense of anger and frustration as the minutes ticked by and I only ever seemed to advance a few paces. I could barely imagine getting to the checkout, which had now become an almost impossible goal to reach.

I felt so sorry for the staff manning the checkouts. As each trolley was offloaded on to the till, it was like a great pile of rubbish crashing down onto the conveyor belt which the cashier had to slavishly pick her way through and start to scan. Each of the cashiers looked stressed and put upon. The friendly bantering exchanges into which they normally entered with the customers were not happening today. Instead, everyone looked grim and cross. Each customer had a look of pent-up fury, as they struggled not to take things out on the hapless supermarket workers. The checkout staff themselves just looked shell-shocked and worn down by the whole thing. Nobody had ever seen anything like it.

Eventually, after nearly two hours, it was my turn to offload my trolley and pay for my goods. I seemed to have a considerably smaller amount of shopping than the people who had gone before me and when I finally got to the till, I felt like I'd almost won some sort of lottery, as if I had won a prize by finally achieving the right to pay. My items were scanned in and I put my card in the machine and paid. What a relief to be able to get out of the place! It was considerably more crowded when I left than it had been when I arrived but the shelves were now woefully empty. What did these customers arriving to shop now hope to be able to buy? There was almost nothing left.

When I got home, I unpacked my items, treating them almost like precious cargo. These few bits and pieces would have to last me the rest of the week, I realised. I certainly couldn't put myself through all that again in a hurry. How awful that even just going to the supermarket was now turning into some sort of major operation, likely to take at least half a day to perform.

I made myself a sandwich to eat while listening to the lunchtime news. The first deaths in London were now beginning to be announced. It was here. There was no escape. What the hell was going to happen now?

Monday morning, we were all sitting in the staff room asking why schools were still being kept open when everywhere else was being encouraged to close. Why us? Was it that teachers were expendable? There was a break staff meeting when extra staff training sessions were announced to help us all to set up "Google classrooms" should a situation arise whereby we might be required to teach our lessons online. This was to be a lunchtime session run by the woman in charge of IT and we were all strongly advised to take advantage of this opportunity.

I went to the session but found it (like so many IT things) to be little short of bewildering. As always when being 'trained' in this sort of thing, I found it almost impossible to pick up even the basics and I was completely lost by the time we got to the "you could do this/ could do that…and if you want to, you can even do this..." while the trainer showed us all the various permutations which Google classrooms was capable of performing. How effortful it all seemed! And would it really be necessary to go through all the shenanigans required to set up all this stuff: a separate 'virtual classroom' for every single group taught? With all the accompanying resources and power points and worksheets and instructions for every single one of my ten different classes? It looked like hours and hours of work and surely things were going to be back to normal in a month or so. Was all this faffing about with technology really essential?

On the other hand, what would happen if we really were going to be closed down and the students weren't able to come to school? In that eventuality, there then would have to be something like this in place, wouldn't there? Didn't we, as teachers, all have a duty to be prepared?

Over the next few days, we all started to go into overdrive, filling every spare minute with the preparation of online lessons. As well as all the newly acquired technical skills this necessitated, every single aspect of what we were now doing in the classroom had to be re-invented and then 'translated' into an online format. Out of nowhere, we had to conjure up meaningful ways of engaging our students and teaching them the skills and knowledge that they would have been taught in a classroom setting via an online resource. Some things, clearly, it would not be possible to do online. In my own subject of Drama, the major portion of the lesson required students to work in small groups and to prepare short performances which the rest of the class would watch and comment upon. The performances would alternate between short extracts from the major classics of World Drama (the Ancient Greeks, Shakespeare, Nineteenth Century Naturalism and Twentieth

Century or Contemporary drama) and the students' own original devised work. The devised plays were short, semi-improvised pieces that they would script and rehearse in small groups on a range of topics (Social Issues, Myths and Legends, Documentary Dramas, for example). How on earth was any of this supposed to happen online? How were students going to plan, rehearse and perform in groups if they were all isolated at home and sat behind their screens? It seemed as if the whole curriculum needed to be reconceived and refashioned in the space of just a few days.

In a blind panic and knowing that I needed to get the material uploaded as soon as possible now, I soon started to feel that I was floundering, not just with the demands of the technology (how to download material; how to save work; how to make sure it got to the students; how to enable them to send in homework; how to send it back to them with comments and marks) but also with the content of what should be uploaded into the "virtual classroom". Who on earth knew what an online drama lesson looked like? Were there any examples of such work? Who was the expert who could be consulted here?

It seemed as if we were just making it all up as we went along. A dispiriting feeling of guilt started to set in. Not only would we not be in school doing our job but it was clear that the 'slim pickings' we were offering on line would in no way make up for what the students would be missing by not being physically in the classroom. All sense of quality control was abandoned. All that seemed to matter was making sure that something, anything, would be there in the virtual classroom so that the students had something they could access in lieu of proper lessons and never mind the quality. It was almost as if we were doing this just to cover ourselves; so that we could say to parents, "Look there's the work. It's up to students to download it. If they don't want to do it, that's not my problem…"

In the end, the only thing I could think of to do with the younger classes was to set them some time-filling project work. Things along the lines of "Go and research Medieval Mystery Plays. Draw a picture of a pageant wagon and find out as much as you can about the York and Wakefield Cycles…… Imagine you are a Medieval peasant standing in the town square watching a performance of Noah and the Flood."

Grim, indeed, but what were the alternatives? (And, of course, within a few days, the Head started sending out furious memos to staff along the lines of "Please do NOT set project work. The students get very stressed by these open-ended tasks and parents say that they take up far too much time. Short and specific tasks with a clear and definite learning outcome only should be set during these difficult times…")

Those days in early March were a time of considerable anxiety. Nobody knew what was going to happen. Figures for infections and deaths seemed to be mirroring Northern Italy in a most alarming way. The government's medical advisers announced that we were only three weeks behind the Italians. If that was so, were the horrific scenes pictured on the news then going to be happening here? Were people we knew going to be expiring on makeshift camp beds in rows on warehouse floors, while grieving relatives were kept away and not allowed to even say "Goodbye"? Were we also going to see those trucks loaded with piles of coffins which we were told the Italian authorities were unable to bury?

As the rest of the UK started to go into lockdown and as more and more people started to work from home, those of us working in schools started to question why we were not being forced to close. Were we expendable in some way? Were we putting ourselves in danger by mixing with large groups of people in confined spaces on a daily basis? Whatever concessions schools made to the notion that we should all keep a 2-metre distance from each other, the fact remained that a school was a place in which social distancing was almost impossible to enforce. At the end of every lesson, corridors would fill as students moved from one classroom to another. Our old school building had never been designed to accommodate over one and a half thousand people rubbing shoulders with each other on an hourly basis. At break times, the communal areas around the school swarmed with pupils talking to each other, eating snacks, finishing off work, knocking on the staffroom door to speak with teachers or just generally hanging out together. The atmosphere was generally boisterous and noisy: noisy with the animation and chatter of young minds exchanging gossip, news, ideas, jokes, plans, moans, complaints, laughter. Similarly, the dining hall, which was almost mobbed at breaktime as students made for the serving hatch, desperate to get a snack to tide them over till lunchtime. Equally so, at lunchtime, when it became the main indoor meeting place, not only for eating but also for socializing, catching up, laughing and generally making contact with each other. A school is a social place. People learn by talking to each other; through discussion and questioning and listening. Students sit crowded together in classes of over thirty in small rooms never originally designed to house such numbers. If what the government medical advisers were saying was true, how could schools be anything other than a breeding ground for the spread of infection on a major scale?

On the other hand, we could all understand what a last resort closing schools would be. Yes, it was happening in other countries but the disruption caused would be unimaginable. Ours was a highly academic school. Almost everything about it was focused on exam success. As the spring term got underway and students entered the final stages of exam preparation before their exams started in May, the atmosphere in school became almost feverish. Even the most hitherto lackadaisical students would gradually begin to become more focused and studious, driven by that need to achieve that all important Grade 9 at GCSE or A* at A-level. Any casualness or tendency to mess about or not pay attention in lessons, had generally by this time in the school year given way to a sharper focus and a desire to buckle down. Students were driven, serious, ferociously competitive, eager to fill any holes in their knowledge in order to get those much-coveted top grades. There was a momentum in lessons as we rode those final weeks towards the all-important public examinations in a couple of months' time.

The thought that this process might now be interrupted or abandoned was unthinkable. It was also true that many students had actually worked quite hard in the weeks since Christmas and almost all were definitely working hard now. They were serious about achieving exam success. The notion that their examination courses would be interrupted at this crucial stage was something that none of us could contemplate. Also, for younger children, there was the whole issue of childcare. If schools were suddenly shut, then the kids would have to be looked after and supervised at home. Parents would have to give up their jobs or try to juggle working from home with having to home-school their children. There were so many factors involved, it was easy to see why the government had been so reluctant to take the dramatic step of closing schools. And schools like ours never closed. When other schools seemed to take "Snow Days" at the slightest flurry of sleet for example, we stayed open. We didn't close. Ever.

As the month of March kicked in there was more and more of a sense that school closures were inevitable. There was too much at stake for them to remain open. Too much potential for the spread of the disease in school: students could infect each other, infect their teachers and infect all of the non-teaching staff (the office workers, the cleaning and caretaking staff, the lab assistants, the peripatetic music teachers, the dinner ladies). Schools were a hub to which people travelled in from all over the local area and then returned home, often to multi-generational homes. Possibilities for infection were rife: on the bus, on the train, in the car to and from school, in the sweet shop or cafe, back home at the family dinner table or on the sofa watching TV in the evening. Close the schools and at least, to some extent, that perpetual potential to spread could be halted.

The Easter holiday was coming up at the end of the month and there was talk that schools would be closed for a couple of weeks before that, so the holiday would be extended by a fortnight. This month off would create a kind of "circuit break" and stop the disease from spreading. That way the country could start to get the thing under control. Maybe things would return to normal at the start of the summer term?

Amongst the students, there was now a slightly heady hysteria setting in. Bottles of hand sanitizer and wipes started to appear on tables and desks in classrooms; a one-way system was introduced for students to navigate their way round the school, supposedly without having to face each other as they walked between lessons. We were all instructed to wash our hands more thoroughly, for at least twenty seconds, and so took longer to get in and out of the staff toilets. The rules against close physical proximity were cheerfully adhered to with much bumping of elbows and pretend hysterical screaming whenever another person came too near. The moment another person sneezed or coughed, there were screams of "Ugh!" and "Isolate! Isolate!" Students started to absent themselves from lessons, claiming that their families were "self-isolating"; staff started to not turn up for the same reasons. Those of us who were still there found ourselves covering for absent colleagues far more frequently than was normal and classes were frequently no more than half full. Closure looked not only inevitable but it was also starting to become desirable under the circumstances.

Rumour and speculation were rife. Would we be closed down this week? Tomorrow? This afternoon? Was that it for this term? Would we be back after the Easter holiday? What if the two weeks weren't enough? Would this run on into the all-important mid-May exam period? Would there even be exams? If not, then how would the students get their grades? It was a very uneasy and unsettling time of great uncertainty and collective panic.

That weekend, I was due to meet my friend Tony to see "City of Angels" at the Garrick Theatre on the Saturday evening. This was a typical part of my weekend routine and had been for years: meeting up with a pal to go and watch a show, then go off for a quick drink and a catch-up afterwards. Nothing particularly unusual about it apart from the fact that it was beginning to seem quite strange as well that theatres were being allowed to stay open when so much of normal life was being curtailed. If close physical proximity was the main way in which the virus was transmitted then surely we were putting ourselves in danger by going to watch a West End show and sitting cheek by jowl next to hundreds of strangers in a cramped theatre auditorium? On the other hand, as I stood outside the Garrick Theatre at seven p.m. that evening watching the audience arrive and bustle into the foyer, none of those confident, stylish and well-heeled audience members looked the slightest bit ill or as if they were harbouring the dread disease. They were the typical Saturday night theatre crowd: loud, a bit flamboyant, self-assured, expensively and colourfully dressed and full of laughter, chatter and their expectations high for the show they were about to see. Rather than being cowed by the fear of infection, there was a mood of defiance in the air, very much along the lines of "We're not going to let this f...g virus interfere with our fun. It can go and get lost!"

Tony had brought a friend along and, as had quickly become the norm, we laughingly touched elbows by way of greeting. This was still a kind of novelty, and we were all a trifle self-conscious about it but everyone else seemed to be doing it and it had become a sort of game, a way of showing that we were "doing our bit" and trying to abide by the new social conventions, for the good of others, of course!

We took our seats down in the stalls. (Tony had managed to get a cheap deal on the tickets and these were better seats than we were accustomed to). Not for a moment did we think about the large numbers of strangers who surrounded us, all in close proximity, both in front of us and behind us and sitting alongside. As the lights went down and the show started, the audience started to become very vocal. This was a sassy American musical, a satire on the Raymond Chandler style "noir" detective thrillers – but with songs. The script was full of clever, witty one-liners and the audience laughed loudly and appreciatively at every punchline. The musical numbers were brassy and upbeat, eliciting prolonged and highly appreciative applause with some whooping and cheering for the big showstoppers. The cast sang and danced with enormous energy, belting out the ballads with all the power that they could muster, the sweat running down their faces as they beamed into the spotlights. If this disease was transmitted by particles in the air, then this show was clearly endangering us all, performers and audience alike.

However, at this stage in the game, I guess most of us were still unaware of the potential dangers of such a gathering. In those early days, there was more of a sense of "This cannot and will not be taken away from us". The pleasure and habit of theatre-going is so ingrained into the lives of so many Londoners, that all we could focus on that evening was a feeling that this was our right and we were entitled to enjoy it to the full. The West-End theatre scene is an integral part of our capital city. It is what foreign tourists flock from all over the world to come and see. It is one of the wonders of the world: that square mile or so of theatre buildings from which the best and most popular theatrical productions ever created are exported all over the world.

There was a sense that evening, though, that this might be the last time we would sit together as an audience in a West End (or any other) theatre for some time. Rumour, again, was rife that the theatres were due to close any day now. In fact, we were lucky that we had managed to squeeze ourselves in to tonight's performance because this might well be our last time watching a West-End show for many weeks or even months to come.

My friend Tony and his mate and I all discussed this notion that tonight was probably the last time for the foreseeable. Somehow, I'm not sure that any of us quite believed it. Also, all three of us being somewhat theatrical types, I have to admit that there was a bit of a sense of revelling in the drama of it all. How foolish that seems now! But then there was, ever so slightly, a sense of relishing the apocalyptic atmosphere abroad in those final days before lockdown; that feeling that we were living through something very momentous and highly unusual and this would be a tale to tell to future generations, a bit like living through the outbreak of war or the abdication crisis or the death of Princess Diana.

We certainly weren't the only ones feeling this on that particular evening and somehow this mood palpably enveloped the rest of the audience in the theatre on that night. In spite of the huge and very vocal enthusiasm with which the opening scenes of the show were greeted, as the performance progressed, you could begin to sense the waves of sadness emanating from the audience. We would not be doing this again for perhaps a very long time. It was as if, by the end of the show, there was a collective understanding that had infiltrated the entire audience; a sense of loss, of grief in anticipation of what was about to be taken away and some doubt that it would ever return. Therefore, the curtain calls, when they came, weren't the thunderous and jubilant ending to the evening which was customary. The mood by this time was almost sedate, resigned. Or was it just that people, like me for one, were starting to realise that what we were about to enter was far more dramatic and extreme than anything which could be conjured up on a musical theatre stage?

At the end of the show, we filed out. The audience were

now markedly more subdued than when they had arrived. Outside the theatre, it was all noise and bustle again as people stood with their companions comparing notes on the show and inevitably all discussing the national situation. Tony's friend had to leave but he and I stood and discussed where we might go in order to get a drink. We imagined that most of the bars would be packed at that time with drinkers all desperate to get what could be their final fixes if the pubs were to close, as rumour again suggested that they might be. We opted, therefore, for a private drinking club, of which Tony was a member. He reckoned that it would be fairly quiet there and that we'd be able to sit down and at least have a proper conversation, unlike in most of the other bars, where we'd probably have to shout over loud music and where we definitely wouldn't get a seat.

As predicted, the private club was more or less empty. We plonked ourselves in a couple of stylish armchairs in an almost deserted room and sipped at our large glasses of red wine. It was only there, in the tranquil atmosphere of that almost silent private members' drinking club that we became aware of exactly how frenzied and maniacal the atmosphere outside in the streets had been that evening. Again, it was that 'end of the world is nigh' feeling that seemed to be everywhere: on the pavements, in the bars and restaurants, on the tube, in the shops… Here all was calm, peaceful, silent. For a few minutes, we talked about the situation, unable to avoid speculation about the forthcoming threatened closures: to our workplaces, our sources of entertainment, to travel. However, as the wine kicked in, we were able to move on from there and to our more usual topics of conversation: the books we'd been reading, the people we'd seen, our parents and families, holiday plans and the usual little anecdotes and stories shared to give each other a glimpse into the workings of our daily lives.

I can't remember much about the journey home that night. It must have been late and was certainly well after midnight. I wonder if I realised then that I would not be having a night out like that again for many months to come?

The following day, I went out and got my paper and spent the morning reading the horrifying predictions for the next few weeks. It was a beautiful spring morning and I felt like getting out for a walk. I fancied driving up to Kenwood and walking across Hampstead Heath and up Parliament Hill. It was certainly too nice a day to be stuck indoors. It took me about half an hour to drive over there and to park in nearby Bishop's Avenue. There were loads of people out and the atmosphere I could almost have described as "jaunty". People were wearing shorts and t-shirts, in anticipation of the warmer weather and there was a feverish buzz in the air. The prospect of an extended Easter holiday certainly seemed to be infecting some with a carefree "holiday humour". The paths across the Heath were crowded and I could overhear people chatting animatedly and speculating about the lockdown arrangements which were due to be announced from Downing Street the following day. We'd all been told to keep 2 metres apart in order to avoid the spread of infection but nobody seemed to be observing this rule at all that afternoon. People were ambling along in large family groups, all very vocal and laughing loudly. I heard Mums discussing their childcare arrangements, dads talking to other dads about their preparations for working from home; older folk bemoaning the state of the country and wondering how they were going to get through it all; younger people still at that stage unable to believe their luck that their exams might get cancelled and that they might get unlimited time off school;

even the younger ones were just thrilled at the prospect of a few extra weeks of holiday. The paths were dusty and the sun beat down, making it seem more like a day in June or July than one from the middle of March. It was as if the whole of North London had decided to get out for the afternoon and later on that day on the news, there was footage shown of one of the London parks which had been similarly over-run to illustrate how none of us were taking the threat of the virus seriously. Scenes like these, of marauding holiday crowds, all taking over the London parks on that Sunday afternoon, were certainly going to prompt the government into imposing some of the more severe restrictions which were then announced later on that week.

After I'd driven back to my flat, I slumped on my sofa to read more of the Sunday paper. I had the windows wide open and enjoyed the late afternoon sunshine streaming in through the window. This was the first really spring-like day of the year and it was impossible, while basking in that glorious spring sunlight not to feel a sense of optimism and almost joy.

The next day, we tried to go about our school business as normal but it was hard not to be distracted by what was happening in the country as a whole. In class, every lesson had to be prefaced by words something along the lines of "We may not be here next week, so if you are told to work from home, this is what you will need to do…" My exam classes clearly were not going to be doing their final exam performances for GCSE or A-level Drama, so I had to tell them that I would assess them on the basis of what they had prepared so far. I asked all of the students to get ready to perform their pieces to the rest of the class during one of our final lessons and I would then give them a mark based on what they had done up to that point in the course. While in theory this was probably fair enough, in practice it didn't quite work because so many of the students were by this point self-isolating. They either had the virus or there was a family member who had the virus or thought they had it. In any case, with the students all working in small groups and with each group working on a different play extract, it seemed that there were almost no complete groups in the class. I tried to get round this by reading in for some of the missing students myself and then assessing the ones who were there but it wasn't very satisfactory. Also, most of them were still at that stage where they were groping for the words and trying to remember their lines so there wasn't much proper "Acting" going on. We did the best that we could.

All through the day on that final Monday, we were constantly checking the news online, each of us desperate for some definite confirmation about exactly what the arrangements were going to be for schools. If we were closing, when would it be? Tomorrow? The end of the week? Next week? Or would they just risk schools carrying on until the end of term. Nobody knew!

That evening when I got home, I had an online meeting for the amateur theatre company of which I was a member. We were meeting to try and plan some of our next productions but as we sat down to try and discuss what we were going to do, the Prime Minister began his broadcast to the nation. This was a significant moment. That night he moved from "avoid pubs, restaurants and theatres" to "all pubs, restaurants and theatres will now be closed with immediate effect". That was it. There would be no theatre performances for the foreseeable future. More significant for me personally, though, was the announcement that schools would be closed from the end of that week.

This was it: these were now our final days in school. It seemed that the government had chosen to extend the Easter holidays for schools by starting them a couple of weeks earlier. At that point we all still assumed that we would be back later on the following month but nobody was indicating any return date. We began to speculate. Maybe we'd be back at the start of May? Maybe we wouldn't return till after the summer half-term in early June? Some were even saying that we would not be back until September...

Personally, I found that prospect inconceivable. If that really was going to be the case, then for me that would mean that the Friday at the end of that week was now destined to be the last day of my school career. I had been due to retire at the end of the summer term. If there was really no prospect of schools returning till after that date, it meant that I would never be going back.

This was a deeply shocking realisation.

I had given in my notice to the Head at the start of March, with the intention of there then being five months of transition, of 'letting go' before I would finally leave the school in July, the end of the summer term. That give me five months to unshackle, to clear out my things, to get used to the prospect of leaving after more than thirty years in the job. That would have given me five months to prepare my final lessons, to say my 'goodbyes', to get my classes ready to be taken over by someone else. Five months for me and others to get used to the idea of parting and of moving on.

Now, suddenly, it seemed that I had only three and a half days for all of this. I felt shocked, stunned, robbed. No longer, a whole term and a half to get used to winding down but now, with almost no warning at all, I was being catapulted out with a violence and suddenness that left me breathless, bewildered and saddened.

The day following the Prime Minister's announcement, there was a full staff meeting in which the Head went through some of the arrangements that would need to be made for this unprecedented period of school closure. We were told not to come into school under any circumstances. The school building needed to be deep-cleaned in preparation for the time when we would all be able to return. We were told to take all our personal items home and to make sure that we had everything we needed in order to be able to teach online from our homes. Further training sessions were offered for those of us who needed to improve our IT skills in order to be able to do this successfully. Because it looked as if there would no longer be any public examinations, various things were said about the forthcoming arrangements for Centre Assessed Grades and the evidence we would each need to put forward in order to be able to submit these. Like so much else at that time, nobody had any idea of precisely what would be required and we kept being told that "At the moment, we just don't know…"

The mood of the meeting was tense and emotional. We had all been instructed to sit 2 metres apart, which was unusual enough in itself. It felt very strange to be gathered together as a whole staff and for us each to be sat in isolation away from friends and members of our departments. It was as if we were each of us already suspected of harbouring the disease and had been instructed to avoid each other for fear of contagion.

We were told to leave the school building as soon as we could that afternoon. There were to be none of the usual extra-curricular activities which generally kept the school busy and open for at least a couple of hours after normal lessons had finished at 3.45 p.m. There would be no sports practices out on the field, no music or drama rehearsals, no clubs or societies meeting, no staff yoga or extra training sessions. Those staff who liked to stay behind in order to tackle their marking or lesson preparation before they left for the evening were discouraged from working in school and told to go home as soon as they could. By about four-thirty in the afternoon the site was deserted and silent – apart from the cleaning staff with their mops and buckets and sprays of anti-bacterial cleaning fluid.

The following day, I relayed the arrangements for the final few days to my form group. This was particularly hard because they were all in Year Eleven. Normally, they would have been entering the last couple of months of their education and been going on to sit their all-important GCSE exams. This would have been the culmination of five years' worth of education and, in a school such as this one, they would all be expected to get the top grades in nine GCSE subjects. By this stage in their school careers, the pressure was well and truly on. Any casualness or indifference to study had, by this point, given way to a genuine studiousness and seriousness of purpose. I had been this group of students' Form Teacher for nearly five years, having helped to initiate them into the school when they had first arrived as small and timid Year 6 pupils five summers before. In those days, they had all seemed so tiny and for much of the time were almost silent. Of course, that initial shyness had quickly given way to a joshing familiarity and boisterous playfulness. They were certainly not silent in form periods now. Over the last five years, they had all acquired the swaggering self-assurance of street-wise North London teenagers. It was almost impossible to remember how they had been during their first few daunting weeks when they'd all been only eleven years old, arriving fresh and scrubbed to take their places at secondary school on their first "Welcome Evening" in late June 2015. Over the years, we had had our various altercations about uniform, punctuality, hair styles and the school rules. There had been moments when they wouldn't be silent for me to take the register in the morning or when one of them answered back in a way that I considered insolent or disrespectful but generally we had managed to rub along relatively harmoniously.

However, we were now entering into particularly unusual and testing times and I felt a strong, almost paternal concern for their well-being. I couldn't help but feel extremely anxious about how the next few months were going to pan out for them. Unlike some of the younger pupils (and even a few of the staff) they seemed to perceive no upside in the imminent closing down of schools. They did not want an extended Easter holiday or to be missing out on their exams. For the most part, they had worked hard during their GCSE courses and wanted to be adequately rewarded for their efforts. Being competitive and generally driven souls, they wanted the chance to demonstrate in a public exam the extent of their knowledge; they wanted to be able to show off their learning. They didn't want their education to be suddenly cut off and to not be able to complete the two-year courses which they had been embarked upon since the September of 2018. As for the extended Easter holiday, they saw no appeal in this. They knew that in the normal course of events, they would be off on Study Leave as soon as the public exam season started in mid-May and so would (apart from coming in to sit their exam papers) be effectively "off school" for the next five months anyway, from May until they returned for the Sixth Form in September. They were well aware that while superficially attractive, the notion of not having to come in every day and do the normal 8.30 till 3.45, would in reality be a bit of a dead time, without much structure and possibly even quite isolating and lonely. Also, young people are quite conservative in many ways and can be as addicted to habit and routines as the elderly. They did not care for this unexpected interruption to their routines, to the normal rhythm of things. I could see it on their faces: a look of apprehension and disquiet; a strong sense of collective anxiety.

We were told that schools would close at the end of that week and that the final lessons would finish at 2.25 p.m. on that day. (We normally finished at 3.45 p.m., so this was much earlier than normal, but it was thought sensible to have a staggered finish with some classes leaving at lunchtime, others straight after lunch and the rest after their final lessons). The day before, the year group (Year 11 and my form) had a Year Assembly in the Great Hall at which they would be addressed by the Head and Deputies and given as much information as was then known about the way the whole situation was expected to unfold...

The Assembly was held in the big main hall at the end of the afternoon on that Thursday. Normally, the students' entry into the Assembly Hall was a bit of a rough and tumble affair but not so on that afternoon. The students arrived seeming cowed and weary. The Hall had been set out to accommodate the new rules on Social Distancing. There were no rows of chairs any more. Instead, there were individual seats, each placed 2 metres apart, with every student and member of staff sat in sad isolation. It felt strange and unfamiliar, adding an eerie and even sinister atmosphere which made people seem divided and wary.

Various members of the Senior Management team addressed the students. Their tone, although intended to be reassuring, seemed funereal. Try as hard as they might, there was an atmosphere of foreboding and dread. It wasn't just the disruption at this crucial stage in their lives and the frustrating uncertainty and lack of information about what would take the place of their forthcoming exams. It was also the unspoken presence of death in this group of normally upbeat and forward-thinking young people. "We will lose loved ones," the Prime Minister had said on television earlier on that week. These young people were old enough to understand that we were living now in close proximity to a deadly threat. Grandparents, older relatives, neighbours and friends were already beginning to succumb. People we all knew were going to die of this. Who even knew how many of us would be safe: the older people in the room on that afternoon; the teachers and the students' families, their relatives, their friends?

For all the anxiety about disruption to exam timetables and the fear that whatever was to take the place of traditional exams might not be fair, it was also the fear of death, of this deadly disease which might strike anyone down at any moment which was also terrifying and so sobering.

Various instructions were given by the po-faced Senior staff about the need to complete all their work for their GCSEs; that even though they would not be in school, every piece of coursework needed to be finished off to the best of their ability. They were told in no uncertain terms not to just sit at home twiddling their thumbs. There would be online lessons in every subject and these they would be expected to "attend" as if doing a normal school day and that any absences from these sessions would be followed up. They would be expected to work and study regardless of the national situation and must not use this as an excuse not to maintain the rigorous work ethic which was expected of them in that school.

Unfortunately, of course, nobody had much information about what was going to happen. It was all just speculation, so all the leaders of the school could do was instruct the students to keep connected via their phones and computers and to respond to any instructions issued. An impression was given that the current crisis would be short-lived (how could it not be? The thought of it going on into the summer let alone the autumn or heaven forbid, next year, was at that stage unthinkable). The school closure had to be presented as a temporary measure; a precaution, possibly even an over-reaction to the perceived dangers and, surely, we would all be back before long?

The students were dismissed on the bell and filed out of the Hall to go home. There was the usual buzz of chatter as they exited but still the mood remained subdued. The teachers were the last to leave the space and we caught each other's eye, each looking troubled, bewildered by this unprecedented turn of events The following day would effectively be the last day of term. We were finishing two weeks before the Easter holiday.

Surely, everyone thought, we'd be back soon after that? Some people started saying that we'd be back after the summer half-term at the start of June. That seemed OK, I guessed. Enough to be able to get this virus beaten and then for things to return back to how they'd always been. Personally, I sincerely wanted us to back at school by then because I wanted to have that final six weeks of the summer term before my retirement. I needed to have that "winding down" time and that opportunity to acclimatise to the ending of my thirty-six years as a teacher (thirty-three of them in that school). I looked forward to a second half of the summer term with all the valedictory rituals of leaving: those final lessons and then the "goodbyes" with all of my different classes; the various social events with other members of staff (the farewell drinks sessions; the valedictory curry for a few selected mates; the delivering of my speech at the staff leavers' "do" with its carefully honed anecdotes and profuse expressions of thanks to the many colleagues to whom I owed a debt of gratitude over the years). Surely by the time we got to the end of the summer term, things would be back to normal and there wouldn't be anything still to disrupt the normal chain of events from unfolding...

The following day, I was due to say "Goodbye" to my form group for what was almost certainly going to be the last time. Normally, we would have said our farewells, before they all went off for their exams, in the second week of May. There would have been a big deal made of shirt-signing, selfies with "Sir", speechifying and all sorts of "farewell" shenanigans. We would have had a big final assembly with funny videos (teachers miming to pop songs and generally sending themselves up to massive cheers from the kids) and then various groups of students would have got up to perform. There would have been a number of student bands; there would have been musical performances from some of the classically trained musicians (a Mozart sonata; a Schubert song); some of the students might have read some of their own poems; one might have got up and shared a "personal view" of a particular issue, stand-up style. It would have been a cheerful, light-hearted, good-natured send-off for the whole year group before they went home and got changed into their finery for the Prom, which was always held on the evening of their last day.

Regrettably, with circumstances being what they were, there was to be no Final Assembly that morning. This was partly because the closure had been pretty much sprung on us and there had not been time to organise any large-scale event. Also, with the new Social Distancing rules, it was felt to be sensible to avoid any situation in which a large group might be brought together in a confined space like the assembly hall. Equally, the final Assembly was by its very nature, a cause for celebration and joy but it had to be acknowledged that there was little of either around now. It did not seem as if there was very much to celebrate. Better to let the students have their own quiet farewells to staff and each other and then to usher them quickly off the premises.

We were allowed a bit of extra time on that final morning for some semblance of the usual 'farewell rituals' to take place. Instead of taking the register and sending the students straight off to their lessons, we were allowed to keep them for a bit longer so that they could sign each other's shirts and engage in a small way in some of those 'closure' rituals which usually marked this rite of passage.

I took the register with them for the final time, feeling very emotional and only just about holding it together. I knew that, as a responsible adult, I had to set an example and give the impression that "normal service" would soon be resumed. However, the fact remained that we had worked together for almost five years but after that morning it was very likely that we would never ever be together as a group again. It all felt very final. There was a palpable sense of loss, even of grief in the air. I felt a huge wave of affection for them all, as if they were my children and that we were about to part from each other for the very last time. It was almost as if we were on the brink of war and that this was it before the lights went out and we were plunged into who knew what horrors.

There were touching little tokens, like cards and sweets and bottles of wine presented by some of my students. While I was moved and grateful for these, at the same time I did not want them. I wanted us to be able to complete the next two months together, not for us to be saying our goodbyes to each other now – so prematurely and with so little knowledge of what exactly the future might hold for us all.

After I'd taken the register, various individuals came up in time honoured fashion and asked me to sign their shirts. I wrote the usual messages wishing them well for their futures. They giggled and laughed as I did so and all too quickly the final moments of our time together slipped away. When the bell went for them to leave, I stood at the door to the form room, wishing each of them well. It felt like being in a movie about the world ending. I wanted to cry, I wanted to bellow but knew I would have to hold onto this until I was in the privacy of my own home later on that evening. As the last of them exited, I cleared some of the envelopes and sweet wrappers strewn around the empty table of our form room. That was well and truly it. They had gone. I was alone. We would never be together as a group ever again.

The rest of the morning I spent in a bit of a daze. I had a final lesson with a Year 8 class, promising to see them all "online" in the virtual classroom the following week and then a session with my A-level students. I decided to keep this as focused and snappy as I could. Usually, final lessons with exam classes in May were somewhat histrionic affairs. We'd generally be marking the end of a two-year association and it was always accepted that the final lesson before the students went off on exam leave would be something of a celebration. I'd usually bring in sweets and cakes. There'd be bottles of fizzy drink, popcorn and snacks. We'd put some music on and usually flash up onto the whiteboard photos from old drama productions, sometimes going back as far as Year 7. There'd be much hysterical laughter at the photo, say, of one of those sophisticated eighteen-year-old drama students dressed as a Munchkin in the school production of "The Wizard of Oz" seven years before and looking absolutely tiny and slightly bewildered. There'd then be a round of selfies and usually some sort of presentation, a nice bottle of wine or some chocs and a card in which they would all have written quirky little messages, which caused much amusement for days after. That particular morning, there was no card or gift from the students and I took in no treats. It did not feel appropriate in the circumstances to turn our last meeting together into a party. Besides, the course wasn't over yet. There was still two months' worth of work to go, as I kept banging on about in those final minutes we still had together. I put power points up of the work still to be covered and tried to be just very business-like and professional. I wanted to give a very clear signal that, while school might be closed, we would all need to try and carry on as normal while working from home and that there was still plenty of work to do. There was the portfolio to be completed outlining the preparation and rehearsal processes they had undertaken for their Performance exam; there were two Set Plays to revise and a sheaf of notes to be turned into probing critiques of the various theatre trips we had been on during the two years of the course. There was loads still to do. While it was all very well for me to stand up at the front of the class and babble on about all the written work to be completed, I was aware of the fact that these students were all budding actors. This was why they had opted to take the course in Theatre Studies in the first place. They weren't necessarily writers but they could all of them very definitely act. I wanted to give them a chance to demonstrate this before we said our final goodbyes. Therefore, I created time, about half-way through the lesson for them each to have a little performance opportunity. They had all been working on scenes which they were preparing to show to the Visiting Examiner at the start of the following term. While these performances had been cancelled, they had all learnt their lines and had worked the scenes up to pretty much performance standard. It seemed fitting, then, that we should end the lesson with a "workshop" performance of each of their scenes. I wanted to see where they had got with these and I also wanted them to have an opportunity to show their work to each other. Most importantly, because it was a Drama course, I wanted them to have the chance to Act. There may not be another opportunity for some time to come, I reasoned, and it was important that we finished on a high.

The students acted their scenes: a sequence from "A Day in the Death of Joe Egg" and some moments from "Night Mother" by Marsha Norman. The students clearly relished this opportunity to show each other what they could do. Their acting that morning was brilliant: full of energy, attack, emotion, fire. It was like watching a troupe of professional performers. There was no doubt in my mind, based on what they had shown me, that they would all have got top grades if they had been allowed to show their work to a visiting examiner. This was high-end, top-quality stuff. I felt very moved and privileged at their willingness to share their work that morning.

Lunch on that last day was a hasty sandwich grabbed on the

hoof while packing bags and tidying up in the way that normally only happened on the very last day of term. I began clearing away the weeks and months' worth of paper from my desk: the minutes of meetings; the print outs of instructions from the exam boards; the pages of student essays; the flyers for theatre productions; the adverts for educational resources. I chucked out old biros, paper clips, glue sticks, post-it notes, plastic folders and filled umpteen black plastic rubbish bags with the detritus of a term. Outside on the playground, the students kicked balls around as normal at lunchtime, shrieking and yelling at each other as they chased around. It didn't seem very different to a normal school day and the idea that we wouldn't be here again on Monday was still difficult to comprehend.

I had a study period straight after lunch, so carried on with my tidying up. I packed several carrier bags worth of books to take home and which I intended to use in the planning of my online lessons. I had play-scripts, theatre history books and books of drama games, knowing that I would need to use these for inspiration if the requirement for online teaching continued.

When the bell went at 2.25 p.m., that was the signal for the students to clear the school. Normally, on the last day of term, this would be a cause for some jubilation and there would usually be some sort of high-jinx perpetrated to accompany it. As staff, we were generally encouraged to make ourselves visible to help usher the students off the premises quickly and efficiently, discouraging any incidents of poor behaviour. On this afternoon, though, it seemed that the students needed no encouragement to beat a hasty retreat. Perhaps they were conscious of the fact that according to the government they should not have been out at all. They needed to be holed up in their houses, Staying Home and Protecting the NHS, as we had all been told to do. They were all gone, vanished, within a few minutes and their exit was quiet and solemn. They knew to make a fast and discreet disappearance, setting out for their homes quickly and with an awareness of the dangers that now lurked abroad.

Staff, on the other hand, had been invited to the staffroom for a "Farewell" drink. I must say, that I was siding rather with the students on this and would have preferred to have beaten a hasty retreat but I was told by some of my chums on the staff that I couldn't be so miserable and that, anyway, this might be our last chance to all be together for some time and that I jolly well needed to go.

Also, I didn't really want to start drinking at three o'clock in the afternoon but then it wasn't a normal day and it wasn't as if we were going to be hanging around for long. It would be a quick glass of wine, then off. And anyway, it would be nice, I reasoned, to have some sort of closure – to feel that we were all in this together and to share the strangeness of this unprecedented truncated term with each other.

When I arrived at the staff room, there were some opened bottles of red and white wine, plus some soft drink options and a crate of clean wine glasses to which people were encouraged to help themselves. I poured myself a generous glass of red and went and sat down with a group of mates. At first, we tried to observe the new social-distancing laws, all attempting to sit 2 metres apart by leaving alternate chairs empty but as the staffroom filled up these strictures were quickly ignored. After a few gulps of wine, the mood started to become quite celebratory. After all, we had effectively been given a two-week extension to the Easter holiday and were "breaking up" two weeks earlier than normal. Yes, we were all expected to be online next week and there would be the usual round of after-school meetings at which we'd be required to put in an appearance (albeit remotely) but at least we would be in our own homes. We wouldn't need to be getting up at the crack of dawn, as on a normal school day. We could make ourselves coffees and teas and drink these while at our laptops and for lots of the classes, they had already been set work, so we wouldn't need to be physically present on the screen for those lessons. The main thing was, though, that we would all be home. We wouldn't be at work. Surely there was something to be said for that?

As the wine started to flow, an atmosphere of hilarity and jubilation began to prevail. There was much bumping of elbows and laughter. There were many little stories swapped of final lessons given that morning and then of incidents in the wider world: outrage at the continued supermarket queues; at the idiocies of the government; at the bluff heartiness of the Prime Minister; at the nerdiness of the Medical Advisers and Scientists. There was the usual speculation about how long it was expected to go on for. When would we be back? Early May or after the summer half-term? Surely not September?

I started to wonder whether this would indeed be the last occasion on which I would sit in the school staffroom. For years, at the ends of the summer term, we had congregated as a whole staff to say a formal "Goodbye" to departing colleagues. These were always hilarious occasions. The person leaving would do a speech, clearly carefully scripted and full of funny anecdotes and stories: the condom which flew across the science lab; the disastrous foreign exchange trip when the plane returning to Gatwick got diverted to Glasgow; the Food Tech lesson in which the whole class got food poisoning; the music concert at which the solo violinist fell off the front of the stage; the Awards Ceremony at which the guest speaker giving out the prizes turned up too drunk to read out any of the students' names. This year, of course, it would be my turn to deliver my farewell speech, something which I had already started to prepare in my head. I imagined myself standing there in five months' time, everyone in thrall at what I had to say and chortling dutifully as I crystalised my thirty-three-year career into a series of laugh-out-loud stories and finished with a heartfelt series of maxims on how to survive in the classroom. As I sat there now, surrounded by people moaning about the imminent lockdown restrictions and telling funny stories about not being able to buy any toilet paper and sharing their recipes for home-made hand sanitizer, I started to become aware of the fact that maybe this was it. Maybe we wouldn't be together again as a whole staff – not next term, anyway. What if this was it? What if there was to be no "Farewell" staff gathering next term and that this really was my final day? This surely could not happen. Here we were, not even at the end of March. The end of July seemed like an age away. Surely things would be back to normal by then? That was an age away, wasn't it?

People started to leave. It was clear that nobody wanted to hang around for very long. Unlike at the end of most staff gatherings, there was to be no group exodus to the local pub in order to prolong the proceedings. This was "Have your drink and go". Again, though, social distancing got forgotten about and people started to hug and embrace the colleagues whom they thought they may not be seeing again for some time. Already, there were some staff off ill – purportedly with Covid-19 – although, as far as we knew, none of them had been taken seriously ill with it. We were, for that reason, a little depleted that day and their absence was a bit of a reminder that illness, potentially life-threatening, was lurking beneath the surface. There were serious dangers to be taken account of and that could not help but impact on the otherwise party atmosphere.

One by one, people left, bravely attempting to stay cheerful, upbeat, optimistic. By about four p.m., the place was almost deserted. I went back to my office and collected my bags and my laptop and piled everything into my car. As I drove out of the by now almost empty car park, I wondered when and how we would all be coming back.

When I got home, I felt strangely deflated. What now, I wondered? It was late afternoon on a Friday. Friday nights were usually for going to the pub or out to a restaurant or round to a friend's house for dinner or out to watch a movie. But no. "Stay at Home and Protect the NHS" was the instruction. I had some food in the fridge left over from the night before. I'd have to heat that up in the microwave and then see what was on the telly: the usual Friday night fare of a double episode of "Coronation Street", a couple of travel programmes, cookery with Jamie and then Graham Norton. None of it particularly inspiring. Then what tomorrow?

To start with, I guess, it all seemed a bit of an adventure. I'd had friends coming over for a bite to eat and some wine on the Saturday evening but, of course, now we had thought it wise to cancel. This was disappointing but there was a sort of ambivalence as well: a sort of smug feeling that we were being "good" and obeying the government's instructions, doing our bit. There was also a kind of novelty value about the whole situation. This crisis was an extraordinary situation and we had to all knuckle down and do what we were told. It would not be forever but for the time being normal life was suspended and we could no longer do whatever we fancied. My Saturday nights were always planned weeks in advance and usually involved a theatre trip or a film or a meal or a pub meeting so there was a kind of novelty value in spending that evening at home, on my own. I even have to admit to a slight feeling of relief at the thought of not having to entertain: not having to go out and buy food and cook it; not having to clean and tidy up my flat; not having to spend the whole evening talking and listening and attempting to scintillate. Instead, I'd have a nice, quiet evening in watching the tv and cooking something tasty for myself and then I'd go to bed early and sober in the hope of a decent night's sleep, for once. So that first Saturday and that first Sunday, I spent completely on my own. There were phone calls, texts and WhatsApp messages and there was a slightly exciting sense of the drama that we were all caught up in. It was a bit like living through a disaster movie. None of us had any idea of what was going to happen or for how long we'd be banned from work or from leaving our homes but for now there was almost a sense of adventure and excitement around.

By mid-afternoon on that Sunday, I suppose I was starting to feel a little flat and somewhat starved of company. At the same time, though, there was a sense of "No, this is what we have to do. It's hard for everyone in different ways and it's certainly no harder for me than for anyone else so just put up and shut up!" By Sunday evening the feeling of "ennui" was running quite deep. On the other hand, it was difficult not to feel a kind of sneaking joy at the prospect of not having to get up at the crack of dawn on the following Monday morning. In spite of the pandemic and the dire situation, it was hard not to feel almost as if the school holiday had arrived a fortnight early.

The start of that week was the first week of online teaching. I had set work for all of my classes on Google classrooms and told them that I would be online to answer any questions. I dutifully logged on at about nine a.m. and waited to be bombarded by student queries. There was nothing. There were the predicted emails from the Head and Senior staff about protocols and the need to keep the pressure on the students until the end of term but very few students contacted me about the work which I had set them to do. That was, apart from the Year 7 students who did start to email fairly frequently with questions about my instructions. They seemed to have a lot of questions and were asking for clarification about how the work should be presented, its length and its format. I answered these queries promptly, keen to give the impression that I was available and willing to support, albeit remotely.

On the second day, we had a virtual Head of Departments meeting in which we were all invited to share how we were coping with the requirement for online teaching. As with many such "sharing" sessions, this became a license for some to just show off and brag in the most fulsome way and I quickly lost interest. Nobody seemed to have any interest in what I had been doing – either because of my imminent retirement, I was already considered to be a non-person or because my contributions were of little value. Either way, the meeting just left me feeling a bit useless and redundant. It was all so new, the technology we were now supposed to be using and full of bewildering numbers of choices and permutations. Some of the dab hands raced through various options they had been pursuing: "You can do this... you can do that... What I find works really well is... Something the students have really enjoyed doing is... I can strongly recommend that you all..."

"Let's try and see this as an opportunity," we were told. "Let's use this experience to develop our skills as professionals... We still need to be providing the highest quality lessons, even though we are no longer actually in the classroom."

It felt like a lot of pressure. It made me feel inadequate and definitely past my sell-by date. In the end, I thought it best just to keep my head down until the end of term in two weeks' time and then try and make a more concerted effort to get to grips with these new-fangled teaching tools at the start of the following term. Hang on till April and then take a fresh approach.

Those last days of March there was a mad scramble to get everything in before everywhere was locked down. The car had to be taken in for an MOT (of course, they found something wrong with the brake pads – so there was an unexpected major expense); I queued forever to get one of the last haircuts at the local Turkish barber and managed to get a modest stash of toilet rolls from Sainsbury's, which then sat for weeks perched on the top of my kitchen cupboards.

For the online schooling, I dutifully logged on at 8.45 a.m. each morning, regardless of whether I had a class or not. There always seemed to be huge numbers of emails to answer (from the Head and Deputies; from students and parents and all sorts of bodies which had suddenly sprung up to offer "support" with online teaching). Students sent essays and work in which needed to be marked and sent back. It seemed quite easy to fill the morning and to finish it with that slightly smug feeling of having been productive for all of the four hours. At one o'clock I'd break and make myself a cheese sandwich and maybe catch the news and then at 1.45 p.m. it was back to the laptop until

3.45 p.m. It really was not dissimilar to a normal working day.

At the same time, there would be WhatsApp and text messages from friends and funny little memes exchanged and forwarded on, all of which helped to lighten the mood. These were all ways of reaching out and reminding ourselves that we were all in it together. The phone proved to be a dependable and very welcome distraction from the drain of online teaching. So it was that the last couple of weeks of the spring term passed by and almost before we knew it, we had arrived at the end of March. We had somehow managed to get through the first couple of weeks of lockdown.

April

The start of April coincided with the beginning of what would in the normal course of events have been the school holiday. This meant that certainly for the next couple of weeks, there was no longer the requirement to crawl out of bed and log on to the laptop at first light in order to begin a day of remote teaching. A different type of rhythm to the day started to establish itself.

One thing I realised very early on in this process was that I would need to keep myself as healthy as possible in order to cope with the challenges of the new regime: I tried to eat well and to avoid all convenience foods; I banned myself from alcohol, tried to limit my intake of sugar and aimed to get as much exercise and sleep as possible.

As soon as the school holiday kicked in, I made myself stay in bed for an hour longer each morning, getting up at 7.30 rather than an hour earlier. I would aim to be in bed by 11 p.m. at the latest and hoped that way I would get my necessary eight hours.

I have always been a great reader and one of the pleasures of weekends and holidays has always been having the time to read more. Therefore, I would always spend at least an hour each morning after breakfast just sitting in my chair and reading a good chunk of whatever book I happened to be reading at the time. First thing in the morning is an ideal time to read: the light is clear and bright and your mind is receptive and alert. It has always felt like one of the most enjoyable of pleasures to be able to immerse myself in a fictional world for an hour or so before the day begins. It feels like a workout for the imagination: the joy of being able to lose myself in a story and a world and characters away from my own life.

One of the most remarkable things about those first few weeks of lockdown, however, was the amazing Spring weather. Every morning that April, we all seemed to awake to radiant sunshine and to cloudless blue skies. Also, the streets were eerily silent. Remarkably, it seemed that everybody was doing what the government had told us to do. People were indeed "staying at home and protecting the NHS" so there was almost no traffic at all on the roads. Living alongside quite a busy road, I was used to the almost incessant thundering of traffic from before dawn to last thing at night. Now, though, cars on the road had almost become something of a rarity. Not only were the roads almost completely silent but you could also now hear the birds in a way that we had never been able to do before. Normally, I suppose, their songs were drowned out by the constant drone of traffic noise but now the joyous chirruping of the bird population seemed to surround and envelop us all. The beauty of these natural sounds, together with the wonderful and warming sunshine and the glorious blue skies made this a spring season like no other.

It hardly seemed to fit with the horrors we were continuing to hear about on the news. The numbers of those infected and then the figures for the dead were rising relentlessly. Footage of crowded hospital wards and exhausted doctors and nurses began to dominate every news broadcast. People watched with a morbid fascination, hoping that things could not possibly get any worse but every day it seemed that they did. The news got grimmer and grimmer but none of it seemed to fit with the spring sunshine, the longer days, the bright blue skies and the summer holiday clothes which people were starting to wear.

In my block of flats, people had taken to opening their doors and spreading out on to the lawns of the communal gardens at the back. Generally, these were deserted by the residents for most of the year apart from for a few odd days at the very height of the summer, when you might see the occasional sun lounger or deck chair left out there. Now, however, because people had nowhere else to go and because the weather was uncharacteristically enticing, people started to set up camp on the lawns round the back. People would put out their camping chairs and beach towels on the grass, settling down for the whole day with a magazine, some snacks and a glass of something refreshing. Being a communal area, people tended to stake out an area for themselves, establishing their own patch of grass if they weren't living on the ground floor, with access to a terrace. This normally silent area started to become quite a congenial and sociable place, as neighbours who had lived cheek by jowl with each other for years but never spoken suddenly started waving to each other and gossiping together. Many of the flats were one-bedroom apartments occupied by people living on their own and most of us were now starting to feel rather starved of company. Having spent days in what was effectively solitary confinement, now suddenly there were people to talk with and some company on hand. Of course, it had its downsides as well. There was a lady on the ground floor underneath me (I was on the top floor). who insisted on sitting outside and chatting on the phone to her friends in a very loud voice that was impossible to ignore. These conversations seemed to go on for hours and, from the sound of it (she was speaking in Turkish so I didn't actually know) there always seemed to be some sort of drama going on that she was desperate to impart to her listeners. There were great intakes of breath and sighs and exclamations and shrieks of disbelief accompanied by loud, cackling laughter – all of which was shared with the rest of us with complete disregard for our privacy or need for quiet. Not only was she extremely loud every time she was talking on her phone, oblivious to everyone else's needs, she also seemed to be a bit of a party girl. Around five p.m. in the afternoon, she'd turn her music on and bottles would be brought out, corks popped, drinks poured and glasses clinked. This would invariably be accompanied by the arrival of a friend, whose car would screech to a halt noisily in the car park and then the two of them would sit outside on her terrace, jabbering away until late into the evening both of them speaking at full volume (as in the phone conversations). It was impossible not to ignore and not to feel invaded by this unwelcome intrusion into the peace and tranquillity of those early spring evenings. (Not to mention the fact that under the new rules visitors just weren't allowed. How was she able to get away with being able to invite a friend round for a night of prosecco guzzling when the rest of us had to sit cooped up in our rooms completely "a seul"?)

I guess it was partly the being cooped up that made me particularly sensitive to noise intrusion at that time. Like many people, I was sitting for hours in my flat on my own and with the arrival of the warmer weather I'd begun opening the windows in order to let in some fresh air, in a way that I had not done all winter. However, with the open windows, I started to become aware of all the different noises that were coming in from outside. On top of the occasional car noise and the lovely, natural birdsong there was also a constant barrage of different sounds from my neighbours. In addition to the Turkish lady downstairs forever bellowing into her phone, there was the sound of children playing up and down the estate and in between the cars in the car park, riding their tricycles, shouting out to each other, laughing and getting told off by their watchful parents; there were the dulcet tones of Radio 2 emanating from the older lady downstairs; the sounds of hedge trimmers from the larger, more affluent houses across the way; the shouted conversations of couples out for walks trudging past the fence just outside my window. The other flats in my block also had their windows open because of the sunnier weather so there was the incessant sound of washing machines, vacuum cleaners, tumble dryers, as well as the sizzling of frying pans, the clatter of cutlery, the slamming of doors. I could hear shouted conversations, heated arguments, hysterical giggling, even the breathy panting of people having sex, on occasion. All these noises, which in the normal course of things would be kept behind closed doors, now made a veritable sound collage all through the day and for some of the night.

One night early in April, I was lying in bed trying to get to sleep when I became aware of group of people sat outside drinking and talking on the lawn at the back of my block. They sounded like they were sitting out there directly underneath my bedroom window. I looked down and could see about half a dozen people all sprawled out on sun loungers and folding chairs, engaged in animated exchanges with each other but in a language that I wasn't familiar with. The Turkish lady seemed to be entertaining. Glasses clinked, there was much laughter and what sounded like heated discussion, but about what I had no idea. The noise they were making was extremely intrusive and I wondered how long it was going to go on for. I tried to read a book but couldn't concentrate. All I could feel was anger and intense annoyance that these people were being so inconsiderate of the other residents in the block. How dare they? I fumed and felt exasperated, belittled, invaded. How the hell could they be so thoughtless?

I tried putting on headphones and listening to music but all the time the hubbub of their conversation intruded. I'd try to listen to the sounds made by the music but all the time, I was listening out for the sounds of the chatter coming from downstairs which seemed to get louder and more heated as more and more drink was consumed. It felt like an assault, an invasion of my privacy and space. Also, how dare these people be communing together when we had all been told so unambiguously to keep ourselves apart?

Eventually and well after midnight, I could hear that the party was starting to break up. However, by now my hackles had been raised and I was then unable to sleep. I lay there for hours wondering what I was going to do. I could not put up with this for weeks on end if these social events were set to continue throughout the summer on a regular basis.

Also, their noise as well as making me feel angry and invaded, made me feel intensely lonely. There was I lying in bed, alone, trying to get to sleep and there they all were carousing and partying and taking over all of the communal space downstairs without a single thought for others. I felt excluded and disregarded, as if I was some sort of "non-person" whose feelings did not matter. So insignificant was I that my presence was not even on their radar. Not for a single second would my existence have even registered with them. These thoughts raced through my mind all night long, completely obliterating any possibility of sleep. My whole body was tense with anger and a kind of ferocity against them all. I wanted to lash out and explode but instead had to keep it all contained and suppressed.

I got up the next morning completely exhausted and raw from lack of sleep. I felt like I had been lumbered with a major problem. If we were to be incarcerated in our homes for months on end, how was I supposed to put up with this if these gatherings turned out to be a regular fixture? Even if they were not, every evening I would now be on edge waiting for it all to start up again; waiting for the noises of conviviality to rise up from outside my window and to invade my own silent space with the noise of others' partying and carousing.

I thought that somehow, I needed to tackle the ring leader of these little get-togethers and I must make her aware of my existence. We had never spoken to each other and I never ever ventured out on to the lawns at the back of the apartment block, which had always seemed to be the province just of the people who owned the ground floor apartments. Perhaps she was oblivious to the fact that there were other people living here? She clearly had no idea that all her party noise might disturb the people with flats just above hers.

Taking my courage in both hands, I gathered a few things together and decided to plonk myself out on the communal lawn. I had a beach towel, some sunglasses, a small rucksack for my phone and water bottle and a copy of "Bleak House" which I had started to plough through a couple of days before. Wearing shorts, trainers, a tee shirt and a baseball cap, I spread my towel out on the lawn and settled down almost as if on the beach for a morning of sunbathing and reading. Again, I was finding it hard to concentrate. I was aware of the fact that I was there on a sort of mission. I thought I would try and speak to the noise perpetrator and to establish some sort of line of communication. I just wanted to make my presence, my existence, known. I felt like a stalker, lying in wait there for her to emerge from her lair and then I would tackle her – or at least say "Hello" and make her aware of who I was and get her to think about whether her party from the previous evening might have created some sort of disturbance. We did all have to live together and alongside each other at this especially difficult time and she needed to be respectful of others' needs.

I was not getting very far with "Bleak House". It was a weighty volume and at almost nine hundred pages was a real door stop of a read. I was lying on my back and trying to hold the book up in front of me but that was extremely uncomfortable. Also, all the time I was rehearsing in my head, what I was going to say to the Turkish lady if and when she eventually emerged.

I was lying on a patch of grass just in front of one of the terraces of one of the unoccupied ground floor flats, the flat next door to hers. This had previously been occupied by another noisy and inconsiderate neighbour who had allowed her dog outside to bark and run around at six o'clock on the morning. This woman had thankfully departed a few weeks ago but her flat had been left vacant and I dreaded the prospect of who was going to take over down there. Was it going to be another anti-social tenant? Another noise perpetrator?

At that moment, the patio doors of the unoccupied flat were flung open by a lady in a smart suit, with too much make-up and neatly cut hair. She was in mid-flow, extolling the virtues of the development and showing round what looked like two prospective new tenants. They seemed to be a young couple. He was in checked shorts and bearded and his girlfriend or partner was in a sort of sun dress.

"Perfect space for entertaining – especially in the summer months." I heard the estate agent lady say.

"Yes, great for a barbeque." the young man added, in what sounded like an Australian accent.

Instantly I was filled with a feeling of dread. Here were what seemed like two more party animals, intent on moving in and inflicting more noise and mayhem on what used to be a haven of peace and quiet. As they stood on the terraced area of the ground floor apartment, surveying the lawns and greenery before them, envisaging the hordes of guests they no doubt intended to invite in order to destroy the sanctuary of my home with their noise and inane chatter and raucous drunkenness.

I put down my Charles Dickens and stared at them menacingly, hoping to ward them off.

"All right mate?" the young bloke said, as he caught my eye. Rather thrown by this, I could only muster a tight-lipped "Yes, fine thanks," by way of response and then had to look away. I didn't want to seem too hostile just in case they did end up moving in to the apartment they were there to view.

The Estate Agent was there for the rest of the morning, giving her spiel to a succession of prospective tenants who marched through the place at fifteen-minute intervals. Surely this wasn't going to be allowed under the new government restrictions? Surely, we could not have new people moving in here with removal men traipsing through the communal areas at a time when we were being told to minimise contact? In my head, I composed an email which I would fire off to the management company later on that afternoon in order to try and prevent such an eventuality.

At long last, the Turkish lady emerged from her ground

floor apartment and threw herself down on a pink beach towel, which she had spread out on the lawn a few feet away from her terrace. Feeling uncharacteristically bold, I thought that I would initiate some conversation:

"Hello... Did you know that they are letting out that flat?" I said, indicating the downstairs apartment next door to hers that the estate agent had just been showing people round.

"Really? ... So there going to be new people there?" she replied in her broken English.

"Yes, it would seem so... I didn't think that people were allowed to move house at the moment. I wonder if the Management Company knows about this?"

She pouted by way of response. I wondered if she was aware of the Management Company and that they existed to oversee the management of the whole building and to see that everyone abided by the terms of the lease (which included not inflicting anti-social noise on others).

"Which flat you live in?" she asked me suddenly. "I never seen you before."

I pointed at my flat on the top floor and counted the four windows which belonged to it.

"We had a few drinks last night..." she murmured. "I lose track of time... Hope you weren't disturbed?"

Wow! I thought. A kind of apology – unsolicited. How should I respond?

I started to mumble, embarrassed that it was almost as if she'd been reading my mind.

"Er... no," I lied – and then thought how on earth could I be so feeble? "But you did seem to be out here till quite late..." |I felt foolishly goofy and awkward, crippled by my usual diffidence and inability to be direct.

"Yea...we had a good time. Was nice..."

Was there going to be any more apology – or was that it?

She continued. "I just not feeling so good this morning..."

Her phone started pinging and she turned to answer it. She then wandered off down the lawn out of earshot. That was probably as much of an apology as I was ever going to get. Nevertheless, at least she'd met me and knew that I existed now and she seemed to show a slight awareness of the fact that her party had gone on later than it should have done. That was a start, at least...

I lay back on my towel and attempted to get through a bit more of "Bleak House", trying to fool myself that I was on a beach somewhere exotic rather than just stuck out on the grass round the back of my flat in suburban Enfield. For all its mundanity, there was something almost magical about the unusually sunny weather at that time and the almost total lack of traffic noise in those early weeks of lockdown. Nothing felt normal. Lying out there on the grass, with the trees coming into leaf, the birdsong and the New River flowing tranquilly by, it was almost blissful. You had to pinch yourself to remind yourself that we were in the midst of a frightening and depressing national crisis.

The television news constantly reminded us of that, as did the daily briefings from Downing Street in which the Prime Minister and the Scientists informed us of how they were dealing with things and alerted us all to the severity of the situation. There were many conflicting feelings in those early days. It was hard not to have a childish sense of almost enjoying the drama of the situation. Here we all were caught up in something catastrophic, with no sense of how we were ever going to get out of it. There were frequent references to this being our generation's 'war' – reinforced by the frequent singing of Vera Lynn's "We'll Meet Again" which was even invoked by the Queen in her broadcast to the nation. People talked about "Doing their bit" when they spoke about signing up to volunteer or going to knock on an elderly neighbour's door to help the with their shopping. It was like being in battle. It was a fight. We all had to 'fight' to contain the virus; 'fight' to stay healthy, to stay sane.

There was one image that I personally found particularly frightening and ominous and that was the footage of the new Nightingale hospitals. These were large converted warehouses or huge exhibition spaces, which had been divided into rows and rows of hospital beds, field hospital style. My imagination could not shake off the sheer misery and desolation at the prospect of ending up in one of those places. They looked like great battery hen farms, in which a human being would be reduced to mere body parts. I imagined the noise and the stench and the suffering. They conjured something from a different era, like the Crimean war, hence I guess the term 'Nightingale' hospitals. I shuddered with horror at the thought of ever being admitted to one but as the numbers of infections rose steadily so did the death toll, I felt that being incarcerated in one of those places was surely inevitable for some of us. Being over sixty and having high blood pressure, wasn't I surely 'at risk'? Was it going to be my destiny to end up in one of those terrifying places? Such a grim fate seemed almost certainly to be on the cards at that time and this prospect cast a deep shadow over those early days. It was as if one was waiting for the disease to strike. It was never a case of would it get me but when and how?

This paranoia and certainty that I was marked out to be taken by the disease was further reinforced when I heard some alarming news about an ex-colleague. For several weeks, since the pandemic had started to run its course in the UK, we had been getting news about a fellow teacher who seemed to have been struck down by the disease. He was one of the first people many of us had known to have been directly affected. His name was Andrew and I had worked alongside him for thirty years. He had retired from our school a few years previously but had since been keeping himself busy by doing various part-time teaching jobs at some of the more prestigious private schools in the area. This man was one of those all too rare 'born' teachers. He had the most extraordinary gift for communicating knowledge and had such astute insights, with a real eye for a quirky detail and a telling anecdote. He was one of those teachers who was universally respected by everyone, staff and students alike, with a passion for his subject and a razor-sharp mind. Andrew was a large man, well over six feet tall and with a huge presence and personality and enormous charisma. He wasn't one of those teachers who needed power points or groovy gimmicks or armfuls of 'resources'. He just brought himself into the classroom and his listeners were enthralled and enlightened by everything he said.

It was with some alarm, therefore, that news started to filter through that he had been struck down by the illness. Few of us knew anyone personally who had suffered with it or, if we did, it seemed that they had only had mild symptoms. His experience of the disease sounded disturbingly severe, however. We heard that he was being treated in Barnet General hospital, which certainly did not sound like good news. Then word came through that he was being put on a ventilator, which sounded extremely serious. Our school seemed to be getting almost daily bulletins and every so often it would sound like there was a flicker of hope or of more positive news but then a day or so later things would start to sound bad again. Eventually, word came through that he had been released from hospital and we all breathed a collective sigh of relief. It was impossible to imagine that such an enormous character could be brought down by this, especially when we were being told by the government that most people's experience of the disease would not be much worse than some mild flu-like symptoms. Anyway, he was now out of hospital and presumably on the road to recovery....

In those early days, it still seemed hard to comprehend that anyone could ever be seriously ill with the virus. Yes, there were news stories and images from hospitals which clearly told a different story but among the people that one knew, they were either immune or just laid up for a few days but not seriously affected. And even Andrew, who had been bad with it, was now out of hospital and presumably on the road to recovery.

A few days later, though, I started to get texts from friends who knew him more closely than I did. It seemed that he had now relapsed. The recovery which we had all been told about seemed to have been reversed. He was now back in hospital. Things did not sound good at all.

Eventually, we got the devastating news that he had died. This was deeply shocking and almost incomprehensible. How could such a strong and charismatic character have been taken by this thing? It didn't happen to people that we knew. How could it have happened to someone so bright, so strong, so intelligent, so wise, so talented?

Rumours started to circulate: apparently, he had been working part-time at a posh school up in Hertfordshire. The girls at the school had all been on a ski-trip to Northern Italy during the February half-term. They returned to school the following week and many of them must have been carrying the virus. He had certainly contracted it not long afterwards as had, so we heard, other teachers at that school. None had been so badly affected as him, however.

His death was a deeply sad and momentous milestone in the progress of the disease. Here was a person of such energy and brilliance who had been just wiped out by it. How could this bastard thing do that to someone like him?

The next few days were overshadowed by this sombre news. Although the weather continued to be like mid-summer, this tragedy cast a terrible pall over everything. I remember, one of my friends from school dropped by while on a cycle ride and we chatted for a few minutes on the lawn outside at the back of my flat. We were both stunned by what had happened. Normally we would laugh and joke together and tell scurrilous stories about the other people that we worked with but that morning there was very little of that. It brought home to us how vulnerable we all were and how tenuous our hold on life was during this uncertain and deeply threatening time.

I felt strange seeing my friend from work again, that morning. Meeting to chat round the back of the flat, outside, our short interaction felt strangely illicit, as if we were doing something that was not allowed. After all, we had been told to keep ourselves apart and not to mix socially but surely having a short conversation, several metres apart but out in the open air was no different to chatting briefly with one of the neighbours on the lawn outside. Was it?

As my friend got on her bike and cycled off, I did not realise at the time, that this would be the last person I would talk to (apart from brief chats across the lawn with one or two neighbours) for some weeks.

Now began that period of intense isolation that was quite unlike any other time I had ever experienced in my life. Yes, I lived alone but for much of every day I was off out working and interacting with (quite literally) hundreds of different people. During the course of my work as a school teacher, I had dozens of different interactions with students, colleagues, non-teaching members of staff, parents, outside agencies. At the start of some days, I was crowded along with everyone else into a massive assembly hall for the beginning of the school morning, all of us sitting in rows listening to some presentation or other as one of an audience of over a thousand. Along with everyone else, I was jostled down the school corridor at the change-over between lessons, fighting my way between the slowly moving crowd of students and other teachers as we made our way between lessons. For most of the day, I was talking and listening and "giving out", verbalising. Giving instructions, information, opinions, insights, views; sharing enthusiasms, cajoling, admonishing, reassuring, reprimanding, clarifying. From 8.30 in the morning through to almost six o'clock at night I was engaged in some kind of talk with other human beings.

Now, however, it was going to be weeks and weeks of just me. Alone in my flat. Occasionally talking on the phone or Zooming but basically on my own and for much of the day, silent. Certainly, nobody would be coming inside my flat for the foreseeable future.

As a working person, used to being out for most of the day, I had relied on a cleaner to keep my home looking presentable and ship-shape. Within a few days of the lockdown starting, she texted me and asked if she could continue to come and clean. I have to say that I had misgivings about this. When we had been told so emphatically that we were not supposed to mix with others or to visit others' homes, I no longer felt very comfortable about having her in my flat. At the same time, I was aware of the fact that if everybody who employed her told her not come any more then she would be left without an income. When we texted each other about what to do, she assured me that she would wear gloves and a mask and that she was only visiting a few other houses and that, as far as she was concerned, there would be no danger to health. I'm afraid I thought that she would say that, wouldn't she? After all, she needed to hold on to her job.

I did not feel easy about this at all. The thought of her going in and out of other people's houses and carrying possible infections with her: the thought of her transmitting the virus to my floors, door handles, surfaces, worktops, bedding, carpets, sinks, taps and all the other potential carriers of the disease in my home was more than I felt willing to countenance. I would have to say "No". She then texted back and asked if she could at least come and pick up some ironing from me once a fortnight, clearly desperate to hold on to at least that meagre source of income. Again, I had to decline.

After that I never heard from her again. This saddened me somewhat, as I had to come to rely on her over the years but these were extraordinary circumstances and I really could not allow somebody into my home on a regular basis when we were all being told so clearly to keep apart. It was the thought of her inadvertently spreading disease which made the prospect just so untenable.

I could tell from the tone of the final texts that she felt angry and hard done by but I wondered what I was supposed to do. Should I have sent her some money anyway, as a kind of "retainer"? But to post a cheque for twenty quid or so just for doing nothing went very much against the grain. And how long for? Every fortnight? For the next however many months? That just seemed crazy. On the other hand, to just stand by and turn my back while the poor woman's income completely collapsed did make me feel like a real heel. 'Heartless bastard' I dubbed myself but at the same time realised that I could not possibly have opened my home up to such a potential risk in the current crisis and, that way, I was able to justify my behaviour to myself.

This did leave me with a problem, though. How was I going to keep my flat clean? Especially as I would be living in it twenty-four seven and would no longer be absent from it for most of the day while out at work. The mess, the dust, the dirt was likely to mount up exponentially. On the other hand, I was going to need things to do in order to get through the long, solitary and confined days. Cleaning could therefore become a new activity, a new way of getting through the hours.

Coincidentally, I watched a TV show just on this very subject around that time. It was one of those 'How Clean is Your House' type shows which dealt with cleaning from the very same perspective: we were all going to be confined indoors for probably weeks, so essential that we all know how to keep our homes 'Germ Free' at this crucial time.

I found the programme very instructive and illuminating. Wearing a plastic apron and rubber gloves, the lead presenter would wipe the surfaces of a suburban living room and then reveal the horrors contained therein. Using a microscope to magnify the various bacteria she had managed to sweep up, I reeled at the wriggling and menacing looking microbes apparently lurking underneath sofa cushions or attached to mattresses or clinging to the inside of washing up bowls. It was an eye opener and sent me off out to stand in the supermarket queue forthwith, ready to fill my trolley with bleach, sprays, cleansers, antibacterial wipes, oven cleaners, drain un-blockers, dusters, jay-cloths, scourers and anything else that could be used in the war against the bugs and bacteria apparently residing in my home.

From that day on, I launched a campaign to get my home "deep cleaned" in a way that it had scarcely been for years, in spite of my cleaner's best efforts. It was a fact that she had whizzed through the whole place in about half an hour and as I began my cleaning marathon, it became woefully apparent that the place had not been cleaned properly for years.

As I began to scrub away at the skirting boards and under the bed and on top of the kitchen cupboards, I became aware of the fact that this was going to be a gargantuan task. It was certainly more than just a couple of mornings' worth of work. As I scraped years and years of congealed grease and dust off the top of the cupboard housing my gas boiler, I realised that my cleaning regime was going to need to be a bit more systematic and thorough. Therefore, I decided to do a room at a time.

I started with the bedroom. The first task was to get right in between the skirting board and the carpet and to really start to scrape away at the grime and dust that had accumulated there. This turned out to be back-breaking and exhausting work. Because of the warmer weather and in spite of having the windows wide open, I found myself breaking into a sweat as I did battle with the dirt. I scraped and scraped away at it and then had to hoover it all up and that was before I even thought about tackling the years and years of dust which lay underneath the bed. For that, I had to heave the bed up on its end and try to get beneath it, completely appalled at the thick layers of dust which lay on the floor beneath. God knows what health hazards I had been subjecting myself to by sleeping only a few inches above this for so many years. I must have been inhaling this stuff every night. Particles from it must have been attaching themselves to my mattress and getting into my sheets and then into my lungs. It was truly disgusting and I felt horrified at the thought of what I must have been subjecting myself to. But it wasn't just the bedroom, it was the kitchen floor, the oven hob, inside the oven, inside the kitchen cupboards, the bathroom floor, the shower screen, the toilet bowl, the toilet seat, the bathroom washbowl and cupboards, the carpets, the wooden floors, the bookshelves, the windowsills...the possible places in which dirt and bacteria might be lurking were suddenly endless. It would take days and days to work through it all and then as soon as the whole place had been done once, I would need to start the whole cleaning cycle again.

This certainly became a project for those first few weeks of lockdown. I developed a cleaning obsession, spending whole mornings on a single room in my flat and deep cleaning every surface and emptying every drawer. Once I had started on this mission, I became appalled at the years and years' worth of muck that appeared to have accumulated. I was now glad that I no longer had a cleaner. What had been the point of her if she had missed so much? Only now was I getting the rooms in my home properly clean for what felt like the first time since I had moved in almost twenty-five years before.

Life began to settle down into a strange new set of routines. The first thing I decided to work on was my sleep. I had always been a dreadful sleeper but now seemed like as good a time as any to start to rectify that. With no online schooling to be done in what was now the equivalent of the Easter holiday and there being no requirement to get up early in order to be showered and breakfasted by 8.35 a.m., it seemed like a good opportunity to practise lying in.

For almost the first time in my life, I made myself at least try for eight hours' worth of sleep. I'd make sure that I was in bed by 10.45 p.m. at the latest and then I would not allow myself to get up before 7.30 a.m. I have to admit that little of that was deep, uninterrupted sleep but I was at least building the principle of eight hours into my schedule. After all, what was there to get up for? The day's tasks and programme were entirely self-invented. There was nobody and nothing saying "Get up because you have to do this…" So, even if I was awake at five a.m., I would lie there and wait for two and a half hours before allowing myself to get up.

Then there was exercise. I had been a scrupulous gym attendee before lockdown. I would go to the gym every single morning before work. I would arrive just before seven a.m. and do nearly an hour on the treadmill or cross trainer or cycling on one of the stationary bikes before getting my shower there and doing my hair and then setting off for work. This routine had faltered slightly in the weeks leading up to lockdown as rumours started to circulate that gyms and swimming pools were places in which the virus could easily spread. I still went but made sure to carefully wipe down the equipment I was using and opted to change at home, arriving at the gym in full kit and then showering at home afterwards. (No hardship really and with the added bonus of thereby avoiding the gym locker room and the associated, hearty but not always welcome early morning "banter" with the other gym users). I persisted in using the gym right up until the last minute, in spite of the frequent warnings about its hazardous nature. This was partly out of habit but also because as increasingly more and more things became forbidden, this seemed like one of the few places where things seemed to be carrying on more or less as normal.

Also, I had always depended on my gym fix each day. I saw those early morning visits as essential to my mental health. It was true, that I was addicted to the endorphin rush; that need to work up a good sweat; to exhaust myself with forty minutes or so of exertion as I pounded the treadmill or pushed the handles of the cross-trainer back and forth. I had always told myself that this was what set me up for the day. It helped me achieve an inner calm and equilibrium. It banished moodiness and little bouts of depression and always left me feeling calm and centred. I certainly believed that I would not be able to function without it.

Suddenly, though, this crutch had been taken away. Along with everything else, the gyms closed and became places that were forbidden. How was I going to manage? Especially at this time, which was going to need great mental resourcefulness in order to get through it. There were challenges on every hand: the fear of mortal illness; the vacancy left by not having a workplace or daily working routine; the days and days of almost total isolation; the monotony of a life more constrained and more circumscribed that at any other point in my life experience.

The challenges of lockdown would require great strength and mental stability. Plenty of sleep, a good diet, little or no alcohol and daily exercise were surely the keys to survival through all of this? There had to be a way of getting the daily exercise fix that would not involve going to the gym. But then I stumbled upon Joe Wicks and thank goodness for him! I gathered that he had started doing a series of daily workouts on YouTube, primarily aimed at children but available to all and for the first few weeks, I logged on and did his daily classes. He had a cheerful "can do" attitude that would pull us all of out of the slothful lethargy into which it would have been so easy to sink in those first locked down weeks. His mantra was "I guarantee that you will feel hundred per cent better" as a result of completing each of his thirty-minute sessions. And it was true. OK, you didn't finish his class dripping with sweat in a way that you did after pushing yourself to do more than half an hour on the gym treadmill, but you did feel lighter and more cheerful and better able to face whatever challenges the day was going to throw at you after taking part in one of his sessions. There was also something about his personality that was extremely engaging. While he did push you to work and exert yourself, he didn't have any of that bullying PE teacher toughness and aggression that had always so put me off physical exercise in my younger days. He had a self-deprecating quality and almost a gentleness that made you feel that anybody could do this and get something out of it. There was none of that macho-mystique that seemed to be part of other exercise videos. He was approachable and genuinely funny, with his rather squeaky voice and his trademark outer London twang. Exercising with Joe quickly became an integral part of my daily routine, taking over from the sweaty gym sessions but also an essential entree into the day.

    I would also allow myself to read for half an hour or so before the day kicked in and this, too, quickly became a habit and a nourishing, much savoured ritual. After my bowl of muesli and mug of tea at the dining table looking out at the New River and the trees outside my window, I would move over to my armchair, make myself another mug of tea and allow myself thirty pages or so of whatever book I was reading at the time. This felt like a real privilege: to be able to immerse myself in some other imaginary world each morning at a time when I would normally have been dashing to work, battling with the traffic and dealing with the start of the working day.

Now I could sit quietly and give myself over to a story and to the feelings and predicaments of invented characters and to the nuances of a writer's vocabulary. What a joy this was! It was like breakfast for the imagination: the chance to just immerse oneself in a fictional world. For a couple of weeks, 'Bleak House' had been my novel of choice with all its quirks, twists and turns and the brilliance of its narrative voice. As soon as I had got through this, it was back to contemporary fiction and then to non-fiction books on subjects like the ageing process or how to become a better sleeper and then back to older classics like 'Rebecca' or 'Brideshead Revisited'. Always at least a book a week and reading with that intensity and sense of immersion that I had only ever managed to achieve previously when I had been on holiday or on a beach. Now this became part of the daily ritual with which to start the day, occasionally picking the book up again later on in the afternoon or taking it out on to the lawn at the back of my flats or lugging it around with me to read in the park. This pleasure never palled and because the books kept changing, there was always a different imaginative place in which to be with each different choice of book. I'd be transported to the beaches of Crete or the colleges of 1920s Oxford or the Hertfordshire countryside of Edwardian England or to Bradford in the 1970s or Berlin of the

90s or the Hackney of the early twenty-first century but always to a different world and time and place. What a pleasure this was and, doing it at the start of every day, what a great workout for my imagination! As my own world became more and more circumscribed and uneventful, it was novel reading which transported me to different times and places, with an intensity that no film or tv show could ever do as powerfully.

Of course, this also became a time of epic telly watching too. Reading was for mornings and last thing at night before sleep. Evenings were for television. Along with all of its other fans, I wondered how on earth "Coronation Street" was going to keep going. How could it continue to churn out six episodes a week on the industrial scale with which it had been doing for the last however many years? And yet, we fans needed our favourite soap to continue in spite of the pandemic. We needed those almost daily episodes to make us feel that life was still capable of going on somewhere with some semblance of normality. We needed that regular contact with the soap's much-loved characters; to hear their catchphrases and to witness their familiar tics and foibles. Ken Barlow and Liz MacDonald and Eileen Grimshaw and Roy Cropper were like intimates and we needed to see them on our screens three times a week. I had often had the morbid thought that if and when life ended, 'Coronation Street' would still be going on. Homes across the country would still be switching it on and listening to the familiar tones of Eric Spear's evocative theme tune. That would continue uninterrupted, whatever happened to me personally.

We fans knew that episodes were filmed six weeks ahead, so it surely meant that there would be enough material to take us up to the middle of May? However, then we heard that they were going to reduce the number of weekly episodes in order to ration them out a bit so we'd probably be OK for at least a couple of months or so. But what then? It was unthinkable that there would ever be a time when 'Coronation Street' would disappear from our screens. Although, if the current lockdown was set to continue into the summer, then that was starting to look like a very real prospect.

This was the time, though, when the iPlayer really came into its own. All those shows that people had missed when they first came out now became a very welcome source of home entertainment. I'd hardly ever used the iPlayer before, either recording shows that I had wanted to watch or managing to seek them out on Catch Up, a few days afterwards. However, when I started to take a closer look at the iPlayer, I realised that it contained a veritable treasure trove of programmes from the last year or so and I started to watch things I would never have dreamed of watching in normal times.

I began with "Killing Eve" which seemed to have garnered a huge number of Awards but was something I had never bothered with before, having assumed it was some sort of "Doctor Who" type fantasy which wouldn't have been of any interest to me. I was quickly proved wrong. I watched the first episode of the first series (there had been three altogether and I had missed them all). I was immediately swept up by the brilliance of the story-telling and the sheer audacious nastiness of it all. Every twenty minutes, some innocuous character like a hotel receptionist or a shop assistant would get bumped off in the most outrageous and surprising way. Even major characters dominating whole episodes never seemed to be allowed to survive until the credits rolled without being splattered to pieces before the end. There was something really horrible about it but also funny and daring and as soon as one episode finished, I was immediately hooked into the next one. Of course, this show had been a massive nationwide hit when it first appeared and quickly became a TV institution but to me, sitting there watching instalment after instalment on my own in those first few weeks of lockdown, it felt like an individual discovery and something that nobody else had quite cottoned on to.

Then there was the adaptation of 'Normal People' which I did not watch on iPlayer but, along with most of the country, watched as it came out in its bite-sized half-hourly episodes. In some ways, this could not have been more different from 'Killing Eve'. Whereas 'Eve' had a surreal, quirky quality and was so violent and extreme in content that it almost seemed to be sending itself up, 'Normal People' on the other hand, was completely Naturalistic, it lingered and took its time. As its title implied, its subject was just an ordinary relationship between a teenage boy and girl as they took their first steps towards adulthood. There were no massive dramas here. The whole thing hinged on nuance and the exploration of the characters' emotions. The effect was slow and dreamy almost. There was very little dialogue, most of the action being conveyed through silences and facial expressions and eye contact and the subtext beneath the seemingly mundane exchanges between the central characters. Everything about it was unremarkable, deliberately so but conveyed by the most gripping and believable acting of the two leading actors. So good were they, that as a viewer you got completely swept up in their predicaments; you lived the events of the story with them; you were there. As viewers, we got completely taken out of ourselves – and I guess this was why the series was such a massive hit at that time. For an hour or so, it enabled us to forget about ourselves and to become these two rather innocent characters, exploring the complexities of love and a relationship for the very first time.

Another show which seemed to grip people's imagination at that time was 'Quiz' – a dramatisation of the story of the 'Major' who may or may not have fraudulently managed to win the million pound jackpot in 'Who Wants to be a Millionaire?'. This had a particularly strong performance from Michael Sheen as Chris Tarrant and was especially memorable for that but James Graham's writing was also gripping. The show was broadcast for three nights over the Easter weekend not long after the start of lockdown and seemed to perform a valuable function in bringing everyone together. Even though we could not see each other at this time when families and households would traditionally come together, we could all be watching the same TV show at the same time as each other and somehow all be connected in that way.

These, and other television shows, certainly provided people with things to talk about because the truth was that there was very little else. No longer going out to work and not being allowed to socialise meant that there was not much material for conversation. Yes, one could moan about the enforced incarceration and bewail the increasing numbers of infections and deaths but apart from this, because nobody was going out and doing anything or seeing anyone there was actually very little to talk about. I guess one thing that did happen is that because now there was more time, people tended to ring each other up more, rather than texting or WhatsApping. It started to become important to hear a living, breathing human voice and a short sentence of text-speak was not the same. There was now time to have those lingering, free-wheeling phone calls which we all used to engage in before texting became the norm and we all got so busy that chewing the fat over the phone with our friends had become a thing of the past. People I hadn't heard from for weeks suddenly started to ring me up. I began picking up the phone and actually answering it, no longer ignoring the landline because I thought it would only ever be sellers of PPI or Double Glazing or dodgy scams on the other end of the line.

In those first weeks, there was a flurry of phoning. Out of the blue, friends would ring up "to just check how you are"; wanting to know that I was healthy and staying sane in spite of the enforced isolation and, of course, managing to keep the dreaded illness at bay. In those early days, there was a kind of unwritten rule that we all had to be rising to the challenge. One must not give in to gloominess or self-pity. One should see Lockdown as an opportunity. Acquaintances rattled off whole rafts of online opportunities for self-improvement and development. One could learn a foreign language, listen to an improving podcast, print off a new recipe, watch an opera from the Met in New York, catch a BAFTA nominated movie, watch the whole back catalogue of streamed theatre productions from the National or from Shakespeare's Globe. The Berlin Phil was streaming recordings of all their most recent concerts; there were endless workshops on Mindfulness and Meditation; loads of people I knew were doing online Pilates or Yoga and even I joined in with the fad for baking banana bread. Rather than bemoaning the dreadful constraints we were all under people started to crow about how wonderful it was to have the time to "slow down" and to "take stock" and many were incredulous at how busy they were with all the new skills and pastimes coming their way. As always, I'm sorry to say, one-upmanship seemed to be the name of the game. The wider the range of new skills and hobbies and interests you could claim to be pursuing during lockdown, the better. People saw it as a badge of honour not to give in; not to succumb to misery or depression or even inactivity. A crammed agenda for the day became a source of pride.

Who knew how long we would have to do this for? As the numbers of infections and deaths recorded started to rise steadily, it became increasingly clear that we would not be returning to work at the end of the Easter holidays. One of my most politically aware friends had said "in your dreams" in response to the Prime Minister's promise to have the thing licked by the summer. He thought we were in for at least three months of enforced house arrest, possibly longer. (At the time, this seemed like a wildly pessimistic prophecy. Little did we all know!).

I thought that I'd better get a project going as well, if only to keep my end up with all those I knew who were learning Mahler symphonies or starting beginner's German or engaging in Advanced Yoga or taking up painting in oils or brushing up on their baking skills. I wasn't sure that I wanted to do any of these things but I did know that I had a half-finished novel in my bottom drawer that I was intending to finish off when I retired and so I thought, why wait? I'd already had a computer engineer come round to my place at the start of the year to get my printer up and working with the intention of being able to print off my creative offerings so now seemed as good a time as any to get cracking with it. I even found a "Novel Writing Competition" online, which was inviting amateur authors to submit their manuscripts by the beginning of June, so that seemed like another incentive to get writing. I am not sure that I ever seriously intended submitting my work for publication. My writing was more like a hobby and an exercise for my brain rather than seriously intended for someone else to actually read.

I wrote in order to satisfy my own urge to continue doing something creative. As a drama teacher, I had helped students to create the plays and devised performances that they had had to produce for their drama exams. I'd also had my own creative blast when directing my two big productions each year, every aspect of which I had been responsible for: the casting, the set and costume design, the technical aspects as well as directing the individual actors. I realised that I was going to miss this twice-yearly creative outlet for my talents, so a return to novel writing seemed like a good alternative. I call it "novel writing" but in fact any writing I did was very thinly disguised autobiography. There was very little that was genuinely creative or imagined about it at all. The people in it were all based on people that I knew and the action was all only a marginally fictionalised account of things that had happened to me. This was another reason why the work was basically unpublishable and was destined to remain forever in my bottom drawer: the characterisations were more or less libellous and not always flattering pen portraits of people that I knew and the action was far too personal and revealing to be broadcast and publicised through publication. What little writing I did, therefore, was for myself. I enjoyed the challenge of filleting and shaping my own experience in order to make a narrative. I liked the trawling through my vocabulary in order to select the write adjective or adverb with which to describe some of that experience. I liked the craft of structuring sentences and of giving them a rhythm; I enjoyed playing with words and selecting the right "colours" almost like a painter mixing different oils on his palette. There was something peculiarly satisfying about capturing moments from my life in words, giving them a kind of immortality and observing how the various parts contributed to the whole.

Therefore, every morning in those first weeks, after my mug of tea, some muesli, thirty pages of the novel I was reading and then half an hour of Joe Wicks, I would turn on my laptop and happily type out words for the rest of the morning until lunchtime. Before I could start this process, I re-read the pages I had written so far in the months, no years, before the pandemic and the lockdown started. I have to say that I was pleasantly surprised by what I read. It certainly seemed to me to be readable, at least. Perhaps no one else would think so but to me it seemed a remarkably coherent (and at times even funny) account of a few key episodes in my life and it was well worth seeing it through to the end. I wasn't quite sure what the end would be but the fragment I had produced so far was certainly unfinished, therefore, completing it would be a little project to take me through lockdown. So as friends bragged about the number of rooms they were going to paint or the number of Hamlet soliloquys they were going to learn, I could truthfully say "Well, I'm going to finish my novel".

For those first few weeks, there was certainly a spirit of optimism abroad. We were all going to get through this and we were going to make the most of our time at home. The enforced confinement had to be somehow made into an opportunity rather than be seen for the dreadful imposition and curbing of our liberties that it actually was. This optimistic outlook was encouraged by the better weather and, of course, it helped having a secure job with a decent income to look forward to each month. It also helped having a comfortable, spacious and light modern flat (now newly cleaned to pristine perfection!) to roam around in and to be able to come and go as I wished, without being answerable to anyone. Things would have felt very different I am sure if I had been cooped up with a fractious partner, both getting on each other's nerves and unable to escape from each other. Or if I had been trying to live in my flat as a member of a family, with small children running around and requiring entertaining or educating or supervising and me having to be answerable to their demands and requirements. As it was, I was only responsible for myself and so in many ways had a better deal than most.

This did not, however, take into account the loneliness of my situation or that of all the other single people who were told to stay at home and not see another person for weeks on end. If I am brutally honest, at first this did feel like a strange kind of relief: no need to arrange things to do or make any effort to see other people. No need to go out to the theatre or pub on those evenings when I wasn't particularly feeling like it. No need to drag myself out to those dinner parties at which I had to get so tanked up with booze in order to be able to pass oneself off as an entertaining guest. No visits to relatives for birthdays or Mother's Day or Easter or for Sunday lunches or picnics in the park. Every single day could be devoted to communing with oneself and cutting out all of the noise, hubbub and distraction of other human beings. The prospect seemed almost blissful; here was a licence to be totally antisocial for weeks on end, with absolutely no tiresome social obligations of any kind. It seemed like a veritable holiday for the soul.

The reality was considerably less enjoyable. Far from relishing the lack of social contact, I realised how very much I needed it and depended on it to make life bearable. I could just about do a day without talking to anyone but much more than that and I just began to feel sad and deeply melancholic. I began to question the wisdom of curtailing my working life if this was what I had now signed up to. No more of that buzz of walking into a place in which you know everyone and everyone knows you. All the shared gossip and hilarity and camaraderie. Now just silence and solitude.

Generally, I found that I could get through the mornings well enough, just about. And then I could busy myself with chores in the afternoon or a walk or just sitting out round at the back of my block of flats in the sunshine... and then in the evenings there was the telly. Quite early on in the day, though, there would be a need to have someone to talk to. I realised how exhilarated I became when a friend chose to ring me in the morning and then we would chat for the best part of an hour. We'd compare our feelings about being "locked down", we'd talk about our strategies for "getting through"; we'd slag off the government and talk about what a rotten job they were doing and how they should have locked down much earlier and why on earth had they not seen the writing on the wall when Italy was so badly affected weeks before? We'd talk about the books we were reading and the tv shows we were watching; we'd discuss how our various relatives or mutual friends were coping; we'd moan about the noise from our neighbours and the supermarket queues and those people we knew of who seemed not be sticking to the rules. These were great opportunities to off-load and I'd finish these chats feeling purged and energised and connected.

However, round about five o'clock in the afternoon, as the prospect of yet another evening completely on my own approached, I would start to sink into a troubling depression. I'd start to feel frail emotionally, as if the slightest thing would set me off. I felt on the edge of tearfulness and indeed sometimes even succumbed to this because I knew of the relief that it would bring afterwards. Let it all out, I told myself, allowing sometimes a torrent of miserable self-pity to have its way with me. I'd feel that I couldn't bear it: the solitary confinement; the uncertainty; the terror and dread of catching the illness; the horrific disruption this was causing to my way of life; the way in which I was being robbed at the very time when I had a licence to go off and do whatever I liked in the form of retirement, now here I was imprisoned in my little flat and confined to the byways and highways of a dull North London suburb.

That, therefore, was my April, the first full month of lockdown. A month overshadowed more than anything else by the tragic death of a highly regarded ex-colleague, a testament to the savagery of this dreadful disease. Also, though, a time of adjustment as habits altered and new rhythms and patterns were established and ways of coping with it all evolved... Most wonderful of all, though, was the glorious spring sunshine and just the peace: the traffic-free streets and the birdsong and the blue skies. That was the first month of lockdown.

May

By the start of May, it felt as though we were getting into the way of it. There was nowhere to go and no one to see, so in order to survive you had to make sure that you had a strict routine for the day. I had this with my exercise regime, my reading and, as the new term started up again, my school work. Evenings were given over to TV, Zoom meetings and ironing. Although it was hard and challenging, it was remarkable how easily one adapted to a life of such limited horizons.

The big change now was with the school-work. While it had been acceptable for the last couple of weeks of the previous term to effectively fob students off with project work and stuff they could supposedly get on with at home, we were now being told in no uncertain terms that we had to up our game. It was clear that schools were going to be closed for some time and that we all needed to provide our students with tuition that would offer a real alternative to being in the classroom. We started to get frantic emails from the Senior Leadership team backtracking on many of the things they had been saying before the Easter break. Then they had said that it was quite acceptable for teachers not to appear online if they did not want to and that there was also no requirement for students to have their cameras switched on either. There had been a load of fuss from the Teaching Unions about the potential dangers of this: the teacher's image being flashed into students' homes was thought to be a Safeguarding minefield. It would enable the students to see into the teachers' houses, to see their kitchen tables and even stray family members in the background. Teachers would need to be correctly dressed to appear on camera and we were warned that images could be recorded and doctored and redistributed in a whole spectrum of alarming scenarios. Similarly, the students themselves were reluctant to allow their images to be beamed into teachers' homes or to be visible to their classmates while they might not have done their hair or have on the right sort of "cool" outfit or could be recorded giving an incorrect answer or looking foolish in some way. The whole thing was rife with potential for humiliation.

In addition, there were all the other problems associated with technology: faulty Wi-Fi connections; interference and dodgy sound; blurred images; not to mention the whole business of getting the right programs installed and up and running on one's home computer. Personally, I found the whole thing completely bewildering.

All the time we were getting increasingly irate emails about how our online provision needed to improve and how we needed to be able to match the apparently brilliant offerings of the local independent schools but there was just not sufficient guidance about how we were supposed to do this. It was just an assumption that everyone knew how to use Microsoft Teams and that one could automatically get all one's teaching resources transferred over to this new method of communication. I, for one though, had no idea at all how to show my power point on Stanislavski's "Method of Physical Action" for example on Microsoft Teams; how to flash it up to my online class and to have it there and visible while I went through it and the students commented on it as I pointed out its most salient features. I didn't know how to take the register on

Teams and to check that everyone who was supposed to be in the class was there (especially if they were allowed to be invisible, without their cameras on). This was a totally new way of working and it sort of beggared belief that we were all expected to be 'tech savvy' enough to be able to just switch to this with only minimal training and support.

During our first week back there was a Head of Departments' Meeting at which everyone was expected to say how they were getting on with their delivery of the new online pedagogy. Of course, this just became another platform for people to show off. It was supposed to be one of those "sharing of good practice" sessions but just degenerated into a bragging session: "This is what I do and it works ever so well..." "Something that has been really successful for me is..." "I find that the students tend to respond really well to..."

I was dreading it getting to my turn, when all I would be able to report would be a couple of faltering sessions in which I didn't seem to be able to get my camera working and the students didn't appear to be able to access any of my lesson materials. Also, there seemed to be a lot of confusion about when the new online lessons were supposed to be. I had, I thought, booked a session with my A-level students, only to be told by some of them that they had already signed up for an "extra English" class at that time or that they were committed to doing a French conversation class with the Language Assistant when they were also expected to be with me.

While the tenor of the meeting had been so positive and when everyone else was claiming to be having such success with their online teaching, I didn't want to pour cold water over the proceedings and reveal myself as the only person who was clearly struggling with this. On the other hand, I felt that I needed to be honest. I needed some help and some advice about how to do this. We did also need a better organised timetable. We'd all been told that every teacher needed to be doing at least an hour a week online with each class but if these were all at random times, then there were bound to be clashes between different subjects. At the moment, it just seemed to be chaotic.

While never as forceful or as strident as some when putting forward my view at meetings, I did manage to convey a need for more training and support, and this seemed to get taken on board. I did also manage to convey the need for a properly and centrally organised timetable of online lessons to be established so that there would be no clashes between different departments each of them competing for students' attention at the same time.

These points seemed to get taken on board and the Deputy Head himself, together with one of the IT support staff, offered to provide some school-based training for those of us not up to speed with Microsoft Teams. So, the following week a small group of us went into school, where we commandeered a classroom for a morning and got taken through the mystifying process of how to do a lesson using this new-fangled resource. As always with computer stuff, it seemed quite simple when someone else was demonstrating but when I started to do it myself, there was always some crucial part of the process that I would manage to miss out and then, of course, it wouldn't work. Like a particularly dense child at these sessions, I would keep putting my hand up and asking for help. What was I doing wrong? What had I missed? Why wasn't it working?

Eventually, with a couple more of these in-house training sessions, I finally got some of the basics just about mastered. However, it always felt very "touch and go" whenever I tried to get a class to log on and work with me online. There always seemed to be students missing or not able to hear and not able to access the work I was providing. When they "spoke" back in response to my questions, their sound was often inaudible or indistinct. The process felt laborious and cumbersome and was often very unsatisfactory. The thought of working in this way for weeks on end did not fill me with joy.

There was a feeling of panic spreading down from the Senior Management of the school in response to a deluge of complaints from parents. These seemed to be equally divided between parents who thought that our online provision was woefully inadequate and those who thought we were all setting far too much work and were making the children feel stressed and overwhelmed. Emails were flying backwards and forwards nearly every day during those first few days of the new Summer Term. These were tense enough times anyway with the daily toll of infections and deaths rising relentlessly. This, combined with a government that seemed to be floundering and appeared to have no idea how to lead us through this catastrophic situation, as well as the daily irritants of having to queue at the supermarket and pharmacy for essential supplies plus the lack of any form of social contact for all those of us who lived on our own, made for a potentially extremely volatile situation. To have to deal with the constant fear that at any moment one might succumb to the dread disease plus having to try and keep oneself from not going completely mad at being cooped up indoors for weeks on end, with no contact with another human being apart from a neighbour casually encountered in the communal gardens and on top of that to have to deal with all of these new work stresses: having to learn how to teach in a completely different way – remotely, using Zoom or Teams or Google classrooms and then hearing that what one was striving to provide was inadequate and not stretching enough or sufficiently rigorous and, therefore, of little value was extremely demoralising. The truth was that we were all effectively making it up as we went along.

On top of this was the looming crisis with public examinations. My school was renowned for its exam successes and this was one of the factors that had kept it continually at the top of the League Tables for however many years. Now, though, we had been told that there would be no exams and that everything was to be decided on the basis of Centre Assessed Grades. In other words, the teacher would decide what grade each student was worth and this would then have to be substantiated by evidence. All the student's marks from the year would be required in order to back up the teacher's assessment, in addition to any coursework which the student might have completed. We were told that any NEA (Non-Exam Assessments) had to be completed and marked so that these too could be used as evidence to bolster the grade awarded by the teacher. Therefore, another extra stress added to these early weeks of what would have been the spring term was the requirement to get from every student a completed version of any coursework-type assignment they might have needed to submit. This would then have to be carefully marked and would need to be available for scrutiny in order to justify the mark awarded. It might also need to be sent off as evidence but, then, who knew because the guidance on what was going to be required by the exam boards seemed to change on an almost daily basis. This was another massive stress factor at an increasingly difficult time.

This meant that all of the exam classes were now emailing in drafts of coursework to teachers on an almost hourly basis.

They were expecting to get instant feedback which they could then act upon as they altered and re-wrote their work in order to get themselves the best possible marks. Keeping track of who had sent in what and finding ways of responding to the work and then adding comments and meaningful feedback created an almost continuous flow of emails all through the day. All this was going on, this constant email exchange between teachers and the exam students, in between teaching the online lessons to the other classes.

The Deputy Head drew up a new timetable for us all so that we could each be seen to be teaching at least one hour a week with every one of our classes. For this hour, we were expected to log on to Teams and to be visible and to do a "proper" taught lesson. Just setting a writing task and telling the students to get on with it was no longer acceptable. We now had to be delivering as near to face-to-face teaching as was possible.

Therefore, the day now became pretty much like an ordinary school day – except that instead of being at school in the classroom one was at one's desk in the spare room, sitting in front of the laptop and speaking into the webcam delivering a "virtual lesson". In between classes, one was downloading students' written work, marking it and adding feedback and then emailing it back to them, as well as reading emails from the Senior Staff and responding to these and attending online meetings at which the various problems associated with lockdown, online teaching and planning for the foreseeable future were addressed and discussed.

This whole new way of working was exhausting and strangely demoralising. There was the sense that however hard one was trying to rise to the new challenges, it was somehow not good enough and a poor second best to the real thing. It wasn't good enough but it was also laborious and curiously draining. And it was incredibly lonely. For all the efforts one was making to establish a virtual classroom and to get one's face up on Teams and to listen to the responses of students and to occasionally even interact with them face to face, the fact was one was sitting alone in a room in front of a computer. One was interacting with grainy images or with muffled and distorted sounding voices for a few agonisingly slow minutes but in fact each of us was in reality sitting in a room alone. There was no interaction with other people; none of the camaraderie or laughter of being in the same building together and bumping into each other in the photocopying room or quipping with each other as we passed in the corridor or catching each other's eye during a whole school assembly or perching on each other's desks in the staffroom during a free period or sharing a coffee and a laugh together at breaktime. You were on your own.

As well as learning how to work in this new way, the new skills acquired seemed to be creeping into various aspects of social life, as well. For example, my sister and I agreed that we would start to use Facetime once a week, as a way for me to have some face-to-face contact with her and her family. This quickly became a Friday evening ritual. Every Friday night at seven p.m., I would log onto Facetime and my sister's image would flash up. She'd be ensconced on her sofa in her house, with her two girls sitting either side of her and her husband, Alan, on a chair just off camera and to the left of the screen. What a novelty this seemed to be, at first. Being able to have sight of my sister and her family at this extremely lonely time was a bit of a tonic. It was lovely to be able to see faces, as well as hear voices. At the same time, the sight of them all sat there together, looking forward to an evening of shared telly, food and drink just made me feel more isolated than ever. It felt cruel that these flickering images of them all together in their home were as near as we were ever going to get to real contact for, it seemed, weeks to come. Something strange also started to happen to our ability to communicate with each other. My sister and I are very close and talk on the phone almost every day. We are usually on for ages, barely ever able to curtail our conversations. In spite of the almost daily contact, we never run out of things to say: gossip about mutual friends, acquaintances and other family members; offloading to each other about various grievances and slights caused by neighbours, workmates, people we know; sharing health worries and concerns; grousing about domestic problems like faulty washing machines and cookers and unreliable plumbers and electricians; sharing views about TV shows and swapping opinions about different presenters and police dramas and slagging off a whole raft of popular entertainers; discussing what we plan to cook and buy and prepare for dinner... we honestly never stop and could keep going all day long. However, with the addition of a camera there were suddenly strange and awkward silences when the normally free-flowing exchanges between us ground to a sudden halt. There were now longueurs and silences as we scrabbled around for the next thing to say. With the nieces, who seemed initially overjoyed to be able to see me on camera and talk to me in this way, for them the apparent novelty seemed to wear off very quickly indeed. They would need to be cajoled into saying something and then would quickly slip away to return to their phones or their own laptops for a more entertaining online interaction. By the third or fourth week, neither of them turned up at all. They were apparently 'up in their rooms' and no longer visible on the sofa in the living room. The prospect of chatting with 'Uncle Nick' for half an hour or so was clearly not much of a draw.

For a few weeks, I really looked forward to these Facetime sessions with my sister and her family. I could not believe how quickly they came around, every seven days. I suppose each week was so uneventful that the days just slipped away, merging into each other almost seamlessly and I was often quite amazed when Friday night came around again and it was time for the family Facetime session.

As I logged off each week, I felt sad that this was what we were now reduced to. I felt sad that the screen encounters weren't more satisfactory. I felt sad that the end of each one marked the passing of another week.

Eventually, we abandoned them. They seemed to have become a chore for the family, interrupting their dinner preparations and becoming something of a tie, while for me I was feeling that they had become a bit of an imposition and a slightly unwelcome intrusion into their family time. Also, I didn't particularly feel a need to be seen on camera with my increasingly unkempt lockdown hair and my rather woebegone expression. Best just to let the Facetime sessions go…and so we did.

Not so with other members of my circle at that time. I had a couple of workmates (one of whom had by now moved on to take a promotion in another school outside London) who quickly decided that regular Zoom meetings would be a good way of keeping in touch. I must say that I had misgivings about this. We were used to seeing each other socially and often met in pubs and restaurants together and always had a thoroughly congenial, if slightly drunken, time. One of our number decided that it would be a good idea if we attempted to recreate one of these boozy nights out by getting together on Zoom while we sipped cocktails or swigged from a large glass of wine and picked at a few nibbles. That way, it would be as if we were all on a night out together. Wouldn't it?

We tried this a couple of times but again a "Zoom social" seemed to me to be a very poor substitute for the real thing. I found it very hard to engage with the conversation for one thing. The normal register of our interactions as a group was generally shared hilarity. Scurrilous gossip and ironic banter normally fuelled our conversations as a group but this seemed very hard to recreate on camera. I was conscious of the fact that we all seemed to be talking over each other in an attempt to be quick and witty, so in the end none of us could hear anything that any of the others were saying. Jokes seemed to be mistimed and scathing ripostes and normally amusing punchlines were robbed of their impact. Humour quickly went out of the window and instead we seemed to be reduced to rather earnest analyses of how our various schools were dealing with the pandemic and appeared to be talking to each other in a completely different tone to normal. We became more like three strangers talking to each other rather than three old mates. To compensate, we'd all start drinking more and more and by the end of the rather wearing couple of hours of forced jollity we would all three of us be feeling quite pissed. Finally, we would all press 'Leave' and close down the conversation, only to be sat there each on our own with a half-empty bottle and a couple of empty packets of crisps. Again, the impact was just to make me feel more alone than ever. I know that, in a manner of speaking, we had been conversing with friends for an evening and being sociable but the brutal fact was that we had each of us really just been staring at a screen. Now that the friends had logged off, I was just sat there on my own at the end of the evening, feeling not a little intoxicated with just a solo glass and an empty bottle in front of me. Not long after, I'd crawl into bed but then, inevitably, would be dragged out of a semi-comatose sleep feeling agitated, wide awake, dehydrated and depressed. Best not to have these Zoom sessions at all if that was always going to be the final outcome, I reasoned.

Slightly more successful were the online activities that I planned with members of my amateur theatre group. These came about because, while devastated that the theatres were closed, and that any prospect of face-to-face rehearsal was completely banned for months to come, we were all determined to keep going in some way and to take advantage of the technology with which we were all now becoming familiar. Somebody in the group (and I think it may even have been me) suggested that we should try to read some plays together online. We could at least read the plays out loud on Zoom and while not the same as rehearsing a full production, it would keep us connected with each other and give us a chance to flex those 'Acting muscles' that would surely go to waste if none of us were going to be allowed to do any acting at all for months to come.

The first play we chose was probably a fairly obvious choice: 'The Importance of Being Earnest'. Nevertheless, there were reasons for this. I imagined (and this definitely had been my suggestion) that most people would probably have a copy of the play lying around somewhere at home and, if not, because it was long out of copyright, it would be easy enough to find the script online. Also, it had the advantage of being familiar, so most people would have at least a rough idea of who the characters were and of how to deliver the lines. The important thing here, it seemed to me, was not to deliver a startlingly original version of the old warhorse but to see what it was like reading a play together using the new technology, in the manner of the new 'normal'; in other words, on a screen with everyone in their own little box and with all the associated technical difficulties of poor internet connections and dodgy sound and people forgetting to mute and unmute and all the rest of it! In the end, it turned out to be quite a success. Yes, it went on a bit (I'd forgotten how wordy the play can be at times) but we had a few chuckles at the lines and there were a couple of good stabs at Lady Bracknell and generally people seemed to enjoy it. Perhaps what people most enjoyed was just the opportunity to see each other on screen and to feel part of something for an hour or two; a heartening antidote to the days of isolation and a welcome relief from the hours and hours of enforced television watching which seemed to occupy most evenings.

As it turned out, the theatre company's online play-readings quickly became a bit of a lifeline during lockdown and they continued for much of the year and into the following April. They worked, partly because it was great just to see each other again but, also, the fact that we were reading a play together gave our meetings a sense of purpose. We weren't just meeting up to have a chat (although there was always a bit of that at the start and again at the end of the readings) but the fact that we were reading a play together gave us a sense of purpose and gave us a concrete activity in which we could lose ourselves for a few hours each week. There was also just the joy of reading together and of being able to 'let rip' when we were reading particularly emotional scripts like a Tennessee Williams or a

David Mamet; there was also the shared laughter over an Alan Ayckbourn or a Bennett or even, somewhat daringly, a Joe Orton. There was that exciting sense of discovery when someone suggested a play title with which we were less familiar, like our large cast reading of 'Inherit the Wind' or a couple of Yasmin Reza plays which people had not necessarily come across before. There was a valuable educational aspect here: we were all learning and finding out about plays and playwrights that we did not know. For many of the group, I am sure, the weekly readings soon became indispensable and, for me personally, they were a welcome relief from the monotony of lockdown. At least on Tuesday evenings, I knew that I would be doing something different. For that one evening a week, I would no longer by slumped in front of the tv for four hours, soporific with the passive ingesting of the usual diet of reality shows, rolling news, crime dramas and soaps. On Tuesday nights, I would be actively engaged and communicating and participating, immersed in my love of amateur theatre. For a few hours, I could pretend to be someone else and let rip, speaking another person's words and emoting and saying all sorts of things that I would never dare to say in real life. For a few moments I had another voice and I could escape.

What with work and my daily exercise regime, plus a serious reading programme and the theatre group meetings and readings, plus the usual chores of cleaning, shopping and cooking, as well as trying to keep up with friends through phone calls, texting, Facetime and Zoom, life was about as packed with activity as it could be.

This was a strange time because there was always a sense that this was a temporary state of affairs: we were being asked to live in this strange and isolated way, to 'lockdown', for what we imagined would just be a few weeks in order to prevent the spread of the disease. There was never any feeling that this was how things would continue for months on end, so throughout there was still a kind of novelty value to this unfamiliar, new, socially distant way of functioning. It was impossible not to imagine that sometime soon there would be a reprieve; that we would have all "done our bit" or "played our part" and that it would have worked. The measures taken would have been a success and then we would all be allowed to bounce back to normal, picking up our lives from where they had been left off. In those early days of lockdown, there was still a relative degree of optimism and positivity around. The general tenor of conversations with people who had not had the terrible misfortune to be struck down by the disease was that we all needed to roll up our sleeves and just get on with it and make the best of things. No point in feeling sorry for yourself. Put your elbow to the wheel; best foot forward, that sort of thing. Therefore, the attitude, when you spoke to people, was very much one of refusing to give in to fear or despair but rather a hearty embracing of the so-called opportunities that lockdown had to offer. Rather than succumbing to the sheer misery of not being able to see anyone or go anywhere or do anything, people tended to almost brag about how much they were enjoying the enforced confinement. People crowed about the number of new activities they were embarked upon; the marvellous use they were making of the time; the relief they felt at being spared from unwelcome social obligations. Everyone I knew was baking Banana Bread for the first time or starting their day with a Joe Wicks PE workout or half-way through a wholesale re-read of the Complete Jane Austen or making headway with the final instalment of the "Wolf Hall" trilogy (all 850 pages of it).

In spite of the compulsory incarceration, everyone was "Busy, busy, busy"

People certainly felt obliged to make the most of the situation. Life as we knew it had stopped for a while but for a few weeks, we could all get off the treadmill, take stock and slow down. You had to try and look on the bright side: the sun was shining and you didn't have to get up and go out to work. It did seem that most people I knew were experiencing an almost guilty enjoyment of this brave new world.

However, there was no avoiding the dismal and frightening truths that we were reminded of every day through the five p.m. Downing Street Briefings that now became a feature of daily life. Each afternoon at five o'clock, the Prime Minister and his cronies, flanked by various medical advisers would give a press briefing from Downing Street and we would all be informed about the dire situation we were in. The disease was rampaging through certain parts of the community, most catastrophically the Care Homes and their vulnerable, elderly residents. There seemed to be no way of halting the relentless progress of the pandemic, especially among older people. While some of us were relatively fortunate in having our own living spaces and an income and had only the relatively trivial challenge of how to best get through the day, it was clear that there were now thousands of people dying in unbearable pain from this disease. Most brutally of all, they were dying completely alone because of the high risks of infection.

This stark reality was there hovering in the background all the time. Whatever spin the government spokesperson might attempt to put on things, and how ever many graphs and slides they attempted to blind us with, there was always that chilling moment when the figure giving the number of people who had died of Covid that day was flashed up on to the screen: 500, 600, 700 – eventually more than a thousand. There was no arguing with these figures and what they meant. They brutally belied whatever attempts might have been made to persuade us that things were not quite as bad as they seemed.

For a while, we could fool ourselves that we were on some sort of extended holiday but every so often there would be something to bring you up short: the sight of an ambulance flashing by; the news that a friend or acquaintance had taken to their bed with a hacking cough, a temperature and breathing difficulties; those awful news stories of health workers or bus drivers struck down while trying to serve members of the public as they went about their daily duties. It was almost as if those of us who had survived unscathed felt duty bound to make the most of our holiday humour because at any moment, this dread thing might reach out and grab you, pulling you down to the hell of an ICU ward and the helpless attentions of exhausted medical teams who knew not how to treat or deal with this disaster. We had a duty to play and make hay while the sun shone because who knew when the thing would creep up on us and drag us breathless, helpless and suffocating towards a hospital nightmare? Every trip to the supermarket was a potential source of infection; every home delivery; every box of vegetables from a Waitrose van; every pint of milk picked up from the Tesco Express; that interaction in the newsagent's to buy the Sunday paper once a week; that petrol pump with the contaminated handle; that scurry into the pharmacy after an hour's wait to pick up a prescription; that squeezing past a stranger on a narrow public footpath while out on a daily constitutional; that trip to the bin store outside my flat, which was shared with more than a dozen different households. Every single one of these was a possible source of contamination; a possible way in which one might unknowingly get infected with the disease. All it took was the touching of a door handle or the inadvertent brushing against a shop counter or lingering too long inside an inadequately ventilated corner shop. It was coming for you and it could get you. Anywhere, anytime.

Yes, I'd come back from buying the newspaper or taking out my rubbish or going on my walk and I would make sure that I washed my hands thoroughly for twenty seconds, as advised... but what if I missed a bit? What if somehow a stray particle had ended up on my clothing or in my hair? What if I'd touched my face or rubbed my eyes or wiped my nose without thinking?

While enjoying the unusually sunny weather and the relief from traffic noise and the reading and the not having to go into work, there was always this fear in the background; this sense that maybe one's days were numbered; that if it had got so many, why would I be exempt? What was so special about me? If others had gone down with it, then why should I be spared?

This was a constant fear and source of anxiety and it was at the back of my mind the whole time but, in spite of this, my main worry was simply about getting through the day. While I would not claim to be learning all sorts of new skills and tackling vast intellectual challenges, I also did not want to feel that I was wasting the time. I was conscious of the fact that these months were more unusual than anything I had ever experienced in all of my sixty-two years. To get through it, I had to try and think of it as a gift. We had been given this hiatus, this break from the normal, this oasis of quiet and it was important to make the most of it in as positive a way as possible.

Of course, I was officially still working at this time. I would not effectively retire from my job for another three months. Therefore, it beheld me to try and remain as professional as possible and to provide the highest quality of online teaching that I could muster. I put time into planning my online lessons. I thought about the quality of the work I was setting and the online provision I was offering. To make these lessons as good and as useful as they could possibly be would take time and effort. I adapted my existing lesson materials to make them work for the "virtual" format. Every lesson needed to be accessible and retrievable by those who, for whatever reason, were not able to get online. This meant making a kind of narrative for each lesson: this is what we are going to do; this is how we are going to do it and this is what you should have learnt by the end. Now, of course, that narrative should be the part of every decent teacher's normal "lesson plan" anyway but much of that is delivered spontaneously in the course of a typical lesson. It's delivered through chat and examples and experimentation. It does not necessarily get written down, word for word, as I found that I had to do now. All of this took time. It became almost like a project in itself and occupied many hours, outside the allotted time of the "virtual" school day. I now found myself working on new lesson materials on most evenings and also at the weekends.

In addition to what seemed like the work required just to effectively do my job, I had also been given another task by the Head teacher of my school. When I had first offered my resignation, she had suggested that I might like to do the Speech for the annual Foundation Day Service that would normally have taken place in the local church at the end of the first week of May. Most years, this was delivered by a guest speaker, some visiting dignitary or other with some sort of connection to the school. It was generally some sort of senior cleric or a journalist or charity worker or even an ex-pupil made good. The speech would be along the lines of "This is what the Founder of the school means to me" and would contain some maxims for how to lead a positive and constructive life.

Quite often the guest speaker would somehow manage to strike the wrong sort of note or to put their foot in it in some way. I guess it was a pretty tough audience to play to: two year-groups from the school (generally Year 7 and Year 10) most of whom were just thinking about the half-day holiday that would follow later in the day after they had dutifully sat through an hour's worth of dreary church service; and the assembled staff and dignitaries, none of whom particularly wanted to be there either, one assumed. Therefore, the guest speaker was an easy sitting target for their disgruntlement and criticism. Twenty minutes of do-gooding platitudes, on top of the hymn singing and the prayers (never thought to be appropriate in a multi-faith North London school) were probably enough to try the patience of the most biddable staff members and many of them traditionally enjoyed laying into the guest speaker on the walk back from the church to the school at the end of the testing hour's church service of commemoration of the school's illustrious founder.

This year, however, the Head was kind enough to invite me to be the guest speaker. "We thought you could say something about what it has been like to have been at the school for thirty-three years… "

Did I detect something of a back-handed compliment there? The way she said it, it sounded like a prison sentence. "Done for thirty-three years…" Perhaps it wasn't something to actually be proud of? Perhaps all those years of service were just a testimony to inertia, to a lack of ambition? A fatal tendency to want to play it safe and stick with "the devil you know"?

No. Those were just the negative voices in my head. Of course, it was an honour to have been asked. I should be flattered that she imagined me capable of having something meaningful and interesting to say. I said that I would "Think about it…"

I thought about it for about an hour. Yes, I'd do it. After all, I had been a Drama teacher and although somewhat reserved and diffident by nature, I never could resist an opportunity to show off or to commandeer a platform if one was being so readily offered.

Unfortunately, of course, there was to be no Church service of commemoration this year. There would be no audience of nearly three hundred students and one hundred staff and dignitaries to whom I could perform and offer my words of hard-won wisdom. This was the year of the pandemic and all public services of commemoration had been cancelled. People could no longer gather in churches to worship together. Hymn singing and communal celebration was no longer allowed.

Truthfully, that came as a bit of a relief – phew! Having originally accepted with alacrity, the whole thing quickly became a major source of anxiety. When we were dismissed from school in March with not much prospect of returning until God knew when, I felt a modicum of relief that at least I wouldn't have the stress of preparing and delivering the big Foundation Day speech.

It was with some alarm, therefore, that at some point a couple of weeks before this event would have taken place, I received an extremely unwelcome email from the Head saying something to the effect that it had been decided to hold the Foundation Day Service "online" and that my speech would be the centre-piece to the event and was I still happy to do it? Damn! And I genuinely thought that I had got away with that one!

Of course, coward that I am, I immediately replied to the Head's request for online content saying that, of course, I would be delighted to oblige and thanking her for the privilege of such an opportunity.

I then went into a complete panic.

The prospect of public humiliation loomed large. What on earth could I say that would merit the entire school population tuning in to listen to my words of wisdom? While the original notion had been that I could share stories and anecdotes about what it had been like to have been in the school for thirty-three years, the sad reality now was that my mind just drew a total blank. What on earth was there to say?

For days and days, I wracked my brain. What was expected here? What would go down well? What would command people's attention and respect?

In desperation, I even emailed the Head for some guidance – forgetting, of course, that she had a million and one other things to do sorting out how to run the school in the middle of a global pandemic and that she had given me this job because it would then be one less thing for her to have to think about. Eventually, in answer to my question asking her what she wanted, she sent back a couple of lines: "Oh just a few funny stories – you know the kind of thing…" Funny stories! Oh no… jokes! I had never been able to make people laugh unscripted and now here I was being briefed to "set the table on a roar" at a time of national catastrophe and breakdown.

Needless to say, I then had many a sleepless night sketching out the content of my speech; writing and re-writing bits of it in my head, desperate to find the right tone, the right tenor, above all the right content. Eventually, it did come to me. In a Eureka moment, I thought "Of course. Just talk about all the things we are missing about the school during this strange period of lockdown..." And that was what I did. Yes, I began with a brief overview of the changes over the years (the fact that when I first arrived thirty-three years before all the "Masters" had worn gowns and smoked pipes and there wasn't a computer in sight...that sort of thing) but I got through that fairly speedily and then got on to a pretty comprehensive list of all the myriad of things every one of us was missing about school while away from it and "locked down". Most of what I talked about was the buzz of being in the building and the companionship and camaraderie among both the staff and the pupils. I paid tribute to the teacher who had died because that was such an awful example of the havoc being wreaked by the disease. I also tried to put my finger on the particular qualities that made the school so special: its high academic aspirations, the range and breadth of its extra-curricular activities; its liberal (and again very North London) ethos; its respect for the Arts and tolerance for individuality and even eccentricity. It really was a very special place and it had certainly sustained and nurtured me for practically the whole of my working life and I felt very strongly the need to acknowledge and pay tribute to that.

After the initial panic and fear that I might not be able to deliver, I started to become very focused and driven. Writing the speech became like a project for me and I began to work away at it almost every day. I knew that I had to come up with something that would be personal, sincere and honest but also be engaging and (I hoped) amusing to listen to. It also had to be something that I would be comfortable delivering, performing even. Given the fact that I had been asked to do this because I was about to retire after a lifetime of service to the school, this would be my Swansong, a great final flourish with which to end, a very public Farewell. I began to relish the challenge, working away at the speech, honing and polishing it, writing and re-writing it in order to get something that would be as near to perfect as I was capable of creating. The autobiographical novel to which I had returned as my current lockdown project would be temporarily shelved in order for me to devote all of my energies to "The Speech". Friends and colleagues were now regularly bombarded with an almost daily commentary on my progress. Some days I thought I'd got it; I'd got the subject matter and had found the 'mots justes' and the witty turns of phrase and the memorable maxims which I thought the thing required. Other days, I felt less positive and would read over what I had written, hearing nothing but a dreary collection of cliches which would be unlikely to hold anyone's attention for even a few seconds, let alone the fifteen minutes or so which I planned to fill.

Eventually, after day after day of quite intensive work on the piece, I had what I considered to be my best shot. There was a bit of personal reminiscence, some reflection and a few 'lessons for life' about all the wonderful things that the school had given to everybody associated with it and which we were all missing during these weeks of social isolation and home working. It was a speech for our times and, I hoped, a morale raiser with a little bit of homespun wisdom thrown in.

The writing was one thing, the delivery of it was another. I gathered that the speech would need to be recorded and then made available via the school website, as part of a number of offerings to mark the school's Foundation Day. There would be the usual selection of Bible readings and of poetry by senior pupils and governors, but my speech was to be the 'main attraction'. Apparently, most of the offerings would be filmed on people's phones and then uploaded on to the website. I tried this but it looked scrappy and amateur. I wanted a more professional gloss for my own offering. Somehow, I managed to persuade one of the IT technicians at the school to set up a state-of-the-art camera and a microphone in one of the school's assembly halls in order for me to make a properly produced film version of my oration.

We selected a day on which to do this. The room was all set up. I changed into a suitably "smart casual" outfit: proper shirt and blazer but no tie (elbowing the jeans and t-shirt which had been my habitual outfit for the last four weeks). I combed and styled my hair in the way that I would normally have worn it for work and made sure that I did a brisk jog round the park beforehand so that I could be buzzing with endorphins and positivity by the time I was ready to perform.

I did a 'dress run' in front of the camera, working out where I was to place my script and how to get my eye level in line with the camera lens and then I went for a take. It wasn't perfect but the occasional fluffed line or hesitant moment merely added to the spontaneity and naturalness of the performance. I certainly felt that to film it more than once would have started to make it seem stilted and over-rehearsed and so the first take became the final one. That was the one that was uploaded and sent out onto the 'Cloud' or wherever these things are stored.

Within a few minutes of putting it out there, I started to get feedback. The Secretary to the Governors, who had been co-ordinating the whole event, immediately wrote me a lovely email saying how much she valued my sentiments and how she appreciated the 'performance' of what I had written. I think she called it a "tour de force" – which pleased me greatly, as that had been my intention.

A couple of days later, the material 'went live' and I am very gratified to recall that the feedback and response I had from everyone who saw it was universally positive, bordering on the euphoric. This absolutely delighted me and provided a real boost in what might otherwise have been a grim and dispiriting time. It was something to do with the fact that even though we were all isolated and apart in those 'locked-down' weeks, the school at least continued to function as a community of which I was still very much a part. The fact that colleagues, students and friends had taken the time to sit through and listen to what I had written made me feel very connected to them all and I felt that my contribution to that world was valued and appreciated. For a few moments, I was at its centre and had been able to articulate something of what we were all feeling during those dark and testing times. The gratification and buzz and excitement of this project had certainly succeeded in lifting me up and out of the lockdown doldrums for a while. Yes, this was a world which I would be leaving forever in a few months' time for but for now, as the longest serving member of that school staff, I was certainly still very much a part of it and this was still something to savour and to relish.

For several days after the material had been made public, I was the fortunate recipient of countless emails and text messages praising me for my contribution. This happened to such an extent and was so unexpected that eventually I became almost overwhelmed by the reactions. The generosity and kindness of everyone was quite unexpected and, again, a reminder of how much I had become a part of the fabric of that institution and what an important part it had played in my life. In all the uncertainty and dread of those pandemic months, my position at the school had given me some stability and a sense of belonging. While every one of us was having to deal with the health crisis in our own way, the fact that we were all part of that great school was a cause for celebration and it seemed like a beacon of positivity during those days of fear and uncertainty. Maybe that was why so many people logged on to watch and listen and even appreciated what they heard there.

Normally Foundation Day was viewed as a rather dull annual ritual, mostly appreciated for the half day holiday that accompanied it, plus the chance to get mildly tipsy on the couple of glasses of cheap wine, with which the celebratory Foundation Day lunch was normally washed down. This particular year, however, it was as if people wanted to be reminded that they were part of a venerable institution that had been around for centuries and that its traditions and rituals were somehow irrepressible; the "ancient foundation" that was the school had been around since the seventeenth century and it would take more than this wretched pandemic to wipe it out. In my speech, I had waxed lyrical about the community to which we all belonged and whose loss we were all so keenly feeling now. Being able to tune into that from home was a way of connecting with each other again; we were able to remind ourselves that we were all part of something bigger than ourselves and that one day this nightmare would all be over.

I was truly amazed at the reaction I received for my little

speech. Yes, I had tried to do it as well as I could but I was still conscious of the fact that all I had done was piece together my thoughts about being in lockdown and away from the hustle and bustle of the daily school routine. I was extremely flattered if in the course of trying to share a few of these thoughts in public, I had managed to say something that people found moving or true. I had no idea that people would even watch it or, if they did, that they would then be kind enough to say that they liked it. The fact that so many sent emails and texts praising my efforts was testimony to the extreme generosity and decency of so many of my colleagues and students. The rush of responses was certainly extremely gratifying and lifted my spirits in what otherwise might have been a very dispiriting time.

All through these weeks, the schools were still being kept open. I am not sure that the general public were aware that significant numbers of teachers were still going into schools on a regular basis. As well as going in to do things like record my speech with the help of the IT technician (which was at least a morning's work!) I'd also been in several times for help with the new technology. There were "socially distanced" training sessions arranged in school for staff who, like me, found it bewildering, unfamiliar and difficult to get to grips with. This was a fairly small group of generally older and more mature staff – the sorts who had never quite mastered the mysteries of the 'interactive whiteboard', for example, and we were all very grateful for those extra sessions arranged in school that were designed to bring us up to speed. In the best pedagogical tradition, the fact that we were learning to do this in a group enabled us to help each other as well as providing some much needed camaraderie in those otherwise bleak and very isolated times.

Another way of keeping connected to the school was doing what became known as 'key worker' supervision. All schools were expected to remain open to a degree in order to provide an education for the children of those key workers who were not able to work from home. Doctors and nurses, transport workers, supermarket assistants, pharmacists and delivery drivers were still able to send their children to school where they would be offered some form of face-to-face supervision in a classroom. Ours being a largely middle-class school, most of the parents were able to work at home unless they were directly involved in health care. Of these, most of the students were thought to be mature and resourceful enough to be able to supervise themselves for the day. Therefore, the offer of schooling for key worker children tended not to be taken up apart from by a handful. Nevertheless, there were still a small number coming in to school all day who needed teacher supervision. The Head asked for volunteers to staff this, generally asking for two members of staff a day.

I volunteered for this, partly because I thought it was the least I could do in the circumstances. In the spirit of wanting to 'give a little bit back', it seemed to me no hardship at all to sit in one of the communal areas of the school with another colleague and supervise half a dozen students while they got on with their online lessons. I could teach my classes from the laptop and then when I wasn't doing that I could get on with my marking and other bits and pieces of work.

The key worker children were a somewhat forlorn bunch, unable to understand why they alone out of a school population of nearly one and a half thousand should have been singled out to come in when all of their mates were at home – having lie-ins and able to play their computer games in between their probably rather sparse diet of online lessons. Their pals could go to the fridge for a snack or two or play about on their phones while they had to slog away at what must have seemed pretty much like a normal school day. They had to wear uniform and ask permission if they wanted to go to the toilet. They were not allowed out except at break or lunchtime and they could not leave until the bell went for the new shortened school day at three p.m. They obviously felt that they had got a bit of a raw deal.

Even so, I enjoyed doing those sessions. In the end, I signed up to do one a week. If I'm honest, it just felt good to have somewhere to go once a week. Above all, it was so nice to see other people: the other supervising teachers but also other teaching and non-teaching colleagues. Some of the office and premises staff were around and there was always a handful of other teachers who'd popped in to collect some teaching materials or because they just needed a quiet space in which to catch up on their marking. Even though we all had to keep our distance and be scrupulous about hand-washing and observe the one-way system around the school building (these were still the days before compulsory mask-wearing), it was great to just be able to exchange a few words of chat with each other, to have a bit of a laugh or a moan: to be able to compare notes on how we were all doing; to swap tips for getting through it and for morale raising activities. It was a chance, once a week, to connect with some warm, friendly and familiar faces. I certainly don't think I was alone in really looking forward to going in to do those sessions.

Certainly, by this time, the phone calls and the keeping in touch with people remotely was starting to fall off. I'd speak to my sister on an almost daily basis, it was true, but to others my phone calls diminished and became more and more sporadic. Like many people during those weeks, I phoned my friends less and less partly because there were fewer and fewer things to say. I did my job (online) went for a walk, queued up at the supermarket, watched some telly, went to bed. The days were unvarying. There just wasn't any news or anything much to tell anyone. Yes, we could bemoan the government and share our feelings about the Prime Minister (shocked when he became ill and was taken into intensive care and although nobody liked his blundering 'posh boy' style, there was not a single one of us who did not want him to get better and certainly nobody ever wanted him to die). Like many others, I supposed I found myself 'scheduling' phone calls. They became something one had to gear oneself up for. One was no longer in the mood for spontaneous chatter and wittering on. The point of booking a call at an appointed time meant that one could put aside time for it, be 'ready' and able to sound reassuring and wise in the way that one thought would best support one's friends. While different friends talked about their sadness or despair or emptiness, I felt I could offer measured and compassionate listening that might make them feel a little better by the end of our conversation. I had to work hard not to get irritated at any suggestion of boasting ("I walked ten miles today" "Just finished 'Anna Karenina' for the second time" "Learnt a new Bach partita this week") and had to rally all my most effusive words of praise, knowing that all they were really doing was trying to give themselves a bit of purpose, trying to stop themselves falling into a desert of ennui and boredom. Good on them. Why not encourage and praise? Be a bit generous for goodness sake!

As the end of May approached, however, we teachers had to grapple with the exams fiasco. If my head had been ever so slightly swollen by the adulation I'd received for my speech, this issue quickly brought me back down to earth again – as it did for all of us. We had been aware for some weeks now that the public exams normally sat by students in May and June were to be cancelled. Instead, they were to be replaced by CAGs – Centre Assessed Grades. In other words, every teacher would decide what each student was capable of achieving and what grade they would have been awarded had the exams taken place. Of course, this meant that the grade awarded by the teacher had to be supported by some sort of evidence. That evidence had to be made available and had to be able to stand up to the scrutiny of an external eye. In other words, as a teacher I needed to be able to produce pieces of paper with students' work on it: essays, coursework, portfolios outlining the rationale behind their acting performances (their research, preparation process, response to feedback, evaluation of their final performance – that sort of thing). However, not content with awarding each student a grade, the exam boards were insisting that we placed the students in our classes in rank order. Therefore, one student had to be awarded the top mark in the group and the rest of the cohort had to be graded below them. Now the sticking point here was the fact that there were numbers of students who were equally good and, in the final external exam, would even have been awarded exactly the same marks. Apparently, this was not permissible under the new system: all students needed to be placed in a strict rank order. This rank order then needed to be justified and supported with evidence. Such 'evidence' was then to be submitted to the Senior Leadership Team in every school and they would then validate, or not, the marks the teachers had given.

It was a palaver and, although supposed to make things fairer, had the reverse effect. As teachers responsible for our students and wanting to credit them as much as possible in this worst of all years, it felt like a betrayal. We did not want to be putting some student 'fourth', for example when all of the students in that class were equally good. They would all, if they'd gone through the normal examination process, have received exactly the same grades. This system seemed designed to create false and thoroughly unfair disparities between equally gifted and talented students. It quickly became a shambles and a system in which none of us had any confidence at all.

Marks went backwards and forwards between the subject teachers, heads of department and the Senior staff while they were tweaked and adjusted in order to fit the twin demands of both the new system and also to provide a fair reflection of a student's ability, work record and academic worth. It proceeded to cause untold stress and anxiety, on top of all the other worries about physical health, mental health, being cooped up, not picking up the disease, trying to get supplies from the supermarket, trying to make best use of the enforced isolation, not going mad at neighbours into whose close proximity we had all been artificially thrown and grappling with the general feeling of helplessness at being governed by fools who seemed to have not the slightest idea of what they were doing or of how to ever get us out of this mess.

It was, therefore, a month of new routines and practices and, although supposedly working from home, school and work was still very much an integral part of daily life, with the weekly visits to the school building and even some face-to-face contact with colleagues. It was not 'home alone' the whole time.

On the other hand, it was as if normality and human contact had become severely rationed. There was no escaping the growing sense of isolation, with only the television and an endless succession of domestic chores to alleviate the tedium, while phone contact with friends became increasingly less frequent.

June

What continued to make life more bearable was the weather. Somehow, it still managed to give us day after day of endless sunshine and blue skies. Air travel had almost stopped so maybe that had something to do with it? We had ceased polluting our skies so for a few weeks they were pure and untainted, while those of us on the ground basked in the sunshine and the summer holiday weather.

Shorts and t-shirt became the norm and for a few hours in the afternoon, sunning on the lawn at the back of my flats was now a part of my daily routine.

June was my birthday month but this year it was also the seventy fifth anniversary of the end of the Second World War. On the 8th June there was to a be a big national holiday, with street parties and spectacular celebratory TV shows but all socially distanced, of course. Boris Johnson and his cronies consistently evoked the Second World War when talking of the challenge we all faced now; of the need to "pull together" and "do our bit"; of facing down the enemy; of making sacrifices for the greater good and other such Churchillian cliches. I suppose there was a tenuous resemblance between the two national crises in that there was danger of imminent death and, in both cases, we all had to give up some of our individual freedoms for the greater good of the whole. I'm not sure that it went much further than that, though. None of us were about to go into armed conflict with a ferocious enemy. Most of us had comfortable homes filled with a plethora of home entertainment devices with which to help us pass the time. We all had phones and iPads and laptops with which to communicate with others. The supermarkets (although severely stretched at the start) were now well stocked with an unimaginable supply of goods from around the world and were positively exotic in comparison with the privations endured by our forefathers. I am sure that many of us were not that impressed by Johnson's efforts to ape a Churchillian leader, which struck many of us as phony and insincere. There was always the sense with Johnson that he was ever so slightly taking the piss at the expense of his audience; that he was doing his best to play-act 'the big man' propped up by his old Etonian bluster and sense of entitlement, convinced that he knew better than anyone else and that he was the one to lead us through this.

Vera Lynn's old war song "We'll Meet Again" was constantly rolled out during these weeks of prolonged separation from loved ones. Almost all of us were doing what we had been told. We were staying at home and "protecting the NHS" by not venturing out of our homes except for our daily ration of exercise. We weren't going into each other's houses or travelling anywhere and, it was true, we weren't having face to face sight of each other. We did have to be positive and believe in the message of that song, that we would "meet again some sunny day" when this whole wretched business was over. Even her Majesty herself made reference to the song at the end of a highly unusual solo address to the nation. There she was on television, praising us for our efforts and our fortitude and reminding us that the privations we were all facing now would eventually end and that we would "meet again". This was a moving television appearance by the Queen; moving in the way that seeing a ninety-four-year-old woman still willing to put herself out there and attempt to rally us all could not be seen as anything other than kindly meant and sincerely intended. Even she, in her castle and surrounded by flunkeys, was basically trapped at home and unable to see any of her closest relatives and was just sitting it out, like the rest of us. She needn't have bothered to make this national rallying cry but she did and I am sure that it was appreciated by the many.

The month of June was also my birthday month. I was born on the 1st June, 1957 and normally the anniversary of this date was the focus of some modest celebrations among me, my friends and relatives. Of course, this year the celebrations would be even more modest than usual, perhaps even non-existent. How was one to celebrate a birthday if we were unable to meet up?

With my friend Deborah, we worked out a way round this. We arranged to meet in the car park around which the crescent of my flats had been built and we intended to sit out on the lawn in the sunshine at around five o'clock (after our online school duties had been completed) and drink a bottle of Cava from some plastic cups and accompanied by pieces of a small cake purchased from M&S. This we duly did. It felt sort of illegal and surreptitious but we did manage to salvage something almost festive from the occasion. It was liberating to be sat outside in the sunshine and to be drinking alcohol. It was also entertaining to be able to watch the neighbours come and go, some of whom had become major characters in my personal mythology over the days and weeks of lockdown in which there had been almost no face-to-face contact with anyone else. One or two other friends had kindly but gingerly dropped items at the door, buzzing on my intercom for me to come down to collect – a bit like a supermarket delivery person. We'd have a few snatched sentences of illegal chatter standing outside the front door and I'd then rush the small gift upstairs to douse it in anti-bacterial spray, so paranoid had we all become by that point.

At the end of that first week of June, the whole nation had been planning to celebrate the 75th Anniversary of VE Day. An extra Bank Holiday had been arranged and events such as Street Parties and a live broadcast from Buckingham Palace had been planned. I doubted that on my modern estate of largely rented out apartments there would be much of a street party. Even though I had started talking to some of my immediate neighbours over the course of the lockdown, we could hardly be said to be a cohesive community. There was no street WhatsApp group, for example, such as I knew friends from other neighbourhoods belonged to, with their frequent exchanges of gossip about the other people on their streets. A few of us did just about manage the Thursday evening 'clap for carers', leaning out of the windows of our apartments and grinning self-consciously at each other as we took part in that weekly ritual. However, that was about as much community spirit as we could muster here, sadly.

That day was another blisteringly hot day and I remember finishing off a long walk that afternoon and making my way home through the backstreets of North Enfield. There, it seemed, the community spirit was very much alive and kicking. In those rows of modest two up two down terraced houses, there seemed to be a number of lively looking street parties in full swing. People had set up public address systems and music from the period (Vera Lynn, The Andrews Sisters, Glenn Miller) reverberated between the houses. At almost every door, jolly looking old couples and smiling young families were sitting out on their front steps or on garden chairs, munching crisps and sandwiches from paper plates and toasting each other with cans of Stella and glasses of prosecco. After all these months of grimness, it was lovely to see people looking as if they had something to celebrate. The carnival atmosphere was infectious and people looked more cheerful than they had done for months. I guess, by that time, there was a bit of a feeling that the disease had done its worst. The numbers of the infected and the hospitalised were starting to come down. Even the daily death toll was falling significantly. There was talk that soon, shops, pubs and restaurants might be able to open again and this alone must have created a more optimistic mood. There was something about that day: the glorious sunshine, the music of wartime with its optimism and sentimentality, the fact that the day seemed to have brought large numbers of people together, that really did make us feel as if we might at long last be turning the corner.

Needless to say, there wasn't quite the same effort being made on my estate, as I re-entered it at about 3.30 p.m. on that afternoon. There were a few kids playing out on their trikes supervised by groups of parents who stood around smoking and chatting to each other in a language I did not recognise (Polish, Bulgarian, Romanian, I guessed?) and then two or three of the old pensioners were sat out on the edge of the car park on plastic folding chairs and sipping carefully from plastic supermarket wine glasses while they reminisced about times past, no doubt bemoaning the ways in which things had generally declined and weren't as good as they once were.

I'm afraid to say, I felt no connection with any of them and just scurried past, avoiding people's eyes and keen to get back to the safe haven of my flat. Also, I was tired after my walk. Walking had become a major feature of each day now. I'd work for the morning, have a sandwich in front of the lunchtime news and then get myself out for at least a couple of hours in the afternoon, returning in time to catch up with any work emails before turning on the tv for the five o'clock Downing Street Briefings to find out about the progress of the pandemic on that day.

With the walks, I became amazed at the sheer variety of places I was able to find to walk to each day. Every afternoon, I would attempt to go in a different direction. West would take me to Groveland's Park in Winchmore Hill, with its lovely lake, gentle hills and woodlands. North would take me up through Enfield Town Park to either Forty Hall or Hillyfields park. South would be down to Palmers Green and Broomfield Park, with its ponds and water features but also with its glorious panoramic views of the London skyline and Ally Pally straight ahead and with the towers of the Canary Wharf and the City on the horizon, which never failed to thrill. Then finally to the East, there was the delightful oasis of the Firs Farm Wetlands, again with its water and wildlife and the enormous fen- like fields that apparently had once been home to a camp for Italian prisoners of war during the 1940s. To the left of this was also Edmonton Cemetery which could be glimpsed through the fence and stretched all the way along the side of the park. At the end of it was the A10 and an underpass which led to another park near Edmonton's Silver Street station but I only ever went there once, finding its atmosphere slightly threatening and somewhat uncongenial.

Along the way, there were all sorts of discoveries to be made. There was the path which ran alongside the New River and could be followed pretty much uninterrupted from Enfield all the way down to Alexandra Palace. There were the imposing Edwardian villas which lined the streets of Palmers Green and Southgate; majestic looking dwellings which radiated a sense of solidity and calm in those otherwise fraught summer afternoons. There were the narrow secret footpaths which could be followed between the rows of suburban houses and would suddenly bring you out on to a playing field or a woodland or to rows of allotments. There were the little convenience stores, tucked away on the corners of roads, with their awnings down to protect the produce against the heat and at which there were no queues (unlike the big supermarkets).

Eventually, almost like children who were to be rewarded for good behaviour, we were informed that there could be some easing of the restrictions which had so constrained our lives over the previous twelve or so weeks. The government announced that it would be permissible for small groups (or perhaps it was just pairs? I can't quite remember the details) to meet outside or to take exercise together or to at least now begin to interact together. This seemed like a big deal but was also strangely anxiety inducing. Having for so many weeks got used to a completely alien, isolated way of living, sustained by strict routines in order to preserve sanity and physical health, the idea that we could now meet with another person instilled a sense of panic and even fear.

For a start, who? Who would be the person selected from out of one's friendship circle to be the "one" that could be met up with? Should it be my father, whom I had not seen for many weeks now? Should it be my sister? Should it be my friend, Deborah, who was the closest to me geographically? What about other friends, who now started to ring up and send texts with tentative requests for meetings?

I think the rule was that you could only meet with one other but if that one other was a different person each time and we both kept a couple of metres apart and arranged to meet outside in the open air, then surely that was about as safe as we could get? Certainly for me, just meeting with one person and excluding all of the others from my friendship circle would not have worked. The way in which I had always led my life was to surround myself with a little circle of different people. I enjoyed the variety provided by my group of friends. I had never wanted to be limited to the company of the same old person. I liked having different personalities in my life and never more so than now. There were at least half a dozen people that I was desperate to see.

At the same time, I had got very used to being self-sufficient during the course of the lockdown. Every day was structured around a carefully organised routine designed to cater to my need for exercise, intellectual stimulation and entertainment. While I had maintained social contact through phone calls, emailing and texting, the thought of now setting aside at least a couple of hours for a social meeting of some sort became somewhat alarming. What would there be to talk about? How would I fit this in around my reading programme, my school work, my creative writing, my domestic chores, my carefully selected television shows? Where would we go for our 'socially distanced' meeting outside? Where would be mutually convenient? What would it be like being with another person again after all of this time?

Eventually, I did agree to meet with my friend Deborah near to the lake in Groveland's Park. True to form, it was another hot, sunny afternoon but I have to admit to feeling anxious and nervous about the meeting. I just did not trust myself to be able to interact normally with another person after all those weeks of being locked down. I felt sure that I would come over as 'odd', as socially awkward, gauche and unpractised in the ways of conversation. That morning, I had done a lengthy jog in my local park in order to get a good rush of endorphins flowing to get me into a more upbeat and sociable mood. I'd left the car behind and decided to walk to the park but, of course, underestimated the time it would take me to get there so ended up being rather late and arrived breathless and somewhat fraught. I also wondered whether I would look different to her. My hair hadn't been cut for months and I was wearing tatty old, badly ironed clothes which didn't present me at my best.

As things turned out, though, of course we were able to pick up where we had left off. It was almost funny seeing each other again after all that time and for the first few moments of being reunited we were just collapsed in laughter. That laughing together broke the ice and immediately we were back into gossiping and chatting away as naturally as if we had only just left each other the day before. We sprawled out on the grass, basking in the sunshine. The last time we had been together (apart from the very brief surreptitious birthday meet) it had still felt like the early Spring but now here we were lolling on the grass in what felt like the middle of the summer.

That afternoon the park was a hive of activity. Joggers, mums with babies in strollers, elderly couples clutching on to each other's elbows, loping groups of teenagers, dog walkers, friends chatting away to each other nineteen to the dozen and, like us, desperate to catch up after months of having been apart. We circled the park at least a couple of times and then ended up on Winchmore Hill Green, at one of its hugely popular cafes where we joined a queue for takeaway coffee and one of their extremely calorific home-made cakes.

For at least a couple of hours, we barely paused for breath, offloading to each other about what it had been like to do our jobs online (we were both teachers), about our mutual friends and how they had all been coping under lockdown; about the epic amounts of telly we'd both been watching and how that had been a salvation during these circumscribed times and how we couldn't possibly have survived without it. We talked about our fears for the progress of the disease and about how it had affected the people we knew; we bemoaned the incompetence and stupidity of the government and their flagrant floundering. I talked through all my worries about having resigned my job and wanted to be reassured that I had done the right thing. Was I going to be OK? Was I going to survive? Was I mad to give up paid employment in order to do God alone knew what? We talked about our feelings of isolation and how lonely we had often felt over the last few months but also how we had managed to survive and congratulated ourselves on our self-sufficiency, resilience and ability to cope in such testing circumstances.

In spite of my fears that I might not be able to get into gear and interact socially again, that afternoon it all seemed surprisingly easy. Maybe all that stuff they kept saying on the radio about how we are all 'social creatures' was true. It certainly hadn't been difficult or awkward to pick up the threads again. I felt relieved and elated as I walked back home. Perhaps I was normal after all? After all those silent weeks, with only minimal social interaction (the one day a week at school, supervising the Key Worker children) the brief exchanges in the supermarket and pharmacy, the electronic encounters on Zoom, it was good to know that I could be with another person for an afternoon and not feel a sense of awkwardness or strain. Maybe normal life would return?

There was now a gradual sense of things starting to open up a bit more. My friend Jonathan and I arranged to meet at a midway point between his home in Greenwich and mine in Enfield. We lighted upon Kings Cross as a reasonable compromise and on the following Saturday afternoon, I drove to a tube station and got on the train to go and meet him. Descending the escalator at Bounds Green felt like a very strange thing to be doing again after all those months of hibernation. Partly, I worried about the safety of it. How could it possibly be safe to be all that distance below ground, trapped in a tube carriage with a load of potential spreaders? As it turned out, I need hardly have worried. The train was virtually deserted and I was able to sit as far away as possible from my fellow passengers. We all wore masks and although I feared sitting on one of the seats and contaminating myself that way, the journey was over in about twenty minutes and I didn't feel that I was putting myself in a particularly precarious position. As well as the trepidation, though, there was also a kind of exhilaration that normal life was slowly returning. I was once again doing what I had done practically every weekend of my life. I was on the tube, being borne off into central London. Transported to that world of metropolitan excitement; to the buzz and glamour of one of the major capital cities on the planet. I can do this, I thought. My heart felt suddenly lighter, more optimistic, after all those months of heaviness and fear, that wearying sense that life was over. Now, everything suddenly seemed possible again.

I emerged from the underground into the blazing sunlight

of the summer afternoon and found my friend waiting for me. We weren't exactly sure where we were going to go. It hardly mattered. What mattered was just to be out and meeting up again after months of separation, in which the most exciting excursion had been a trip to the local Tesco's. We made for the Regents Canal. Again, as in the local park the weekend before, the towpath had what I can only describe as a carnival atmosphere. Everyone was out in their most colourful summer clothes, all in shorts and brightly coloured t-shirts and sunglasses. People were laughing and whooping as they greeted each other. We weren't the only friends celebrating a reunion after months of separation.

It was important to find somewhere to eat and crossing the canal by Granary Square there seemed to be a number of places open for takeaway sandwiches and drinks. We stood in line at a trendy snack bar and ordered a couple of enormous baguettes, dripping with mozzarella and basil and olive oil. Jonathan ordered a beer but I stuck with coffee (my favourite lockdown tipple) which we then took to some steps over-looking the canal where we joined a very hip and happening young crowd. The steps were covered in artificial grass and we felt like an audience for a play as we watched the barges on the canal below pass by, while the various cyclists, joggers and walkers competed for space on the tow path.

It felt suddenly extraordinary to be out, to be in central London, to be eating and drinking outside on that summer afternoon, in the hub of all those chattering and stylish young people. Just as the tube journey in to town on that day had given me a bit of a lift, had buoyed me up and made me feel optimistic and that life had got the capacity to return to normal, I now felt similarly positive about the future. We must surely be through the worst of it now? We had paid our price, done our penance for whatever crimes against the planet this terrible disease had been punishing us for. Now we were starting to re-emerge. There was a summer. There were friends. There was a social life again. There was food and drink in the sunshine. There was chatter and laughter and views and opinions and stories to swap. Life was returning...

It had been some months since I had last seen my father and as soon as we were permitted to meet outdoors again, I thought that it would be OK for me to go over and at least sit in his garden for a few hours. It had felt like a terrible dereliction of my duty, not seeing him at all from the middle of March until the height of the summer. However, I was merely doing as instructed. We had been told to stay at home, to not engage in any but essential travel. The news had been full of care home catastrophes in which waves and waves of the elderly had all been infected and struck down with the disease and I felt that it was right and proper that I stay away while the pandemic was at its height. He did have carers going in to his home twice a week as well as a cleaner and regular visits from my sister, who lived closer to him than I did. While we were aware that her thrice weekly visits were probably against the rules we were also equally aware that without this regular contact from her, he simply would not have survived. It was a question of choosing the lesser of the two evils. After all, she had not mixed with anyone apart from her family and they had all been holed up at home for months, not seeing anybody outside the family circle so as far as she was concerned, my sister thought that she was very unlikely to infect him. On the other hand, if she had not gone over as much as she did, he would have seen nobody and had no one to do his shopping or washing up or change his sheets or help him to get into fresh clothes. She maintained that what she did was pretty minimal but I am sure it was the key to his survival during this very difficult time.

Before Covid had struck, my father had managed to get himself to a council run lunch club once a day which was held a short bus ride away from his home and which gave him the chance to mix with some other elderly people as well as providing him with a hot meal every weekday. Of course, this was one of the first things to go, as soon as lockdown loomed. We immediately tried to get some sort of "meals on wheels" service for him because by this time his dementia was so advanced that he was no longer capable of cooking even the simplest meal for himself. Even operating the microwave and taking a TV dinner out of its packaging would have been beyond him.

Finding a 'Meals on Wheels' service was easier said than done. Needless to say, the council no longer provided this service and many of the private companies which advertised something similar were either far too expensive or did not deliver to the area in which my father lived. Eventually, after what seemed like hours of being put on hold and transferred from one department to another, I managed to track down a company which would deliver a two course hot meal to my father's door each day for just under seven pounds a time. Seeing that this meant that nobody would have to go out shopping for him or cook, this seemed like a bargain to me. The food would be delivered to the house, piping hot and ready to eat. Result.

Of course, the quality of the said meals was not great. The meals were packaged in tin foil cartons and enticingly labelled with titles like 'Cumberland sausage and mash' or 'Beef in Red

Wine' but, according to my dad, the meals all tasted and looked very much the same. They seemed to be a sort of brown mush – but they were hot and they were delivered by a cheerful chap who rang on the door and left the meal helpfully positioned on a tray on the chair by the phone in his hall – so at least there was a bit of human interaction along with the daily delivery of the food.

I decided to drive round to him for that first visit, during that gradual easing out of lockdown. Normally, I would have travelled over to him by public transport, using the tube, overground train and a bus but now that felt too dangerous. Three possible sources of contamination and I also needed to bear in mind that at the age of ninety, he was most definitely at the top end of the most vulnerable group. My sister and I had often reminded ourselves that he could well have been in a care home and chances are, had he been, he would not have survived. The care homes had been ravaged by the disease. Not only had it swept through the entire care service for the elderly but the conditions in which the very old were now kept were approaching the inhuman. They were forbidden visitors and were frequently pictured on the news looking tragically bewildered while desperate relatives attempted to communicate with them via Facetime or Zoom – but almost always to no avail. We had, in fact, considered a care home for him a couple of summers before when he seemed to be losing his short-term memory and could no longer boil an egg or even dress himself properly. Then it had seemed to be almost inevitable. But I had taken him off to visit a couple of local ones and we had quickly reached the conclusion that while he was struggling to look after himself and found living by himself extremely lonely, it would be better for him to maintain his independence than to end up incarcerated in one of those places. Yes, the staff there were all caring and friendly types but it was more the sight of the other inmates that put me off. Most striking were the glimpses into their rooms. The inmates all seemed to have the doors of their rooms open as we walked along the corridors. Although it was the middle of the day, we passed a number of rooms in which there was just a comatose looking figure stretched out on the bed, clearly only days away from death. Could I really condemn my father to an existence surrounded by such sights? He might have to go into one of these places one day but for the time being it was better to keep him out of there and in the real world, my sister and I reasoned.

That Sunday morning, I got into my car and drove along the North Circular and over Kew Bridge and through Richmond down to Teddington. What was remarkable was the ease of the car journey on that day. Normally it would have been stop start all the way but on that particular day it was something of a breeze. I guessed that most people were still staying at home and avoiding the roads. It certainly made a huge difference to my journey.

When I got to my father's small modern house in a neat little cul-de-sac, the sun was shining and it was a pleasant summer's day. I rang the door-bell and could see him through the glass door shuffling towards the entrance. If I had expected an effusive and histrionic welcome after all of our months apart, I would have been disappointed. He gave no indication that we had been separated for more than twelve weeks and his welcome was no different from what I would have received if I'd just dropped in the day before. I couldn't help but feel a little disappointed and let down but then that had always been his way. He had never been demonstrative. It was part of his brusque Northern way to be "unimpressed" and he would never have claimed an emotion that he did not feel. Maybe my absence from his life for all those weeks had not bothered him.

I followed him into his living room. In spite of it being a warm summer's day, the windows were firmly shut and the room smelt stale and musty. It worried me that we might be cooped up together in this unventilated space so I quickly swung open the sliding picture-window glass door to allow a bit of a breeze in from outside.

As soon as I could I went into the kitchen and made us each a coffee or, rather, a coffee for me and a tea for him ("Don't care for coffee but you have one" was his usual response if I offered to make him one. He'd always been strangely suspicious of coffee, seeing it as some sort of decadent non-English import loosely associated with either Italy or the USA; certainly, deeply suspect on both counts). I felt that I needed to take control in some way, as well as being desperate for refreshment after my journey which, although relatively smooth, had still been at least an hour in which razor-sharp concentration had been required to dodge in and out of the traffic lanes and negotiate the various crossings and junctions of a route which was almost an exact diagonal line across London.

I managed to find the remains of a packet of ginger nuts in his ancient biscuit tin and took a plate of these through to him, to accompany his cup of tea.

"How are you then?" he kept repeating, sadly showing no interest at all in any kind of reply that I might make to this enquiry.

The conversation soon petered out after I'd asked a few basic questions, along the lines of asking him about what he'd had for his lunch and what he'd watched on TV the night before.

It was a warm enough day so I told him that I needed to go and sit in the garden.

He didn't understand when I told him why.

"I need to sit outside. We've got to be careful. I don't want you to get the virus"

"What virus?"

"You know, the Corona which is killing so many people at the moment"

"Well, I haven't got it!"

"I know you haven't but I need to make sure that I don't give it to you…"

"You haven't got it, have you?"

"I don't think so but we need to be careful."

I moved a wooden chair from his dining table to the patio outdoors.

"What are you sitting out there for?"

"I've just told you. I don't want you to get the virus…"

"What virus…?"

And so it went on.

In the end, I sat outside on the patio a couple of metres away while he stayed sat in his armchair, which was facing his television in the middle of the room. I thought, in vain, that he might want to turn his chair round so that he could at least see me but he didn't. He remained facing away from me, his head leaning back against his chair as he closed his eyes and dozed off.

Perhaps unfairly, I started to feel angry. Angry that I had made the effort to drive all the way across London, putting myself at risk and actually flouting some of the lockdown rules, only to be met with his apparent disregard for my company.

There really didn't seem to be much point to my visit, if he was just going to sit there facing his television screen with his back to me and making no attempt to turn round and engage with me.

I fired off a grumpy text to my sister, needing to vent my anger on someone: "No point in my being here. I'm in the garden and he's just sitting inside. Pointless!"

Having put up with his irascible moods for months almost single-handedly, she was not that sympathetic.

"Think I might just leave." I then texted provocatively.

She told me that I couldn't. I'd only just got there, she said, and she was sure he appreciated my being there even if he didn't necessarily show it...

Trying to make the best of it, I tried to reason with myself that at least I could enjoy the garden and the sunshine and the peace. Telling myself, Buddhist-like, just to appreciate the moment, I tried to stop fuming and just appreciate the peacefulness of his small patch of suburban garden.

While he was slumped in his chair, with his eyes firmly shut, mouth wide-open and sound asleep, I told myself that at least it was an opportunity to catch up with the Sunday paper, so I went and fished it out of my bag and spent the next hour or so reading through the Culture section.

Eventually, he stirred. For a moment, I thought he might turn himself round and acknowledge my presence but no such thing. All I could hear were some long and rueful sighs. He must have forgotten that I was there.

Deciding to make my presence known, I shouted through and asked him if he fancied a walk out.

"Can if you like," he answered. "Where do you want to go?"

Seeing as the choices round there were extremely limited, I

found myself again suppressing my irritation. Truth was, I didn't particularly want to go anywhere. I was offering the walk for his sake and to break up the monotony of the afternoon. There were really only a couple of options: a bit of park adjacent to the river Thames a few hundred yards down the road or alternatively, a bit further away, Bushy Park. I thought Bushy Park might be better as it would take a bit longer to get to and would eat up more of the time. By the time we got back from there, he'd be ready for his tea. I'd make us some sandwiches, we'd eat them and watch the six o'clock news and then it would be time for me to go.

Bushy Park was not that far away but the walk there seemed quite effortful on that sultry afternoon, mainly owing to the heat, I suppose. The sun was beating down fairly relentlessly and my father was not that steady on his feet. Catastrophic scenarios involving falls, ambulances and lengthy waits in A and E played through my mind as I accompanied him stumbling up the pavement in the direction of the park. Perhaps we had been too ambitious? On the other hand, it would surely do him good to get him out for a couple of hours and away from his armchair in which he appeared to spend the whole day. I couldn't just allow him to fester there, locked in behind that glass door. Part of the point of my visit was to encourage some sort of modest activity, I told myself.

In spite of the stumbling and the staggering, we eventually made it through the back streets of leafy, well-heeled Teddington and across the railway bridge to a road crossing adjacent to one of the park's entrances. Once there, we didn't have to do very much. We could find a bench and sit on it for half an hour or so before attempting the return journey. It has to be said that the park was beautiful at that time of year. A little less tended than some of the other royal parks, Bushy Park has a very particular kind of beauty. It seems very flat and stretches for what looks like miles; it is normally very green, with great plains of grass stretching as far as the eye can see (although this particular summer, having had so little rain, it had the parched look of an African safari park). Cyclists and joggers frequented the paths but we perched ourselves on either end of the wooden bench and watched the various groups trundle by: the fractious Mums pushing their buggies along the paths; the very talkative young dads sounding off to other young dads about their work, their kids' schools and whatever football team they supported; the giggling pairs of teenage girls gossiping about clothes and boyfriends; the sulky looking youths plugged into their headphones; the slow moving elderly couples out for their Sunday afternoon strolls. It was a bit of entertainment for us and we watched the passers-by in silence, occasionally both nodding off in the close heat of that midsummer's afternoon. Every so often, my father would let out the occasional long sigh but apart from that there was almost no need to speak. It was strangely relaxing to sit there together in the sunshine in virtual silence, me knowing that he was just grateful to have the distractions on offer and appreciated the company provided by my physical presence, even though I made no effort at all to make conversation. To use my sister's favourite phrase, "that ship had sailed". In his demented state, conversation was not something in which he could any longer engage.

It must have got to about half past four before we roused ourselves from our afternoon lethargy and made the slow trek back from the park. We passed the local Co-Op along the way, where I nipped in to get some supplies: some bread for sandwiches, some corned beef and a bit of chocolate cake.

"Glad to be back," my father muttered, as we walked through his front door. It was by now getting on for tea time, so I busied myself in the kitchen making a pot of tea and getting our sandwiches ready. When we turned on the TV, there seemed to be something of a furore. The "shit had hit the fan" about Dominic Cummings breaking the lockdown rules with a trip to Barnard Castle and the media was having a feeding frenzy. He appeared to be giving a press conference in the garden of Number 10, attempting to smarm his way out of the journalists' sharp questions and making out that he had done no wrong. The journos were in uproar. Why should he be allowed to get away with breaking the rules when the rest of us had endured months of incarceration, obediently abiding by what we had been told and not going anywhere and not seeing anyone? There was something particularly repellent about Cummings's smug replies: the self-satisfaction, the entitlement, the belittling of those who dared to question him; his hideous scowl; his game playing; his apparent bewilderment that the whole nation did not empathise with his position. Somehow, the lush garden setting made it all the more hypocritical. Especially for those of us who had been holed up for months in tiny flats, with no outside space. OK, the garden wasn't his but it was his milieu and betokened the support and high level of protection that he would be granted. The man was clearly unassailable.

I watched the broadcast from the garden, with the patio door open and my father sat in front of me, also facing the television but still with his back to me. I wondered how much of this he was taking in. I made occasional attempts to canvas his opinion about what we were watching but got little or no response.

When it got to about seven o'clock, I decided that it was

time to brave the North Circular again and to make my journey home. I washed up the plates and tea things and tried to leave his kitchen in a state of reasonable order. As I left, he stayed sitting in his chair and I wondered to what extent he registered my departure.

At least the sun was still shining as I made the journey up across Richmond Bridge and down to Kew, before joining the North Circ. It was then that the traffic started to slow down as I joined the lane with all the other drivers who had been out visiting relatives for the day and were making their way back to the various suburbs of North London. It's not a relaxing journey and I had to keep my wits about me. Thankfully, there were a few interesting things to listen to on the radio: Feedback, Last Words and a play on Radio 3.

I started to feel rather sad and lonely on the long journey back. I just longed to be in my flat, relaxing in front of Sunday night TV and looked forward to a long soak in the bath, to unwind after the stresses of the drive. It was Monday again the following day and therefore back to more online lessons, but I was conscious of the fact that the weeks were slipping by and that this was my final term as a teacher. Four more weeks or so and I would be officially 'retired'. What a strange and bewildering thought that was.

A couple of weekends later, I managed to arrange my first meeting for many months with my sister and her family. We knew that we were not yet allowed to meet in each other's homes, so the usual invitation to Sunday lunch was off. Instead, we worked out a place to meet that would be about half-way between our homes, mine in Enfield and hers in Staines and we decided on Chorleywood Common in Hertfordshire. I had recalled, from childhoods growing up in Watford, that there were some lovely open spaces up there, not far from the M25's junction 18, and I suggested to my sister that providing we could get parked, it was as good a place as any at which to meet.

We'd said that we'd rendezvous at about one o'clock in the afternoon in the car park and decided that we would each bring some picnic items. I don't think that we had ever been separated for so long. It had been nearly four months and it was bizarre meeting again after all that time. Of course, within seconds it was as if we had only met the day before and I suppose there had been frequent phone calls, texts, emails and even Facetime meetings but it certainly felt momentous being in each other's physical company again after a separation of so many months.

Wandering away from the car park, we found a lovely open stretch of ground on the other side of the common and set out a picnic blanket for lunch. It was another glorious, hot summer's day and the sun was beating down. There was something particularly lovely about the weather that day and we were grateful that it had not let us down on the day that we were all to be reunited.

Sister brought various items out of her M&S carrier bag: sausage rolls, smoked salmon sandwiches, scotch eggs, fried chicken wings and set them out on the blanket, encouraging us all to help ourselves. I'm afraid my contributions were a bit more basic: some Hula-hoops, Haribos, marshmallows and Jaffa cakes but they were still appreciated and between us we made short work of the food on offer. Enjoyable as it was, there was nevertheless still a slight sense of danger lurking in the air. We were all wary of touching anything that might have been handled by someone else, for example. Each of us was careful to hand sanitise before picking up a sandwich and we made sure that fingers were wrapped in a paper napkin before taking a chicken wing from its plastic packaging. We were careful to sit the regulation two metres apart and tried hard to avoid any physical contact – not that easy when we were all desperate to give each other a hug or an embrace. Difficult as they were to sustain, though, we were all keenly aware that these constraints were a price well worth paying in order to get back to some semblance of normality. Certainly, it was a great treat: being able to meet up and share food again, albeit while being almost forensically scrupulous about not touching anything that had been handled by another. Perhaps we were emerging from this testing crisis at long last?

After our picnic lunch, we packed away the debris in our cars and crossed the busy main road adjacent to the Common and wandered down to the River Chess, which sits in a lush, green valley at the bottom of the Chiltern Way. The sun continued to shine and we laughed and joked as we walked along, the nieces gossiping about their friends and teachers and my sister and I exchanging news about our mutual acquaintances and other family members. It was lovely to be outside and together in that undulating pastoral landscape. However, it had to be necessarily short-lived. The rules at that time, if I remember rightly, specified that these outside meetings in small groups needed to be kept short and we were also all worried about traffic on the M25 getting home. It had been adventure enough just meeting to share some food together and way beyond the scope of anything else that we had done recently in terms of both travel and social contact, so it felt right to curtail things after a couple of hours.

We said our reluctant goodbyes but were pleased that the plan to meet had been successful and talked of doing it again in a few weekends' time. I drove away feeling a little sad and realising how much I had enjoyed their company; how easy and unforced it had been and how that felt like my natural state – not the grim enforced silence and solitude of the previous three months.

When I returned home, there was a van parked outside the entrance to my block of flats and some strangers were carrying furniture through the lobby into one of the flats on the ground floor. Instantly, I had a feeling of dread, wondering what new horrors of noise pollution and intrusion were going to be visited on me by their arrival. The hot weather was all very welcome but it had encouraged a form of 'outdoor living' from the other residents on my estate that could be noisy and boisterous and I assumed that the newcomers would inevitably add to that.

And we weren't even half-way through the summer...

July

As we entered the month of July, it seemed hard to believe that we were now approaching the end of the school year. We had first gone into lockdown in March and now here we were with little indication that the schools would ever go back before September. This was beginning to create a national outcry. If the pubs could start to open, the shops, the museums and the restaurants, then what about the schools? As staff members, we had had to complete individual Risk Assessments detailing our fitness to return to work. I noted on mine that I had "extra points" for my age. I'd also been taking medication for high blood pressure for years and that too needed to be acknowledged as my fitness to work was ascertained. Nevertheless, as far as I was concerned, I didn't feel myself to be particularly 'high risk' and signed myself off as "fit to work" before emailing the form to the Head. She was busy trying to work out whether she had enough staff to be able to reopen the school effectively when the time came.

Personally, of course, I very much wanted to return. I wanted to be back in harness for the last few weeks of my career. To not be there would make me feel cheated. How could I possibly have the grand send-off which I thought thirty three years at the school merited if the school was still going to be shut?

Thankfully, there did seem to be some movement towards re-opening, at least for some students. Also, I was still continuing to go in to school once a week to do the key worker supervision and on those occasions, I would usually bump into the Head or one of the Deputies and they would assure me that there would definitely "be something" to mark my departure and to celebrate all my years of sterling service. There was talk of a 'socially distanced' barbeque, outside on the school field. Possibly with limited numbers in order to make it as safe as possible but I was promised that this was a definite plan. Staff were canvassed about their willingness to return to school for an afternoon towards the end of term for the said barbeque, speeches, presentations and socialising planned and I was told that there had been a resounding response. Apparently almost every member of staff wanted to attend. I could hardly flatter myself that this was just in order to say "Goodbye" to me. Rather, it was the opportunity to catch up with each other that I guess people were most attracted by and who could blame them? After all those months of being cooped up and isolated, here at last was a chance to get together and to have a laugh and a natter and a moan. Of course, when asked if they would attend a big social at the end of this strange and isolating time, surely everyone was going to say "Yes"?

Much more importantly, though, it did look as if schools were going to be able to open to pupils before the start of the long summer holiday. Whatever the state of the pandemic, this was now being seen as a major priority. There was much talk of the dangers to young people's mental health as a result of all these months of home schooling. There were also many question marks over the quality of the online provision in many schools. Of course, sitting on the other end of a computer screen could not possibly replicate the experience of being in a classroom with a teacher and as the months went by, it was clear that the quality of online provision in many schools was starting to drop off. Yes, there had been a furious burst of creativity and invention in the early weeks of the pandemic as many teachers rose to the challenge of trying to instruct students in a "virtual" form but as the novelty had worn off, so too did the quality of what was being offered. It was, therefore, with a great collective sigh of relief that we greeted the news that some students were going to be allowed back into schools before the end of the summer term.

Of course, this would necessitate an almost military operation in terms of keeping schools safe and adhering to all of the new rules and regulations. Desks needed to be set at least 2 metres apart; rooms needed to be cleaned between each lesson; hand sanitiser and antibacterial sprays would have to be provided at every turn. Students needed to be kept in bubbles, and only minimal contact with others outside those bubbles allowed and teachers would need to come in, deliver their lessons and then leave. There was to be no social milling about; no meeting in the staff room at break for coffee and a moan; no gossiping in the resources room while queuing to use the photocopier; no lengthy chats in the staff toilets. It was going to be a highly regulated new regime and, as it turned out, involving fairly minimal teacher/ student contact.

Eventually as things unfolded, it seemed that only 2 year groups would be permitted to return to school before the end of that term. None of the eleven to fourteen year old students in Years 7 to 9 would be returning. Also, the exam classes in Years 11 and 13 had effectively finished when the teachers had awarded them their Centre Assessed Grades, so it was deemed that there was little point in them coming back to school, either. Therefore, it transpired that the Year 10s and the Year 12s –

both groups still being in the first year of their exam courses – were the year groups thought to be most in need of some live contact with their teachers before schools shut down again for the summer. It was decided that, each of these year groups would be given a fortnight in which to have at least one lesson with each of their teachers. I had no Year 10 class, having handed that group over to my immediate colleague when I thought that I might possibly be retiring at the end of the year. I did, however, have a Year 12 class so I would at least see them and have one 'proper' lesson with them before I left the school forever.

As the time approached for the re-opening of schools (albeit to limited numbers of exam classes only) school seemed to go into overdrive. There were endless emails and Zoom meetings about protocol under the new 'Covid safe' regime. We had Heads of Departments meetings about how to make best use of the time we had been granted for our single face-to-face lessons with our students. We had to submit details of work we intended to give to our students for the long summer holiday so that they would come back fully prepared and raring to go in September. (Although I, of course, would no longer be there at the start of the next autumn term). This was an issue which I needed to address. How would I communicate to the students that I would no longer be teaching them in September? Not only had I not taught them for almost half of this academic year (owing to the pandemic) but now I would have to tell them that next term, I would not be teaching them at all. This was going to be hard. I worried that they might be rather disgruntled that I was abandoning them. Even more, I worried that they might not care at all…

That final lesson was a somewhat strange affair. I felt that I needed to consolidate all the stuff we had been trying to do online over the last few months: the work on the set plays, which demanded close textual analysis and knowledge of a wide range of context and background materials; the work on the theatre practitioners we had studied, whose influence they were supposed to show in their forthcoming practical work in Devised Drama (which they would tackle the following term). However, the idea of having my drama students sat down for the whole hour and twenty minutes of our allotted time while I rabbited on and talked them through an audit of what we had supposedly covered over the last five months seemed uninspiring and unfair. After all, they were drama students. They were people who wanted to get up and Act. It was clear to me that what they needed was a completely practical session, in which they were "getting up and doing" rather than passively listening. We had all had more than enough of all that over the last few weeks and months. So that was what we did: a few warm-up games to create a bit of humour and silliness and then some relatively stretching practical exercises looking at a range of devising techniques, which I hoped would be useful to them the following term.

Planning the session that way meant that our last lesson together was fun but also productive and, I hoped, engaging. They were a talented bunch and quick on the uptake and I appreciated their willingness to get up and throw themselves into the activities I'd prepared. They didn't mind making fools of themselves and happily discarded their inhibitions, as I encouraged them to make machine (and other) noises and to throw themselves on the floor and to bounce around the room. Five minutes before the end of the session, though, I called them all to order, got them to sit round in a small circle, took a deep breath and told them that this was the last time I would ever meet with them. They seemed genuinely shocked and surprised and a part of me was mildly flattered that they looked so taken aback. I had to go through the slightly dreary explanation about having been at the school for thirty-three years and that it was now time to move on (though to what, I had no idea) and they seemed to find that a reasonable enough explanation for my intended departure. As the news sunk in, I regretted the fact that the carefree and uninhibited mood of the earlier part of our final lesson had now dissipated. Instead, I suppose there was a slight awkwardness between us. What this was to do with, I wasn't quite sure: to do with the fact that I had been harbouring this "secret" for so many months and was only now divulging my position; the fact that I was leaving them at what was for them a very difficult time when, it could be argued, they needed me most; perhaps they thought I was being selfish and only interested in my own comfort and security. I do not know. The fact was, they were genuinely sad and I did feel guilty at inflicting such a blow on top of the many others which they had experienced during this strange and highly unusual year.

Normally, exam classes leaving their teachers in May before going on Study Leave and then embarking on weeks of examinations in the main Hall would celebrate in some way. Teachers would bring in snacks and soft drinks to share with the students and there would be a bit of a party atmosphere as shirts were signed, cards and small gifts handed over and the class would reminisce about the highlights of their two year exam courses. Sometimes we'd play video footage of performances that the students had done or we'd do parodies of some of the scenes that the students had acted in for their practical exams or the students would ask to play some of their favourite drama games. The mood would be celebratory, irreverent, occasionally sentimental and often very silly. It was a rite of passage which all students expected at the ends of their exam courses.

This year, there was to be no such ending. The pandemic had thrown us all off key. Time-honoured rituals like these had been abandoned.

"If you'd told us, we'd have got you something." one of the students said, half-jokingly. But I wondered how I might have told them. It wasn't something I wanted to deliver through an email. It wasn't something that I would have felt comfortable saying over a Zoom call either. Like with so many other things in this unsettling and completely unique year, there were no precedents for how to behave. How do you tell a class of students that you are leaving them when you haven't met with them for more than five months? Also, when I'd only got an hour with them for their final lesson, I had wanted to use it productively and creatively. I didn't want to spend it ruminating over my intended departure.

As they left the room with their valedictory comments, slightly awkwardly and obviously still in shock, I stood by myself in the empty classroom and wondered what had just happened. That had been my last lesson. Ever. After thirty-three years at the school, that was it.

Normally, after such a momentous event, I'd have dashed over to the staffroom and off-loaded to whoever was sitting there. But needing to adhere strictly to the Covid protocol, we were no longer permitted to congregate in the staffroom together. In fact, it had been made very clear that as soon our lessons had finished, we needed to vacate the premises.

So I turned off the light in the classroom, went into the

drama office, packed my school bag, turned off the computer and locked the door. I ambled along through the playground to the almost deserted car park, got into my car and drove through the school gates. That was it: a very quiet, very solitary, rather sad "goodbye".

A couple of weeks before this, I had arranged to go into school to do two days of clearing up. I needed to empty my filing cabinets, clear my bookshelves and generally dispose of my thirty-three years' worth of stuff. There were rows of ring binders of ancient lesson resources; box files with minutes of meetings going back to the early nineties; there were boxes and boxes of photocopies of playscripts, old school play photos and programmes; samples of students' work from way back kept to provide examples for future generations of how things should be done. There were folders of old schemes of work, drawers full of past exam papers and sample answers. There were videos of past school plays and old bits of now defunct technical equipment: decrepit looking mics and leads and tripods and old video cameras and boxes of junk now loosely referred to as "props". These items filled bag after black plastic bin bag which I then piled up in the lobby of the drama department, hoping that eventually one of the caretaking staff would appear to cart it all away. True to form, though, there was something tremendously therapeutic about getting rid of it all. I got into a state of quite manic activity, determined not to leave a trace behind of my existence or of my career of all those years. The 'getting rid' turned out to be strangely enjoyable – a wonderful cleansing but almost physically enjoyable too. It was great to be doing something practical after all those months of sitting about. To be now heaving bin bags around and taking stuff off shelves and carting it all out to be dumped felt exhilarating and liberating.

I felt little nostalgia or sense of loss as I filled another bag with student essays from ten years ago. Why had I kept them so long? The exam boards had changed, the questions were different, the set texts were no longer the same, the material examined had constantly been updated. What on earth had been the point of hanging on to all this stuff? It felt great to pour it all into a bag and to chuck it out!

It was about this time, though, that I heard rumblings from various friends on the staff that the proposed end-of-term Retirement Do to which almost the whole staff had signed up, might not be permitted to go ahead after all. The numbers of people who'd signed up to attend were starting to create a major Health and Safety concern. It was now illegal for people to meet in groups for fear of spreading the virus, so the prospect of nearly one hundred staff members all gathering together for an end-of-term social event was something that could no longer be countenanced. Also, there were worries about how such an event might be perceived by the parents. If staff had not been coming into school for all those months, partly out of fear of contagion, how was it now apparently acceptable for them to gather together for a big social event? If they weren't able to come in to school to teach the children, how come they were all able to turn up for a barbeque and a free glass of wine?

No, it was clear that the promised staff social and the official farewell event could no longer be allowed to take place. If I wanted some sort of party or send-off, then this was something that I would have to organise myself, away from school premises and with much smaller numbers.

Luckily, I was able to rope in a couple of friends from the staff to help me bring this about. We each undertook to do a bit of research, approaching various pubs and other venues, trying to find somewhere that would serve as a suitable setting for my retirement do. Unfortunately, we kept running into the same problems over numbers. Nowhere would accommodate more than six people but I certainly wanted more than six people to be there. We were told that we could get round this if more than one person booked a table but then one of the pubs did warn me that if we were seen by other punters as being obviously part of a larger group (of say, three or four tables, all of whom were known to each other and part of the same gathering) then this would cause problems. "Especially with funeral parties" I was told, because those mourners would also want to be able to have larger gatherings. Naturally, they would resent the sight of a large group of carousing teachers, who were apparently all able to congregate together, even though family groups of the bereaved were not permitted to commiserate with each other in a pub setting. I could see their difficulty.

In the end, the day was saved by my friend Barry, who offered us the use of his garden for the occasion. We agreed that I would be able to invite a select group of colleagues to come and have a drink in his garden and that I would supply some modest "nibbles" and plastic glasses. We'd then ask those invited to bring a bottle so that they could each have a drink and we would gather together for a couple of hours or so on the afternoon of what would have been the final afternoon of term. That way, I could at least deliver a leaving speech to a small group of soon to be ex-colleagues and together they could help me to achieve some sort of 'closure'. That, at least, was the plan...

A couple of weeks before this event, a small group of my closest pals on the staff (my second in the drama department,

Jo; the Head of Music, Jim and our lovely departmental cleaner and staunchest ally, Lesley) were all invited to Barry's house for a small informal 'farewell' before the bigger event a couple of weeks later. Barry and his sister Diane (who had also been a big part of the shows we'd all worked on over the years, always taking on that essential role of backstage supervisor, which had become so important in our increasingly Health and Safety obsessed age) hosted a lovely supper and drinks party and provided a platform for us all to reminisce about the decades of drama productions which had been so much a part of our time at the school together. If I am absolutely honest, too, I have to confess that this was the part of my school life that I was going to miss the most and it was important to have a chance to say goodbye to those wonderful creative experiences which we had all shared together over the years. Of course, in the normal way of things, there would have been a big whole staff event to mark my (and others) departure. Over the years, we had had a whole range of different events to mark this important rite of passage: the retirement of long-standing members of staff, providing them with an opportunity to give a formal goodbye surrounded by the colleagues with whom they had worked sometimes for the whole of their working lives. These events had been held at a variety of different venues over the years: the local golf club; a boat on the Thames; a function room at one of the more upmarket local pubs. More recently, we'd had a marquee on the school field with a barbeque and then a 'disco' in the school canteen, enjoying the fact that the event was then self-contained and could only ever be attended by our own people. I have many fond memories of those rather drunken summer nights, sat out, for example, on the steps of the local cricket club, munching a burger from the barbeque and chatting away to another member of staff before bracing myself to hit the dance floor and bopping around manically to 'Dancing Queen' or something equally retro. Because these shindigs were always held on the last night of term and at the end of a gruelling school year, everyone was very excited at the prospect of six weeks of summer holiday stretching ahead. At the same time, these events were also tinged with a sadness that we were bidding farewell to long-serving and much-loved colleagues who had been a part of the fabric of our daily lives for years and that somehow the staff body would never be quite the same again. Music would be blaring out of the sound system; people would be dancing frantically, abandoning themselves to the rhythms of the cheesy retro pop songs; there would be raucous laughter and loud and animated chatter coming from the non-dancers at the bar and it would always be a sweltering summer's evening, with most of action taking place outside under the stars. The passing of the school years was invariably marked by these occasions.

Of course, there was to be no such 'do' this year. Gatherings in large numbers were not allowed for a start and any communal eating, drinking and dancing was strictly forbidden. Therefore, we made our own small celebration around Barry's dinner table at his house in Enfield and, somehow, I felt that this was better: more personal, more bespoke but also less fraught and frenetic. The chance to chat quietly and reminisce around a table rather than the pressure of needing to "work the room" and shout conversation over a deafening sound system was much more congenial.

I dressed up a bit for the evening, putting on a smart jacket, shirt and tie. It was the first time I had worn "office clothes" for many months. Barry's house was only a fifteen-minute walk away and that added to the enjoyment, being able to stroll round on foot rather than having to get a bus or a train or a taxi to the venue.

When I arrived, most of the others were there already and I have to say that I felt extremely comfortable with the assembled crowd. They were all friends and colleagues who had worked with me for years: there was Lesley, our lovely cleaner, who used to greet me each morning when I arrived for work. She'd always been the first person I saw each day, forever ready with a warm greeting, a lovely smile and a scurrilous story or two. She had always lifted my spirits and made me laugh and it was totally fitting that she should have been with us on that evening of valedictory celebration. Then there was my wonderful colleague, Jo, always so warm and giving and funny and such a contrast in style and demeanour to me but the perfect complement to my more reserved style. She was never not up for a party and I knew that her effervescence and extrovert nature would guarantee that the evening's events would go with a real swing. Then there was Jim, the Head of Music at the school and the man whose musical brilliance had enabled us to produce all the greatest hits from the golden age of Broadway musicals over the years. His expertise and thoroughness were always a joy to work with and his good sense and calming personality was a great foil to me – especially in those moments when the show was starting to either unravel or push us to the limits. His aura of calm at all times was a life saver. Then there was Barry himself, who had been the technical manager of our productions. Always totally reliable and, again, full of common sense and incredibly generous in his willingness to work tirelessly behind the scenes and to do everything he could for the good of the shows. He had a great 'can do' attitude and somehow managed to solve all of those problems which others might have found insuperable. What a terrific team we had been over the years. How sad that we were now about to disband but how wonderful that we were all able to come together to mark our parting of the ways and to celebrate a lifetime of work together, in spite of all the restrictions of Covid.

Quite early on in the evening, after the swapping of news and inevitable discussion of the national situation along the lines of who could ever have predicted that it would have gone on for so many months; what it had been like being back in school and teaching those odd single lessons to the Year 10s and Year 12s; who else had we seen while we were in; how marvellous that the weather was continuing to be so summery; how sad not to have a big whole-staff get together to mark the end of the school year…after that, Barry asked for our attention "before you all get too drunk" (!) and pointed his remote in the direction of his TV. There was a flickering of the screen and for a moment or two I thought we were going to start looking at some highlights from recent school musical productions. (This had always been a bit of a ritual with us at the end of school shows, after we had been to the pub and had a few drinks to wind down: we'd then usually repair to Barry's house for a take-away curry and then settle down and watch some old videos of school productions, reminiscing and comparing what we had done in the past with the show we had just finished. For example, watching a "Nancy" from the school production of "Oliver!" twenty years before and comparing that performance with the Fraulein Maria in "The Sound of Music" which had just had its final performance a few hours before). Therefore, I was fully expecting to watch something similar at that moment. A compilation of 'greatest hits' for example – choruses from

'South Pacific' and 'Les Mis' and 'The Boyfriend' with maybe a couple of individuals featured in solo numbers. I was slightly taken aback, therefore, when the DVD started to play and it was not that at all. What I saw were some 'talking heads' beginning to talk about a person; this person had been a "huge influence", had given them "so much", had been "a terrific teacher and mentor"; the speakers would be "forever grateful" for everything they had learnt and been taught. It took me some time to cotton on that the speakers were all actually talking about me...

 I watched in almost jaw-dropped silence as speaker after speaker came on and said how much they had enjoyed working with me; how hugely important the big shows we'd worked on had been in their lives and what a major part of their school experience they had been. Some talked with real delight about how much they had enjoyed learning about drama with me; about the skills they had learnt and the knowledge that they felt I had given them. There were ex-students, ex-colleagues (including a Head Teacher and also the Director of Music from a few years back, who had also been a terrific pal and colleague on production after production), even some parents. Some of the speakers were now making their way in the world of professional theatre and gave heart-felt tributes to all that they believed I had taught them.

 It was a profoundly moving experience watching that film with all those heart-warming tributes. I felt incredibly touched that they had all been willing to have their thoughts filmed; that they had taken the time and the trouble to do this. I was also extremely grateful that my friend Barry had spent so much time compiling, editing and collating the film. That seemed such an incredibly generous act, not to mention the technical expertise and investment of time that it must have required of him. It seemed to be the most astonishing act of friendship and I will be grateful to him forever.

For much of the time watching this glorious film, I was stunned in to almost total silence, unable to say much apart from to gasp with pleasure at some of the lovely things that were being said. Some of the contributors were now much older than they had been when I'd first worked with them. Tim Muffet, for example, although now an eminent BBC television reporter and journalist, was no longer the black haired, slightly truculent young man that I had remembered from his school days but was now a silver haired and utterly charming, hugely competent media performer. How could that child have turned into this middle-aged man, upon whom I had apparently made such an impact? As student after student took their turn to appear, from the 1980s, the 90s, the 00s and the last decade, it was as if the years were rolling past. There was certainly no denying that I had done a good stint at that school. I had been there for thirty-three years, after all. Not a bad innings at all, a lifetime in fact and whatever doubts I may have harboured about not being quite ready to go, this was testimony to the fact that I had been there for a long time. Maybe it was better to leave now, while I was still clearly so fondly remembered and feted, rather than to hang on for another couple more years and risk acquiring a slightly more tarnished reputation?

That was a sobering thought and it did bring home to me the finality of what I had done. I was definitely leaving. What I was leaving to do, I knew not but the tributes were testament to the fact that my work at that school was now finished. It was time to move on, to find pastures new and there could be no looking back.

Inevitably, this made for a slightly subdued mood over the dinner table as we tucked into the meal which Barry had prepared. His generosity and kindness really did know no bounds. Not only had he spent hours making the video (contacting people; telling them what was required; collecting the material from them; putting it all together) but he was now about to serve us a magnificent feast at his dinner table. He now started to run around his kitchen, pulling dishes out of the oven, pouring fresh glasses of wine, making sure that we all had full plates and glasses of water and cutlery and serviettes. What a tremendous host!

I realised that I could not allow myself to drift into a nostalgic reverie as I replayed in my head all the lovely video tributes and reminisced about the shows that each of them had brought to mind. I needed to snap out of this and engage with my lovely companions: to chat and laugh and sparkle. Luckily, the wine helped and after a few more refills the mood became a bit more boisterous and, at times, even raucous. What we talked about then, I have no idea, but the party atmosphere kicked in and we were certainly in no mood to tear ourselves away by the time it got to midnight and our carriages/ taxis arrived to carry us all home. (In fact, I think I walked back with Barry's sister Diane, who just lived around the corner from me).

The following week was the final week of term and the last few days of my thirty-six-year teaching career. On the Friday afternoon, we were to have the small garden party (again at Barry's) for me to deliver my (much-anticipated!) leaving speech and to bid my final farewell to some of my other nearest and dearest colleagues on the staff. The days before were consumed with preparing for this event and with me winding up my remaining classes on Microsoft Teams as I delivered my last ever lessons as a teacher. Did I ever dream that I would be finishing my teaching career peering into a laptop from my desk at home and just about getting away with it as I burbled on in response to the modest contributions of the students, while they attempted to perform various bits of drama on camera, with what can only be described as "limited" success? I could hear myself sounding like some Victoria Wood parody of a teacher: "Yes, that was a most interesting interpretation, Bhavid... Loved the way in which you decided to deliver the lines in a monotone. Was that a deliberate choice...? Yes interesting the way in which you decided to speak at such a low volume, we had to really concentrate to make out what you were saying. That was a fascinating effect! Yes, I liked the fact that your character chose not to use any words in that scene. Just a nod of the head or blink of the eye can be strangely powerful — as we all saw, didn't we?"

What rubbish it all was really! Bending over backwards to make out that the students were doing something interesting and creative when we were all aware of the fact that, in reality, we were just filling in time; making out we were doing something, anything in order to drag ourselves to the end of term and could make out to the parents that we really had been delivering high quality lessons when, in fact, it was hard not to feel that we'd all been just treading water for almost half of the school year.

Luckily, though, the end of the school year was approaching and the whole ghastly charade could be allowed to wither and die.

Maybe if it had been a normal summer term, I would have felt some sadness as the end of that final term approached but, under these circumstances, I have to say that it was just relief. Relief that the floundering on Zoom and Microsoft Teams could be allowed to peter out and that the onerous responsibility of having to try and provide something worthwhile to occupy my students could finally be abandoned.

As Friday afternoon and the much-anticipated Garden Party approached, I realised that there were some preparations to be made. I'd asked people to bring bottles but I thought that I ought to make some contribution myself, so I went and bought a few bottles of bubbly from the supermarket, plus some multi-packs of crisps and paper plates and serviettes. It all looked rather meagre but then we weren't really supposed to be doing it at all and the whole thing wasn't expected to last much more than a couple of hours anyway. I also wanted to order some flowers for some of my immediate colleagues, the people who had stood by me day after day, over the years. These I ordered from a local florist and arranged to collect at lunchtime on the day of the party.

That final morning, I went into school to hand over my security pass, my keys and my school laptop. Relinquishing these items marked the end of my time at the school. They were the official markers of my identity. I was expecting to see the Head in order to say a final "goodbye" but I was told that she was busy interviewing a new member of staff for September. Instead, I was approached by one of the Deputies who handed me a small package. This contained a glass tankard with the school motto and crest engraved on it and was obviously intended to grace the mantlepieces of long serving staff members. I was also given an envelope with a cheque from the governors to mark my long years of service, These were handed over without much ceremony and would normally have been presented publicly, in front of the whole staff and accompanied by applause and public adulation. Not so on that morning. Just as I was stood in the school hall clutching these items, the Head appeared from her office and so I handed over my school lanyard and the keys to my office and my school laptop and carrying case. She joked about how she was going to keep the rather snazzy key ring and the carrying case and have them for her own. We all made hasty and rushed "farewells" and then I scurried out to the car park, clutching my tankard and cheque and thinking more about that coming afternoon's garden event than of what had just taken place. It was a strangely perfunctory "goodbye".

I drove round to the florist to pick up the various bouquets and got changed into a suitably 'smart casual' outfit for a summer's afternoon. Then I walked round to Barry's and started chatting to the handful of people who had arrived early.

I had my speech (carefully rehearsed and endlessly edited and re-written) in my jacket pocket but resisted the temptation to down a proffered glass of prosecco as I knew that I needed to keep a clear head. I also didn't want anything to take the edge off my energy, knowing that it would have to be delivered and performed with everything that I had: full voice, razor sharp comic timing, good breath control; sweeping gestures and a not too hammy range of facial expressions.

We got into the speeches fairly quickly, realising that people were all on the minutes and being the start of the school holidays, many were anxious to escape and get away. My colleague Jo delivered her tribute first. As my second in department and 'right hand woman' she had known me at my very worst and through many ups and downs. However, she spoke with real love and appreciation and with a genuine affection for my foibles and eccentricities. It was a pen-portrait to treasure and I was hugely appreciative of everything she said.

This was followed by my own farewell and my tributes to the many colleagues and friends who had made my working life so intensely pleasurable and satisfying. I tried to throw in a few jokes and funny asides and these were met with the laughter I'd intended. I felt great warmth and appreciation from all of my friends there that afternoon and realised in those moments that it was unlikely that life would ever get any better than this: standing there in the golden July sunshine in my friend's lovely south-facing garden surrounded by about thirty dear companions at the end of a working life well lived. This surely had to be the pinnacle?

Afterwards, I allowed myself a good guzzle of prosecco and then set about working the room (or, in this case, the garden) making sure that I said something particular to each of the friends who had made the effort to come along. Everyone was in 'holiday humour' and all in hats, sundresses, shorts, t-shirts and Ray-Bans. It was that incredibly precious time when the whole of the summer holiday was stretching ahead and not even Covid could dampen our spirits. We laughed, chatted, swapped stories and everyone expressed their envy that I was "getting out" and their disbelief that I was old enough to retire and wished me well for the future.

Soon enough, people started to leave until there was just a handful of us left. For a moment or two, as we talked about holiday plans and travel arrangements, it was easy to forget that this was my retirement do and marked the end of a personal era. It could have been the dying moments of any summer barbeque or lunch party and I started to wonder whether I should be feeling sadder or experiencing something more momentous. As even the last few guests drifted off and there were just a couple of us left, I didn't feel much more than a need to be able to walk back home and have a bit of a lie down. It had been a tiring day and now I just wanted to slump in front of the TV quietly and absorb it all.

I walked back through the streets to my flat in the late afternoon sunshine, with some sense of anti-climax. I supposed that in more normal times, there would have been a big pub crawl planned or something a bit wilder and more climactic – but no. This was much more of a slow fade. This was my ending.

That evening, I'm afraid I just parked myself in front of the telly, as I had done for so many nights before during this strange time of enforced domestic captivity. The afternoon boozing, the sunshine and the sheer emotion of the last few hours had left me drained and not a little jaded from too many glasses of lukewarm prosecco. By about seven o'clock I was feeling extremely sluggish and not really capable of doing anything apart from staring open-mouthed at the usual Friday night TV fest: a double helping of "Coronation Street" and then Graham Norton and celebrity chatter later on. I knew that one of my friends from the afternoon was going out drinking in Walthamstow later on and another was having a rival party in a nearby park, which was going on at that very moment, so there were other places I could have gone to. But I had already slipped into that retirement mindset of What's the Rush? There's plenty of time. No need to go dashing out again. Just take it easy. And so I continued to slump and the evening just gradually faded away.

A few days later, I was off down to Devon to stay in a cottage that I had booked a few miles from where my brother lived in Ottery St Mary. I knew that I would need the change of scene and I was certainly looking forward to getting out of the hot and by now oppressive city. The idea of a few days near the coast and surrounded by trees, fields and greenery was deeply appealing.

As in previous years, I decided not to take the car. Apart from anything else, my eye-sight had been troubling me for some time and I doubted my ability to read the road signs clearly. I needed to book another optician's appointment and would do that as soon as I returned from my time away. In the meantime, I thought it best to take the train, in spite of the fact that it did not seem to be a particularly safe way of travel at the moment: being cooped up in a railway carriage with a load of strangers and potential virus carriers was not appealing. On the other hand, I guessed that not many people would be travelling at that time and it seemed less risky than negotiating a lengthy car journey with dodgy eye sight.

I packed a small suitcase and made for Waterloo, where I would catch the train down to Exeter. I had done the journey the year before, again at the start of the school summer holiday, but that time I had had my dad in tow. He was by that time in the grip of the dementia which had been getting worse and worse as the months had gone by. I remember him being completely bewildered when I'd turned up at the door saying that we were going down to Devon that morning. "News to me" he had said, as I started to chivvy him out of the door and into a sudden downpour as we made for the bus stop. I don't quite know how I managed to get him down there at all but I did and we passed a reasonably pleasant week, although I do remember thinking that it was unlikely he would ever be able to stay away from his home ever again. The disruption to his routine had just been too unsettling, although I still believe that the change of scene and the fresh sea air had done him some good.

This year, however, I was travelling solo. The train carriage was pretty much deserted, apart from some 'lads' who seemed to be part of a cricket (or even rugby) team and kept up a loud stream of banter with each other throughout the journey. We had been told that we all had to wear masks and that was something of an endurance test, being masked for the whole trip. Nevertheless, I was glad of mine then and it did give the illusion of a measure of protection. It felt strangely liberating, though, to be sitting in that railway carriage, allowing myself to be whisked off out of London and towards the lovely Devon countryside. I had a book that I was half-heartedly reading but I was more interested in looking out of the window, especially once we had got beyond Reading and were starting to plough through the lush green meadows and landscape of an English high summer.

After what seemed like a very quick journey, I got out at Honiton, where my brother's fiancée Lindsay had kindly offered to meet me and drive me to my accommodation. My brother was working from home and could not leave his desk until after five p.m. so we drove back to their house to pick him up and then they took me off to the Waitrose in Sidmouth to pick up some supplies for my stay. In previous years, the cottages I had hired had always had a 'Welcome Pack' to greet us on arrival but this time (I guessed because of the pandemic) there was no such offering so I had to go and pick up my own milk, bread, butter and cereal before opening the door to my temporary home for the week.

It was odd getting out at the Waitrose car park with my brother and Lindsay while we all fished around for our masks and put them on. I still was not used to seeing people I knew in masks and the effect was always disconcerting and not a little disturbing, as if we had all somehow been drawn into a strange science fiction drama in which we were all unwittingly playing a role.

After the Waitrose shop, my brother suggested that we go to the pub for a drink. At that time, pubs were allowed to open but people had to be sat outside and it was table service only. We tried to get into a couple of places on the sea front at Sidmouth but because we hadn't booked anywhere, we were turned away. However, we did manage to get into one of the town centre pubs with a large beer garden and sat there over a couple of pints catching up on news and bemoaning the horrors of the national situation. I also shared with them a new ambition that I had only lately started to harbour: my intention to move house. For years, I had lived in a modern two bed flat that had served me well enough while I had been working but now, I felt that I needed to find somewhere a bit closer to the centre of town and with some outside space, at least with a balcony or even a small garden. It just so happened that one of my ex-colleagues was in the process of selling a house just round the corner from me. It was actually a half house, which had been converted out of one much larger house but it had been completely refurbished and modernised. My friend had showed me round when the refurb had been finished and I'd fallen in love with it. At the time, though, I did not think that I would be able to afford it. However, now I found myself in receipt of a lump sum as part of my pension on leaving teaching and that made me wonder if perhaps I might be able to afford it after all. It also seemed like a wise thing to do: to put the money into a house rather than just allow it to get eroded away in a savings account. At the moment, the house was under offer to someone else but I had expressed my interest in it to my friend the seller and she had said that if the current deal fell through, I could have "first refusal". I was quite excited by this idea and shared it with my brother and Lindsay. They were also looking to buy a new home and for at least an hour we talked excitedly of our property ambitions.

Leaving the pub, they dropped me off at the little holiday cottage I had chosen to rent for the week. It was a charming place: tiny but ideal for one person. It stood in a row of three and was sandwiched between a couple of other larger holiday homes, all kitted out in a similar style. Mine had a fetching little kitchen diner with a table, sofa and TV and then upstairs was a large bedroom underneath the eves of the cottage, with a bathroom on the same floor. It was small, manageable and cheerful and I looked forward to spending the week there and unwinding after the stresses of the year.

Because I had had a couple of pints of strong local "real ale" in the pub with Tim and Lindsay that evening, my sleep was fitful, as it always was after even a small amount of alcohol. Therefore, I did not experience the deep sleep and profound rest that I had been craving. Nevertheless, when I decided to get up the next morning (I can't say "wake up" because I'd been awake for hours) the sun was shining and the birds were singing. It did feel lovely to be away and to be somewhere different after all those months of being cooped up in my flat at home. As always, I decided that I needed to start the morning with some sort of physical exercise, so I pulled on my jogging gear and set off for a run down the road. This was a bit easier said than done: the little development of holiday cottages was in a turning off a busy main road and when I jogged onto that there were no pavements. The early morning traffic was hurtling by and it actually felt quite dangerous. I tentatively picked my way along a grassy slope by the side of the road and made for a muddy looking track about a quarter of a mile away. Once on that, I felt a bit safer, although it wasn't a great place to jog, with its uneven surface along a steep uphill path. I followed the winding country lane for a few minutes, eventually arriving at the edge of a modern-looking housing estate, through which I picked my way in order to arrive back out on another main road. In the distance, I could make out what looked like a green or playground and I headed for that. I thought that if I did a circuit or two of that then that would probably be enough and I could then turn round and make my way back to the cottage for breakfast. Because I was on unfamiliar territory and wasn't really sure of where I was going, I momentarily lost my concentration and almost bumped into a rather irascible gentleman riding on one of Sidmouth's many mobility scooters. He was zooming up the path that led across the green as I continued to run towards him. The man on the scooter was then forced to veer off the path and move on to the green itself in order for me to jog past on the path. The man cursed me as I ran past and immediately, I realised that I should have stopped and moved aside to let him pass but I had just felt flustered and unsure of how to behave. A bit of a black mark for me there, I guess.

When I got back to the cottage, I showered and made myself some breakfast. I guess because of Covid, there were no toiletries supplied – no shampoo or soap, so I would have to seek out a chemist as one of my first tasks of the day in order to kit out the bathroom, I decided. There was no rush, though. I had not arranged to meet my brother until later in the day, being conscious of not wanting to impose myself too much and realising that they all had busy lives and would have things they needed to do. Therefore, I had a more or less free day until mid-afternoon, when we had arranged to meet for a coffee and then to go back to their place for supper.

As had become my habit, after breakfast I settled down to read for an hour or so, enjoying playing at being a house owner and lounging about on the sofa of the cottage, with book in hand and Radio 3 playing quietly in the background. I was reading "Rodham" – an extremely convincing fictionalised account of the life of Hilary Clinton – and enjoying it very much, finding it extremely plausible, and loving its audacity. Amazing that something as cheeky as this could get published without getting its author sent to prison on libel charges!

By about 10.30, I thought it was probably time to wander down to the town, to buy those bathroom necessaries and to have a mooch about the shops and sit for a while on the promenade, maybe taking in a spot of lunch. I also needed to see how far it was to walk from the cottage in to the centre of Sidmouth. I knew that it was about a thirty- minute walk, which was fine as I had walked at least that every single day since the start of the pandemic.

Again, it meant negotiating the busy main road with no pavement and that somewhat precarious scramble up the grassy bank by the side of the road. Eventually, this did give way to a pavement and from thereafter, the walk became quite enjoyable. It was another hot, sunny day and it was lovely being able to see trees and meadows on either side with, finally, a glimpse of the sea up ahead. I approached the outskirts of the town, with its houses and small industrial buildings. These gradually gave way to well-kept bungalows and family homes and then eventually the small hotels and guest houses which lined the streets on the entrance into the town. It was a fairly substantial walk but I didn't mind. It was great just to be out and about and away from the usual sights and sounds of Enfield.

As I entered the town, I passed the summer theatre, which I had visited on previous occasions. Clearly there were no productions scheduled for this year, which was disappointing. The Agatha Christie thrillers and Alan Ayckbourn comedies had always provided a reliable source of entertainment for at least one evening on visits in previous years. I made my way through some of the backstreets until I eventually found a branch of Boots where I would be able to stock up on shampoo, shower gel, soap and other essentials. As I entered the shop, I was told by the lady on the till that I risked being fined for not wearing a mask. Horrified at the oversight and caught rather off-guard, I quickly grabbed a packet of masks and added them to my purchases.

After that, I made for the seafront, drawn to it by the sounds of the seagulls and their ceaseless shrieking cries. The promenade was busy with many holiday makers taking in the sea air. It was mainly elderly couples and one or two young families and a few sad looking widows. I felt slightly out-of-place and conspicuous. I wanted to find a bench on which I could sit down and watch the people passing by but every single one was occupied. I leant on the balustrade separating the pavement from the pebbly seashore and I looked out at the sea. It was a calm summer's day so the sea was almost flat. There was just a mild breeze blowing. For the most part, I felt contented and untroubled. Looking at the crowds parading up and down the promenade, it seemed that the world was returning to normal after all those months of lock down and fear and the enforced incarceration in our homes. It felt good to be relieved at long last of the burden of work; to not have the constant stress and anxiety and that never ending drain upon my time and creativity. While it had been painful letting go, it was more the making up of my mind to do so than the actual severance which had caused me the most grief. The leaving itself had been relatively painless. It was now on to the next chapter and this was the first page. That felt good. The world was my oyster. Well, it would be once the Covid restrictions were lifted and it did look as if we were starting to win that battle. Things were opening up again; the numbers of infections were dropping; the numbers of deaths were certainly way below what they had been. There was a cautious optimism about the future and this was compounded by the cheerfulness of the scene around me at that moment: the jolly holiday crowd, all intent on making the most of the great summer weather and of being by the seaside. There was a mood of optimism and hopefulness in the air.

I needed something to eat, so went and bought a jumbo-sized locally made pasty and a take-away latte. I did then manage to find a bench but just kept to one end so that others could also use it if they wished. I munched on my pasty and continued to observe the constantly trawling crowd, wondering what their experiences of the previous year had been and thinking about what they might have had to endure in order to get to this moment.

The hours passed and I wandered back up to the cottage to wait for my brother who had said that he would collect me at about three p.m. It was nice to get into a car when he arrived and to be driven down the little country lanes as we made for his house which was in a tiny hamlet about six miles away. I know it was selfish to expect him to drive me about but I knew that I would not have been able to drive along those tiny narrow roads with any confidence at all, so I was relieved that he seemed happy to do the driving.

My brother's house was a rented modern house, attached to another similar home in what appeared to be the middle of nowhere. At the back, the view stretched for miles, with not another house in sight. It was idyllic, although I doubted that it would have suited me with my addiction to the buzz of city life.

We went and sat out at the back and drank a couple of glasses of prosecco. It felt like a blissful retreat from the world and I just sat and relished the absolute peace and the beauty of the surroundings. As the afternoon turned to evening, we moved indoors and then had some food. We chatted away, partly about house buying again but then we moved on to talking about my dad, my sister, my brother's daughter and her family (amazingly, my brother is now a grandad. What did that make me, I wondered?).

It got to about nine o'clock and not wanting to outstay my welcome, I suggested to my brother that it would be OK for him to drive me back if he didn't want to be out driving too late and he agreed. The country lanes seemed even more treacherous at night but again, he seemed not to mind them, saying that the headlights of approaching cars gave warning of their imminent arrival and therefore made it easier to drive at night than during the day…in some ways.

I was quite glad to get back and watched a bit of TV before crawling into bed in my single-person's cottage. It was so nice to be away and free from all the usual stuff back home.

The following day was a Sunday, so for much of the morning I mulled over the Sunday papers while downing endless cups of tea and slices of toast. I then did a quick walk down to the sea front and another walk along the prom before meeting my brother and his family for an excursion to West Bay. Three of us (me, my brother and his stepson Eliot) were to be dropped off in an adjoining bay and then we were to do the five miles or so of coastal path before joining Lindsay in one of the car parks at West Bay, from which we would go in search of some fish and chips and ice cream. Sounded good to me! The walk across the cliffs was bracing and invigorating, although also quite strenuous because there was a lot of up and down and some of the climbs up were unusually demanding. It was wonderful to be walking so close to the cliff edge, though and the sea was at its most alluring. It was yet another perfect summer afternoon. A couple of hours or so later, we met with Lindsay near to the harbour wall at West Bay and then went in search of our fish and chips. There were quite a number of stalls parked up along the sea front and we chose one of the vans on the end, in view of a house that had recently appeared in the second series of "Broadchurch". I think it was the house in which the character played by Charlotte Rampling was supposed to inhabit, an oddly glamorous association in this slightly rough and ready small seaside resort.

We got our fish and chips from a man serving the food from a van and sat on benches in what seemed to be his garden. I guess it all had to be outside in order to comply with Covid restrictions and I did have a momentary flicker of concern about hygiene as the unmasked fish and chip fryer handed us our food. On the other hand, there had been very few cases in Devon and it was almost as if the disease had somehow passed it by. The food tasted extremely good, partly I imagine, because we were consuming it in the fresh air, breathing in the smell of the sea emanating from the harbour which was close by and also because we had worked up healthy appetites from our five-mile coastal walk and were all extremely hungry.

After the fish and chips, it was then time to seek out some ice cream and, again, there were plenty of options to choose from. Because it was so hot, our hands got very sticky with the melting ice cream and I think I had to bin mine before it was finished because it just became impossible to eat.

We eventually wound up the afternoon's excursion and then drove back to my brother's house for some TV and a drink. It was the usual Sunday night fare; some sort of murder mystery or cop show but mildly entertaining and I felt easy and comfortable watching it in semi-silence with my brother and his family. At ten p.m., he kindly drove me back along the little country lanes (by now pitch dark) and I felt slightly guilty that I was forcing him out of his home at that time of night but he didn't seem to mind.

The next couple of days were working days for my brother and his family, so we didn't see each other. On the Monday, I got the bus to Beer and enjoyed sitting on a deck chair on the beach there for the afternoon. I was careful to make sure that I got the 4.30 p.m. bus back, though, because I don't think there was another one after that. The bus driver seemed to have nerves of steel. The roads were extremely narrow and barely wide enough to let the bus through. Every so often, he would come across another vehicle approaching from the opposite direction and the other driver would have to reverse back into a passing space in order for the bus to drive by. I admired the driver's determination and skill when sharing those tiny roads with other users. He seemed completely unphased by it.

When I got back that evening, I passed the time much as I would have done had I been at home. I made some food, watched the news, sent a few texts and emails and then settled down to watch whatever was on TV before retiring to bed to read at about half past ten. Yes, it was an uneventful evening but relaxing and, anyway, I was on holiday…

The following day, I had arranged to meet one of my great pals from work, Nicola, with whom I was to rendezvous in Lime Regis. She had been staying in Poole and because she knew that I was in Devon at the same time, we fixed on Lyme as a reasonable near half-way point. (Well, probably considerably nearer to me than to her but she gamely offered to cycle over…)

Again, I travelled there on the bus and met with her in a harbour side pub. It felt strangely decadent ordering alcohol in the middle of the day but it was also intensely enjoyable and we passed a couple of hours gossiping about our mutual acquaintances before venturing out on to the Cobb and re-enacting some of our favourite moments from 'Persuasion'. We took photos of each other, posing as Meryl Streep in 'The French Lieutenant's Woman' pulling our hoodies over our heads and making grotesque and unflattering faces, which made each other laugh. I must have got the bus back at about five p.m. – again, surprised by how infrequent they were even in the height of the tourist season and so different from the almost continuous stream of buses that we are so used to in London.

When I got back to my cottage, I fell into that post-lunchtime boozing lethargy and slight depression and knew that I'd probably be in for another night of broken sleep – which I was.

Therefore, the next day I resolved to take it fairly easy. I'd arrange with my brother's family that they would come round early evening for take-away pizza to be eaten on one of the picnic benches in the grounds of the three cottages. I also had some wine which I would serve and thought we'd all have a glass of red to wash it down. Part of the excitement here was around whether the pizzas would be delivered on time. I had ordered them from a shop in the town and wasn't convinced that they'd know how to find us, so I was pleasantly surprised when the boy rode up on his motorcycle with a Margarita, Vegetarian and a Hawaiian for our enjoyment. It was fun eating pizza outside that evening as dusk slowly descended and made even more enjoyable by the fact that nobody had had to cook. Afterwards, we all went indoors to watch some tv until the time came for them to hit the road just after ten o'clock.

On the final day of my stay, my brother and his stepson arrived late afternoon in order for us to walk from my cottage through the fields and along the banks of the river Otter back to their house. It was another breathtakingly beautiful evening and there was something particularly special about the countryside then as it bathed in the early evening light. It was also unusual for me to do an inland walk in that area. More often than not, walks were by the sea and along the coastal paths but the fields and meadows we walked through that evening had a very particular beauty of their own. I also felt a great closeness to my brother in a way that I had not felt for years. I suppose it was something to do with the time we had spent together that week which fostered an intimacy that we didn't usually enjoy, generally only meeting infrequently and for more formal family occasions like my father's birthday or getting together for tea on one of their occasional visits up to London.

Again, we arrived back at their house and had some food and enjoyed another warm and companionable evening. I was due to leave the following day to go back to London so took my leave of them that night. It had been a welcome and very refreshing break. It was also good to put a bit of distance between myself and the ending of my school career by getting a change of scene and just being with some completely different people.

As I crossed London on the return journey, going from Paddington and back up to Southgate, the city felt once again to be hot and oppressive and I was very grateful that there had been a chance to escape its intensity. I just needed to work out what I was going to do to get through the other five weeks of the summer holiday before the schools all returned at the start of September – by which time, I assumed, I would need to be finding myself something to do.

August

There was certainly one thing for sure this particular August: it was not going to be a normal one. This was for a number of reasons. Firstly, we were still in the grip of the pandemic and normal life was not about to be resumed. True, we seemed now to be able to go to restaurants and to some pubs but we weren't able to get on to planes and the normal gadding about all over Europe was definitely off the cards. There was also, for me, the fact that my working life was over now. This meant that there wasn't quite the same frantic scramble to fill every day of August with summer holiday fun before the dreaded "return" in September; that sense that the moment needed to be seized because in a few weeks' time it would be back to the treadmill and the daily grind. Now there was no necessity to fill the month of August with travel and excursions and adventures because these could just as easily be had during the autumn. Also, travel outside the school holiday was likely to be considerably less expensive. There would be fewer crowds, too, as one would no longer be competing with all of the other summer holiday makers forced to squeeze their fun into that same single month.

Therefore, the pressure was off to some extent. In previous years, I remembered it often making me feel quite stressed and almost ill. This sense that I needed to be making the most of the time; had to be jetting off and gallivanting in order to have something "to show for it" by the time school reconvened at the start of September. Planning that time and filling it had always been a source of considerable anxiety: finding the right people to do things with; not clocking up huge debts on flights and hotels and treats that would then take the rest of the school year to pay off; making sure that there were definite plans made, places visited, adventures undertaken.

Now, because of the change in my circumstances, there was really no need to do anything at all this August. I could, for the first time in years, take a genuine summer holiday. With now no obligation to even prepare online lessons or to mark any students' work, I could sit back and enjoy my leisure time unencumbered. This would be an August summer holiday in which there would be no new set books to prepare and research; no new schemes of work needing to be written; no big autumn drama production to prepare for. For the first time in years, I could spend the summer months relaxing and doing my own thing, unencumbered by guilt or the feeling that I ought to be doing something to prepare for the autumn and the return to work.

In spite of the fact that the schools had effectively been closed since March, I had still had many school duties to carry out and much of the time had therefore not been my own. There had been all of the online lessons to prepare; material to upload on to the computer; meetings to attend; work-related emails to respond to; documents to write and amend; school policies and procedures to follow. For all the fact that we were not physically in school, the last few months had been pretty 'full on' workwise, right up until the end of that final week in July. After that, I had escaped down to Devon and it was only now at the start of August that I was, for the first time, sitting around without a clear sense of how I would need to fill my day.

Luckily, I had enough routines from the months of lockdown to sustain me for much of the time. I still started each day with some reading (a novel; a non-fiction or history book or biography; the occasional pop psychology tome) and, of course, I was still very committed to my daily exercise routine. I'd also dabbled with some creative writing and was trying to work on that (a semi-autobiographical work of fiction) for about an hour each morning. These three elements became the pillars of my morning routine: reading, exercise and writing. After that, it was time for lunch (a sandwich in front of the one o'clock news) and then I'd generally take a walk to a local park or hop on the train to somewhere a bit further afield. Sometimes there would be phone calls to friends to make or even meetings in pubs and restaurants and that way the August days quickly passed. If they seemed uneventful, then I was able to persuade myself that this was still the school holiday (I would be paid up until the end of August) and was, therefore, entitled to take things easy. There didn't need to be any big plans or adventures. This was well-earned 'down time'. These were, and always would be, holiday weeks and it was perfectly legitimate to spend them relaxing and frittering away the hours.

Even so. Although I had effectively left school, I still could not escape the usual "elephant in the room" which always haunted the second part of August: the publication of the A-level and GCSE exam results. Throughout my teaching career, these had always dominated the last weeks of the summer holiday: it was impossible not to wonder what on earth the students in one's care might have achieved – or not. What were they going to get? Would they do as well as expected? Would they have made some terrible mistakes and fared far worse than they should have done? Whatever happened all of us on the staff knew full well that we would be judged on the quality of our exam results. These were, and nobody could ever disagree with this however hard they tried, an objective assessment of our ability to teach. If we were good, then our students would do well and come out with top grades. If we were crap, then the students' grades would reflect this. These were a stark and brutally revealing testimony to the quality of our worth. For years, I had always felt how bloody unfair this was, that right in the middle of what should have been the relaxing August holiday we always got this dreadful summons back to reality. You could be lying on a beach in some far-flung part of the world but know that any moment there would be an email winging its way across the planet with a terrible judgement on your worth attached: your students deemed to have failed or to have triumphed or to have met expectations. In all ways, it was a judgement on you which there was no escaping. And cruellest of all that it should come slap bang in the middle of the summer holidays, when school matters should have been furthest from our thoughts. Very cruel.

I had hoped that this particular year, I would not be subject to that awful rising sense of foreboding which generally began in those first few days of August. Surely, because I was retired and could no longer be held accountable, it wouldn't bother me? I would not need to frantically log on to the school website at eight a.m. on the results morning in order to find out the worst? There would not be that terrible pressure this year, surely?

Also, this year there had been no exams. The teachers and the schools themselves had awarded the grades so surely there could be no surprises? There would not be that dreadful, harrowing despondency as your eye skimmed down the list of grades awarded and with shocked disbelief clocked the "D" grade awarded to someone you had banked on as being an A star student. That certainty that there must have been some mistake but also that awful, niggling suspicion that may be the grades are right. Maybe they did all just mess up? But surely this can't be right? It must be a clerical error? And then that dreadful sinking feeling when you started to envisage the long-drawn-out appeals process requiring a whole epic palaver of form filling and the need to seek all sorts of different permissions from the Head, the parents, the students themselves (invariably all of them now on a gap year in some far-flung part of the world and so uncontactable) in order to meet the deadline for a re-mark. Then, only to get the student's script returned and to find that the marking was absolutely spot on; that their answer had just missed the point or was all just waffle or just plain wrong. You'd look at the Exam Board's mark scheme and realise, to your shame, that there were things that you had forgotten to teach them or that had not occurred to you and that in the end, the "D" grade was unfortunately all too accurate a reflection of what they had supposedly not learnt.

Those days and weeks leading up to the publication of exam results were a maelstrom of paranoia and anxiety and catastrophizing. I'd have nightmares that the whole cohort had mis-read the questions and had all been failed; that mine was the only department in the school in which nobody had achieved a pass grade; that single-handedly I had pulled the whole school down from the top of the national league tables to somewhere near the bottom; that the results were so appalling that my resignation would be called for immediately and that my presence would no longer be required in September; shown the door and banished with ignominy and shame.

Although these were fantasies concocted in my head in the dread run up to results day, they were not as far-fetched as they might seem. Quite often, the exam boards' marking seemed mystifying and irrational. Good students sometimes appeared to do very badly and indifferent ones surprisingly well. There was often no rhyme nor reason to it. This was especially true of the marking in a subject like Drama, which was often all over the place. The marking was capricious and completely bonkers some years. But that was little comfort to me who would then be forced to account for the marks to the Senior Staff at those gruelling post-results interviews that always took place in the first few days of September. The prospect of that particular interrogation always loomed over what was a grim enough time as the days shortened and the autumn chill in the air started to make itself felt.

For some reason, in spite of the facts that I was no longer a part of the institution and that the students had not had to make their knowledge (or lack of it) known within the confines of a formal three-hour examination paper, I still felt a kind of crippling horror at the thought of 'Results Day', which was now starting to loom. In fact, the dread seemed worse than ever. Maybe it was something to do with the lack of activity and of distraction. If I'd been wandering around an art gallery in a European capital or out having dinner in a French provincial town or fly-driving down some American highway, then perhaps my mind wouldn't have been so focused on worrying about what the students were going to get in their exams.

I eventually realised that the only thing for it was to be out of town on the day that the results were published. Quite often, I would have gone into school to help with the distribution of the results but having made my farewells in the middle of July, I really did not want to be creeping back in there a month later. I knew that my fear would be writ large on my face and I didn't want to be seen shuffling in looking sheepish and terrified. After all, I was supposed to have 'escaped', to be starting my new and ever-so-fulfilling-and-exciting-new-life. I didn't want others to see that I had clearly been sat at home worrying myself into a state of acute turmoil about the frigging results for the last two or three weeks. Get a life!

Yes, the best thing was to escape but where on earth to? Airports were banned and I really did not fancy just going and lying on a beach somewhere. I'd have felt too awkward and conspicuous. I didn't want to go moping about some city, trawling round some provincial art gallery and then wandering around a cathedral before plonking myself in a tea shop and wondering how the hell to get through the long evening ahead.

The Sunday papers seemed to be full of ideas for 'Staycations' as they called them so I flicked through those, trying to see if they would give me some inspiration. Eventually I came across an advert for a company called "Footpath Holidays" which arranged independent walking tours for groups and solo travellers. I certainly did not want to be part of any group but quite fancied some solo, "self-guided" walking. I went on to their website and looked at some locations and prices. Their charges seemed quite steep seeing as all they did was send you a map and arranged some hotel bookings but I guessed that they took the hassle out of it and if I went just for three nights or so, then it wouldn't cost much more than £500.

I wanted somewhere I could get to quite easily but which I hadn't visited before. I noticed that they organised a walking tour of the South Downs. Now that was somewhere I'd always wanted to visit but it was also relatively unfamiliar territory.

Why not give it a go?

I phoned the company and talked to a lady there. It all seemed to be a bit more complicated than I imagined, partly because I had left it "so late" (well, only two weeks before I wanted to go) and then the usual complication of me being a "solo traveller" and there not being many single rooms available in the hotels that they used. She made it seem as if it would be quite a feat to be able to get me sorted but I left it with her and eventually she phoned back, telling me that I was "lucky" because there had been some cancellations and there was one hotel which might just be able to squeeze me in. At first, I thought the price was far too steep just for three days. On the other hand, I knew how essential it was that I managed to get myself away on the results day and for its aftermath, so somewhat reluctantly I agreed to pay what seemed like a pretty exorbitant cost for a holiday I could easily have organised for myself at half the price.

When the day came around, I was glad to be lugging my bag down to Southgate tube and then getting the train from Victoria down to Eastbourne. Again, it was great just to be getting away. The dullness of the days at home and the boredom of the routines I had set up in order to get through were starting to get to me. It was invigorating again to have a bit of a change.

The train was mercifully empty and I really appreciated the greenery of the Sussex countryside after we got past Gatwick. I had to alight at Lewes in order to get a local train and then a bus to Alfreston, where I was to be accommodated for the three nights. Unfortunately, the buses were extremely infrequent. Even though it was only about half past four by the time I got there, I appeared to have missed the last one that day so had to get a taxi. That was fine and it meant that I wouldn't be scrabbling around at the other end trying to find the guest house but would be dropped outside the door (a good thing, seeing as the guest house was right at the other end of the village, along another road with no pavement).

When I arrived at the B&B, I was met by a slightly grumpy owner who told me immediately that I needed to put on my mask. He didn't seem that welcoming and was perhaps suspicious of a single middle-aged man who had booked to stay for three nights at what must have been very much the last minute. The man took me up to my room: a sizeable one on the first floor of a large Victorian house. It looked out on to some fields and a cottage garden at the back and was comfortably, if unstylishly, decorated. He told me to come back down to the reception area as soon as I had settled in so that I could place my order for breakfast – which struck me as a little strange- but I suppose they needed to make sure that they had enough of everything (if all the guests decided to order sausages, for example, then these would presumably need to be procured the evening before – or removed from the freezer and defrosted... That seemed to me to be the rationale, anyway). After I had ticked off the various items I imagined requiring in the morning (tea/ orange juice/ bacon/ egg/ toast/ marmalade etc etc) and handed my tick box sheet to the man, he then proceeded to give me the lowdown on where to eat that evening. Apparently, all the local eateries got very heavily booked in the summer months and I wouldn't be able to just turn up. I didn't listen very carefully, telling myself that I would find a local supermarket and get a few things from there and take them off to eat them outside somewhere, so that I could make the most of the late summer evening.

Deciding that I needed to go and explore, I unpacked and

then headed down the road in the direction of the centre of the village. A busy main road passed through it and, once again, I had to be very careful to avoid the traffic, especially on those sections of the route which had no pavement. The village was a little further away than I thought and when I got to the only store it was way past six o'clock and was therefore closed. I had forgotten that this was not London. We weren't in the land of the convenience store or corner shop. This renowned tourist centre had one village shop and at six o'clock in the evening it was closed. (It shut at mid-day on a Sunday, I noticed). Thwarted in my quest for food, I went in search of a garage or somewhere else where I might be able to buy at least a sandwich. The garage had nothing except a few packets of crisps and some Mars Bars. I went into a pub, which advertised "bar snacks" but was met by a rather aggressive owner: "Have you booked?" No I hadn't. "What is it you want?"

"Just a sandwich"

"Oh no. We don't do sandwiches in the evening…"

Cursing the lack of charm and of customer service, I left hurriedly and thought that I would try elsewhere.

Remembering that the man at the B&B had said that there were a couple of pubs in the next village that did food, I thought that I would try them. I think he'd said that they were about a twenty-minute walk in the opposite direction. Not wishing to walk along the busy main road again, I decided to follow the river which wound through the town and looked particularly alluring in the golden early evening sunshine.

The river walk was beautiful. The path was almost deserted apart from a few sheep and cows in the fields nearby. As I followed the path out of the town, the traffic noise receded and all I could hear were bird song and the gentle flow of the river.

It felt so refreshing to be out of London and in this charming Sussex countryside. I almost forgot that I was in search of sustenance but managed to spot a small number of houses some distance from the river path in what seemed like the next village, so made for them in the hope that I might be able to get something to eat there. However, if I'd imagined that these places were going to be less crowded, I was wrong. One of the pubs had an enormous pub garden but it was packed. Every table had a large family group, drinking and waiting to be served. A couple of harassed looking teenagers carried out plates of burgers and chips as they shouted out table numbers. It all looked a bit rowdy chaotic and I imagined that if I tried to order anything now, I'd be waiting for ages. Also, I didn't want to sit on my own in that crowded and noisy place. Everyone else was in a big group and sitting there waiting for a plate of indifferent food was likely to just make me feel sad and lonely.

There was another pub nearby but it was exactly the same story so I followed the river path back to the hotel, telling myself that it certainly wouldn't cause me any harm to do without for once. I'd get a big breakfast in the morning and could certainly stock up on toast and stuff then, so it wouldn't be the end of the world if I went to bed hungry on that particular occasion.

The next morning, I got up early after the usual fitful sleep and wondered about how I was going to maintain my usual exercise routine in this unfamiliar setting. Having survived since March without visiting a gym, I had always managed to do something whether it was a Joe Wicks exercise video (PE with Joe or one of his twenty-minute workouts) or a somewhat breathless jog round two circuits of Enfield Park. Today was a bit different, however. I had a long walk planned, which would count as my daily exercise fix and there was nowhere obvious to jog around there. There weren't any pavements on the road outside the hotel and I hadn't seen any parks nearby when I had been out the previous evening. Surely it would be OK to forgo exercise just this once?

I wasn't convinced about the wisdom of this, knowing full well that without the accompanying endorphin rush produced by thirty minutes of vigorous exercise first thing in the morning, I was likely to feel sluggish and not a little depressed for the rest of the day. On the other hand, I really couldn't face putting on my kit and going in search of a suitable exercise venue that morning, so I decided to risk it. I was supposed to be on holiday, after all.

Leaving my room and descending the surprisingly grand staircase at my B&B, I made my way to the breakfast room on the ground floor. My host was bustling about officiously, clearing away plates and dishes and chatting heartily to the other guests about their plans for the day. There weren't many others around. It was mainly middle-aged couples all preparing for either a leisurely drive around the local beauty spots or walkers like me gearing up for a lengthy day's hiking. My pot of tea for one arrived, together with some toast. I helped myself to fruit juice and some Cornflakes and ate them staring into the middle distance, hoping not to catch the eye of any of my fellow guests. I hadn't banked on this part of my stay: that uncomfortable business of having to eat breakfast in a public place at a sad-looking table for one, surrounded by much married couples all eating in companionable semi-silence.

Eventually, the owner's wife appeared in a full vizor and face mask, her hands encased in white rubber gloves, with a plate piled high with the Full English Breakfast I had ordered the night before. She bustled in and out and seemed very capable, if a little tense. She asked me about where I was planning to go that day and I told her that a cab would be arriving for me in an hour or so to take me to the starting point for my day's walk. She seemed impressed that I was intending to walk for the whole day and joked about me needing to stock up with a hearty breakfast. I simpered encouragingly and appreciated her attempt to be friendly and humorous.

After breakfast, I went back to my room and gathered my things for the day: a map, some water, sun cream, sunglasses and a small rucksack. In my water proof walking trousers, thick blue woollen socks and hiking boots, I certainly looked the part.

Going back downstairs, I sat out on a wall outside the house and awaited the arrival of the taxi that would take me to the starting point for that day's walk. These were the so-called "Jack and Jill Windmills" on one of the highest points of the South Downs. From there, I would walk the ten miles or so along the tops of the Downs and be back at the hotel by late afternoon.

The taxi was an enormous people carrier and I had to wear a mask while I was inside, as did the driver. For some reason (nervousness and not feeling that in control as a result of not having had my daily endorphin rush from exercise) I mistakenly sat in the front seat. I never normally did this with taxi drivers, always preferring to sit in the back so that I could avoid having to make conversation. Sure enough, this driver took it as a sign that I wanted to speak so I had to engage in fairly half-hearted small talk for the duration of the forty-minute journey.

It was a relief to arrive at my destination and to not have to think of things to say anymore. He deposited me in the car park in front of one of the windmills. These were obviously a bit of an attraction in the surrounding area but the car park was almost completely deserted. Hard to tell why when it was another beautiful day of bright sunshine and blue skies. Maybe people who came to this area were keener to visit the adjacent seaside resorts on a day like this: Brighton, Eastbourne, Hastings. Anyway, it seemed as if I was going to have the Downs to myself that morning. The route was easy enough to follow: a white chalk track right across the top with staggering views on either side. It was all very green and very 'Southern' in comparison with, say, the spectacular cragginess of the Lake District or the Yorkshire Dales, with which I was rather more familiar. There were no mountains or lakes here. It was more rolling green hills, often with the sea in the distance and those white cliffs, of which the Seven Sisters were the most famous example. Nevertheless, it was all still spectacular and lovely in its own quiet way. It was also easy walking. The path was clear and more or less flat, the heavy climbing having been done in the taxi when it climbed up the hill to the windmills from where I had started the walk. It was also almost deserted apart from occasional walkers who I passed and shyly acknowledged along the way.

I strode on, making good progress and only taking occasional breaks for a swig of water or to check my phone. There was something very exhilarating about being out in the open air and up high on the tops of those downs with the whole county of Sussex spread out on either side. It really was a most enchanting county and its proximity to the sea added an extra allure. The sluggishness and slight depression of the earlier part of the day soon lifted and I started to feel quite buoyed up from the sunshine and the fresh air and the peacefulness of it all. Only the faintest and most distant traffic noises, with the occasional bird song or tractor sound from far away could be heard. After all those months of lockdown, it was certainly extremely energising to be outside and striding along, with not much to worry about or trouble me and most of my attention just on getting to my ultimate destination. The hours passed quickly and by about two o'clock I had completed the whole walk. I got back down to Alfreston by following some winding paths which led through a rather posh looking housing estate and back to the centre of the village. The shop was open now and I picked up a few basics, a sandwich for lunch and some salad bits and pieces for my evening meal later, if I decided not to bother with a restaurant.

When I got back, I felt that I had certainly had a good walk. My legs were aching and my feet were sore, so I ran a very hot bath and soaked in it for a good hour or so. I then lay on my bed to read and must have dozed off for a bit. One of my friends had recommended the Ben Elton novel "Identity Crisis", a satire of some of the dafter aspects of contemporary life which I was enjoying enormously but even that couldn't hold my attention and so I allowed myself to drift off. I must have woken at about five and thought I'd go and investigate some of the local restaurants. Could I face sitting at a table for one for an hour or so and ordering some food? Maybe.

I must have walked up and down the main street in Alfreston for at least an hour but I couldn't decide on where to go. Even at that hour (late afternoon) everywhere looked very busy and I couldn't imagine myself eating in any of the places I had seen. The staff all looked hassled and unwelcoming. This was clearly the sort of little country town that only really came to life for a couple of months in the summer, during which time it was completely overrun with tourists and outsiders and all their various demands. The people working in any of these places probably barely had a day off during the tourist season and all of them looked overworked and disgruntled. No – far better just to go back to my B&B and have a little picnic outside in the garden and savour its peace and tranquillity.

That was what I did, trying as best I could to relax and enjoy my cold pieces of chicken and my slightly cheerless accompanying salad and bread rolls while trying as hard as I could not to think about the exam results, which would be published first thing in the morning...

I had another not very satisfactory night's sleep. Always before Results Day my sleep was dreadful anyway as I subjected myself to the various nightmare scenarios in which every single one of my students had failed and I was to be had up before some sort of Educational Tribunal for gross professional incompetence.

I had brought my iPad with me so that I could log on to the school website first thing and put myself out of my misery. The results were usually posted at dawn and were available for staff to see wherever they might be in the world on that particular morning in August.

As I waited for my iPad to start up and update, I turned on the TV news. As always on this particular day, the A-level Results were the main story of the day. What a horrid jolt this always was, dragging you out of any holiday mood that you might be in at the time (on a beach, or sun lounger or airport or one of any number of exotic locations) and bringing you back down to earth with the most alarming jolt. This was a reminder that however hard you might have tried to escape, the 'RESULTS' were there to signal your professional competence (or not) and these were the foundations on which every other pillar of your life rested. Yes, you could be sipping a Bacardi and coke on a Caribbean beach but this was a reminder that this had all been financed by a job in which you were expected to deliver. If you didn't get the grades, then the cocktails and sun loungers might be no more.

Clearly this morning, though, there was something deeply wrong. The news story went on and on. Normally, it was just a few shots of grinning students opening their results envelopes and then some educational pundit commenting on "yet another sharp rise". This time things seemed very different.

Apparently, those results that we had all sent off to the Exam Boards in good faith had all been altered. The students were not getting the grades which the schools had awarded. There was something called an "algorithm" which had adjusted all of the teachers' grades and in some cases the grades finally awarded were nothing like what had been expected. The news now featured groups of tearful looking students and their families all appearing shocked and bewildered at the baffling results they had received. There were weird inconsistencies which nobody appeared to be able to account for. One girl, who had been predicted a string of A stars by her prestigious, expensive and extremely exclusive private school, had opened her envelope to find herself given an "A" and two "Ds". The girl sat there on her sofa wailing and blubbering in disbelief while an angry father vowed to fight the whole system and get this aberration investigated and overturned. There were countless scenes like this. There was something clearly catastrophically wrong. Somehow, a computer appeared to have overturned all of the teacher predictions and hardly any child in the country seemed to have been awarded the grades that they had expected.

There was anger, outrage, disbelief. It was a major story and dominated the morning news to the exclusion of all else. It was clearly a national disaster, on top of all of the other disasters which this government had been responsible for.

There was also something wrong going on at my school. The results, which should have been available by now, had not appeared. Instead, there was a strangely ambiguous email from the Head saying something along the lines of all Heads of Department would need to make sure that they had their evidence to hand in order to launch the Appeals Process on behalf of every student. She had clearly chosen not to publish the results that had been received because they (as in the examples shown on the tv broadcast that morning) in no way reflected the true talents and abilities of our students.

Somehow, eventually, I did manage to see what my tiny cohort of students had been awarded for Theatre Studies and (miraculously in the circumstances) their grades were exactly what I had submitted to the exam board. Apparently, though, this was not unusual: "smaller" subjects had been more or less waved through, while larger and more crucial grades in subjects like English, Maths and the Sciences had all been doctored and in almost all cases lowered way beyond what would have been expected.

There were clearly going to be some horrific days ahead for all Head teachers and Heads of departments in major subjects while the exam results were challenged and, it was hoped, then re-assigned. I did not envy those engaged in this process and could tell from the frantic, erratic tone of the school emails which were now filtering through that we had been plunged into a period of deep crisis. Not only had schools weathered the most unsettling upheaval for years with the months and months of school closures and all of the horrifying threats to health and well-being, now here they were being thrown into the hell of completely bewildering examination results with all their effects on League Tables, students' futures and their university places and to teachers' careers and their professional prospects. All of this had been thrown into total disarray and chaos.

Having now left the profession, I realised that I had little part to play in un-scrabbling this awful mess. I hadn't predicted that this would happen. Like everyone else involved, I just thought the Exam Board would rubber stamp the teachers' grades and that there would be no horrible surprises. How wrong I was, but also how glad I was not to be around and to have to deal with this disaster. I could imagine the tears and the hysteria and the wails of disbelief. Thank God I was away from it and out of the eye of the storm, I thought, somewhat guiltily.

Well, there was nothing I could do about it now and I had deliberately chosen to absent myself from it all this year by choosing not to be around. That was the main reason why I had booked this trip away in the first place. I had to leave them to get on with it and concentrate on making the most of my time away.

That day's excursion was another segment of the South Downs way, starting this time in Rodmell and finishing in the market town of Lewes. Once again, I went down to breakfast and tried to make myself as inconspicuous as possible amidst the chattering married couples and fractious family groups who otherwise occupied the breakfast room. Again, the owner's wife scuttled around between the tables, looking like something out of a science fiction movie with her enormous dome-like visor and her rubber gloved hands. She appeared to be working far harder than her husband and seemed to go backwards and forwards between the tables at least a dozen times, while all he seemed to do was walk among the guests making enquiries about their plans for the day and dispensing his rather pompous "largesse". Thankfully, I was able to escape after a couple of slices of toast, went up to my room, used the toilet and brushed my teeth, packed my bag for the day and wandered out to the drive at the front to wait for my taxi. It was the same man as the day before. I felt that I'd already used up my limited store of conversation on the forty-minute journey the day before so was only able to make very half-hearted attempts at chat as he drove me through the busy summer holiday traffic to the start of my second day's hike. He dropped me outside the pub at Rodmell and I gave myself a few minutes to explore the village before setting off on my route. This village was famous for being the country home of Virginia Woolf so I took few moments to locate her house and to then walk around the grave yard of the village church. This was an idyllic spot and was exactly what you would imagine an English country village to be like. I envied the peace and tranquillity of the lives of its inhabitants but couldn't forget that Virginia Woolf had gone out from here one spring morning to drown herself in the nearby river Ouse. In spite of its appearance of blissful calm and order, it was clearly a place in which a soul could still be in torment and driven to madness and suicide. What lies beneath…

Nevertheless, that day it was another bright and already hot summer morning and I had a lengthy hike to complete. Locating the path that I thought I was meant to follow, I began the climb up from the village on to the South Downs way and began my day's trek. Somehow, the scenery wasn't quite as attractive as it had appeared to be the previous day. Part of the track was concreted over and seemed to be a road for farm vehicles. There was also a field that I had to pass through with a "Beware of the Bull" sign, which made me rather nervous, especially as there were no other walkers in sight. The more I walked, the more I felt that I had perhaps taken a wrong turning. Something about it did not feel right. I was supposed to be heading in the direction of Lewes but the little villages in the distance were clearly not that busy market town. Maybe I had gone wrong somewhere? I pulled out the map for another look, having blithely set off with only a cursory glance at the route, which had seemed quite straightforward at the outset. No. On closer examination, I could see that I was walking in the opposite direction from where I was supposed to be. No wonder the landscape had not seemed as appealing as it had done on the previous day. I was walking in the wrong direction and had been doing so for at least a couple of miles. Retracing my steps and again keeping a watchful eye open for the bull which the sign had warned me about, I returned to my original starting point and realised that I had taken a wrong turning. I had gone right when I should have gone left. A world of difference! I now set out on the walk which I should have been doing in the first place and, yes, the views were once again very pleasing. Different from yesterday; less panoramic but more undulating, with little streams, hillocks and copses but still charming and captivating. This route took me along the banks of the Ouse for a stretch of it and I wondered how near or far I was from the sight of Mrs Woolf's fateful plunge into its cold and uninviting waters. At one point along the way, I passed a hostel which had a deserted snack bar serving teas and coffees and snacks so I stopped off there for twenty minutes or so before another upward climb which led me across the tops of the Downs once more and eventually down into the outskirts of Lewes.

By now the sun was boiling hot and I needed to find somewhere for a drink and some lunch. It must have been about two o'clock and once again, I must have completed the walk in record time because my cab was not due to pick me up for another three hours. Making my way to the central square, which was dominated by a rather lovely but extremely elaborate war memorial, I scoured the map of the town centre. I rather fancied sitting by a river or in a park for a couple of hours with my book and dozing in the sunshine. Thinking that I had located what looked like a suitable spot on the map, I made my way towards what seemed to be the main shopping area, hoping to pick up a few provisions for my supper. There looked to be a Waitrose not far away so I made for that. The central shopping area of the town was pretty standard, although there was a rather attractive bridge over the Ouse, which led into a more 'arty' area of coffee shops and antique dealerships, which I wandered around for a while. I felt drawn back to the river, though, and followed some signs to a 'River Walk' which seemed to run alongside an enormous retail park. There were a number of empty benches along the river bank and I decided to plonk myself down on one for a while. I had been walking for ages in the hot mid-day sun and felt that I needed a bit of a rest. Also, after a couple of days of solo walking, I was now starting to feel a little lonely and sad. In spite of the change of scene and the challenges of finding the right route to follow on the walk, my mind was still filled with the exam results fiasco. It was impossible not to think about it and I was now regretting not being around and on hand at school for my students and colleagues, as I had been in previous years at this time. Luckily, I knew that the students in my own particular subject were OK as far as them getting the results they'd been predicted in my subject were concerned but I was well aware of the fact that they might have been seriously disappointed in some of their other grades and I wished that I had been around to offer counsel and support.

I sat on the bench overlooking the river and watched it flow by. The Ouse looked very different here to how it seemed out in the more open country. Here it was flowing through a town, with small industrial buildings and warehouses on either side of its banks. The river looked tainted by its surroundings and now seemed grubby and unappealing. The built-up nature of this part of town was oppressive, stifling even, especially in that blistering hot weather.

I looked at my watch. It would be another two hours before I was due to be picked up. What was I to do to fill the time? I'd done my supermarket shopping and I had stopped off for a coffee and a glass of water. What else was there to do here? There certainly wasn't any leafy park nearby in which to lie down and read my book.

All of a sudden, I had had more than enough of my own company and needed someone to reach out to. I knew it would probably be irritating to her and that she would no doubt be busy and I would inevitably be interrupting something but I had an overwhelming need to speak to my sister. At least with her, I wouldn't have to pretend that I was having a whale of a time. With her, it would be fine to make her aware of the fact that I just needed to hear a familiar voice and that I was by now more than fed up with the voices inside my own head.

I dialled her number.

"What do you want? I'm busy…"

"I just needed to hear your voice"

"Are you OK?...Are you having a great time?"

"Yes, not bad, thanks. I'm just sitting on a bench by a river..."

"Oh, very nice. Where is that?"

"Lewes..." I knew that she had once had a boyfriend who had come from Lewes and that she had visited his parents with him there many years previously and that the town would therefore hold some associations for her.

"Oh..." she answered, as I heard her mind flicking through those memories. What might have been...

Not wishing to pursue that, as I wouldn't have wanted a partner from years back resurrected at that moment either, I swiftly changed the subject:

"What do you think of the exam results fiasco?"

We started to talk about it and she reassured me that by having opted to retire from teaching the month before, I was now "well out of it..." However, with school aged children herself, she could understand how disastrous the whole situation was for all concerned and we chatted about that for a few minutes.

We then talked about our different plans for the evening; the food we'd be eating and the TV we'd be watching, as we always did. I felt grateful for those few moments of connection and reassured by her familiar tones. I thanked God for the contact.

After the call, I wandered along the river bank a little more and then decided to make my way back to the more interesting part of the town: the old town square and, beyond that, the castle which was where I was due to be picked up by my taxi man later in the afternoon. I felt very sluggish and rather exhausted from two days of long-distance walking. Trekking back up the hill and out of the modern shopping area, I wandered around some of the backstreets and wondered what it might be like to live in this sleepy little place. I could not imagine it somehow. Even though it was the middle of the afternoon at the height of the tourist season, it was strangely silent and almost deserted. I don't think Lewes was somewhere I would wish to end up myself.

I found the castle and climbed up the hill to survey the views. There was something quite un-English about it. I felt as if I was in Normandy or some part of northern France rather than in the quintessentially English county of Sussex. Then, with thirty minutes or so to kill before my lift arrived, I went into a nearby Pret for an iced coffee and observed some of the locals, trying to put my finger on exactly why they seemed so very different from Londoners.

My cab arrived and I was whisked back through the rush hour traffic to my B&B. Any sense of a tranquil rural idyll was quickly dispelled here. There were traffic jams and honking horns and road rage-possessed drivers all along the way. Driving through a tunnel, we hurtled along at break-neck speed, while other drivers sped towards us with murderous impatience. These so-called 'country roads' seemed no different to the North Circular at a similar hour.

When I got back to my room in the guest house, I ran myself a hot bath and soaked in it for a while. The long morning's hike and then the tiring afternoon of mooching about in Lewes in the baking summer sunshine had left me fairly whacked and I certainly didn't fancy doing very much that evening. Another quiet night in seemed hugely desirable.

I turned on the six o'clock news and, of course, it was dominated by the exam results debacle. Ministers were interviewed, head teachers, education experts, disappointed students and their parents...it just went on and on. After having made such a mess of the whole pandemic and then the economy, this seemed to be yet another disastrous set of decisions made by our government and the national mood seemed to be one of outrage and hostility. On and on it went; the news, the One Show; Panorama; Tonight; the nine o'clock news, News at Ten, Newsnight. There was no end to it. Checking through my school emails, however, there seemed to be surprisingly little, just ambiguous statements about how things were going to be investigated and warnings that we should not have any direct contact with either students or parents. Clearly everyone was hoping for some sort of volte face and a reversal of the disastrous decisions that had been made.

I went downstairs and sat outside on one of the picnic benches in the garden of the guest house and ate my solitary meal of some slices of Waitrose quiche and a bit of salad. It was all eaten in a few minutes, after which I just sat and watched the sunset as it fell over the lush green valley below. It was certainly a most fetching and attractive place but would I ever come back? Maybe not. I'd been there for three days and that somehow was enough.

The next morning, I had another taxi to take me to the station and then felt a sense of huge relief as I slumped into a seat on the London train and allowed it to carry me back to Victoria. Although only 60 miles or so from where I lived, there was something about the little Sussex towns and railway stations that felt stifling and alien. Yes, I know that I had recently retired and could hardly be said to be a spring chicken myself but there was something about all these places that just felt very ageing. They felt "small time" and oppressive in a way that London never does. No. Get me out of here. Get me back to noise and energy and diversity and excitement and high culture. Now!

I must have been in my flat again well before midday and what a relief it was to be back. The break had been nice enough, I guess, but three days were sufficient. It was always the same with me. However pleasant it was to get away, I found myself missing the excitement and the cosmopolitan edge of London. That provincial smugness and gentility was not for me, I reminded myself, as I trundled through the tunnels of King's Cross pulling my overnight bag behind and caught my tube back up to Southgate.

I gathered that most of my colleagues were now preparing sheaves of evidence with which to appeal their students' devastatingly inaccurate exam grades. In my case, I would not be required to do this so I decided to stay out of it for the time being. I followed it all on the news, though. Apparently, now the results were all to be recalled and re-assigned. This was a good outcome in lots of ways but it also meant that the agony was to be prolonged again for some. Where would it ever end? And then it was all to be replayed the following week with the publication of the GCSE results, which would presumably follow a similar pattern and then the whole ghastly scenario would be played out again.

It was all just too agonising to contemplate so, for much of the time, I just sank into my own familiar routines and tried to concentrate on preparing myself for my first full month of proper retirement in September. When the new term started, I would no longer be required to deliver online lessons or go to Heads of Department meetings on Zoom or to fill in my Exam

Results Analysis – because I would no longer be there.

My friend Barry picked up on the mild anxiety I was experiencing about the autumn and suggested that the best remedy for it would be to plan a trip away. He even offered to come with me. Of course, at first, I dismissed the idea, thinking that if there was to be any kind of trip undertaken in September, it would definitely be on my own. On the other hand, this would be no ordinary September. It would be the first one in almost forty years when I had not been at work and, however onerous working life might have become, I imagined that this would be a very disconcerting change of rhythm and routine. Maybe it would be a good idea to go away at this time with a companion and who better than a companion who had recently undergone the same process; the same process of unshackling from a career which had consumed his whole life, almost even more so than it had mine? Barry would know what I was going through. We'd be able to share our thoughts and experiences with each other and I knew that he would understand in a way that perhaps others might not be able to do. It suddenly seemed like a very good idea to take Barry up on his offer to be a holiday companion for a trip to be taken in those first days of September. He knew, he said, that I would be thinking about school and about my friends and colleagues all returning to a place that I had now left. He reckoned that I would find this hard and he understood that the transition from working life to retirement was not necessarily going to be smooth. It seemed like a very good idea to say "Yes".

We agreed that we would depart the day before the start of the new term so that we could be "somewhere nice" on that first morning, while our friends from work were going into their first staff meeting of the new term. We hadn't quite decided where we would go. I had a number of suggestions for somewhere that might involve some walking, such as the Peak or Lake District and Barry agreed to give it some thought and come up with some suggestions of his own.

More and more, as the last few days of August rolled by, this plan seemed like a good idea. It was definitely sensible to have something planned for the start of the new school year. I certainly did not want to be just stuck at home wondering how it was all going and musing on whether or not I was being missed.

We decided not to go away for a whole week. The important thing was to be away for the first few days of the school term. It would probably be OK to be back by the end of that first weekend. Let the term get underway, with us as far away from it all as possible and then return and get on with trying to make as good a job of Retirement as possible.

I also had another couple of issues. For some time now, I had been suffering with poor eyesight. Driving a car was becoming nigh on impossible because of my increasingly poor vision and at night, in spite of some very thick lenses in my specs, reading a book or a newspaper was more or less beyond me. I would seek out the brightest lights possible and keep shifting the angle of the book I was reading in order to get the maximum amount of light on to the page but all to no avail. I realised that even before my "Retirement" began, this was something I needed to rectify. I did not want to be going into it with such poor eyesight that reading (one of my principal pleasures and something I hoped to do a whole lot more of now) became a trial. I needed it to be easy and pleasurable and didn't want to be constantly orientating myself in order to just about get enough light to read by.

I had visited an optician at the start of the summer, having had several visits in which I had complained to him that my spectacles were no longer effective or doing their job. After several tests and different visits, he eventually diagnosed an unusual form of cataract and he suggested that I arrange to have it removed. I was excited by the thought of this solving my sight problems and decided to be treated privately in order to get the operation performed as quickly as possible. (Under the NHS, I would have had to wait for over a year, partly as a result of the backlog created by Covid). Of course, it would cost me: something in the region of £5,000. Although, if this could improve my sight and make reading pleasurable again instead of the strain and source of stress which it had now become, then it would be worth every penny.

I had various tests and meetings with the ophthalmic surgeon in August but the operation itself would be scheduled for the 10th of September. Therefore, whatever trip Barry and I planned for the first week of the month would have to be over by then.

Barry had been a particularly good pal to me over the last few weeks: hosting my various "leaving" events and then now offering to be my holiday companion in order to ease me into the first unfamiliar days of full-on retirement. I was starting to feel that I owed him one. Therefore, with my assistant Jo (who had also benefitted several times herself from his kindness, generosity and thoughtfulness) we planned to take him out for a "Thank You" dinner in the West End.

This was planned for one of the last days in August and we chose Balans in Soho as the venue. We wanted somewhere lively, fun and a bit exotic and Jo and I had certainly been there together many times before and it never let us down. Therefore, this was picked as the venue for our "Barry night". We must have drunk quite a lot (well, Jo and I certainly did) and unsurprisingly, because we had all worked there together for so many years, the school became the focus of much of our conversation.

Inevitably, perhaps, I started to get rather sentimental about it and, in a slightly drunken way, began to bang on about how much I was going to miss it and how much I would envy them all returning in September. I started to reminisce about the camaraderie between the staff and about the sense of purpose and freshness that the start of the new school year always engendered...until Jo (quite rightly) weighed in and effectively told me to "get a life."

"You've done it!" she shouted over at me, albeit in a slightly hectoring way. "You did it really well for all those years but now it's time to move on! You really don't want to be going back to do yet another year of more of the same, do you? You've got the whole of the rest of your life ahead of you. There are so many things you could go and do now. I am so jealous! If I had the opportunities that you have now got, you wouldn't see me for dust!"

That was me told and of course, she was absolutely right. I'd done it. Time now to do something new...

September

Up until this particular year, September had always been a month that I had dreaded. It was forever associated with the end of summer and it signalled the time to knuckle down and behave again after six weeks of pleasing yourself and doing just as you liked: six weeks of foreign travel, of hotels, of trains and long car journeys and airports; of restaurants and too much wine; of sea and sun and tanning on a beach for days at a time; of being with friends and laughing together and drinking together and exploring the world. Come the last few days of August, though, there was always that sense that the temperatures were cooling, the nights were starting to draw in and the leaves on the trees were beginning to turn. The long summer holiday was drawing to a close and it was time to go back to work. And the autumn term was always a "tough gig": four months of pretty relentless slog. New classes to get to know, new topics to teach, new exam specifications to get one's head around and all requiring that extra spurt of energy and focus that the long holiday just gone was supposed to have delivered. "You've had six weeks off. Now it's eyes down and get on with it. No complaining" A fair cop.

I'd always struggled with the first few days of the new school year. That sense of the holiday becoming a distant memory and now no excuses for not buckling down to work. The business of those first few days: the new timetables and lists of students' names; the endless meetings and "target setting"; the dreaded "Exams Results Analysis" when you had to trawl through each student's exam performance and analyse whether they had performed better or worse than expected and then account for any shortcomings in the way that they might have been prepared was invariably a trial. There was always a bustle and business-like atmosphere about the school in those first few days. No shirking or malingering allowed, everyone expected to be back and at the top of their game after the six idle weeks of the summer holiday.

How glad I was not to be part of that anymore.

This year, of course, my poor ex-colleagues would all have the added complexities of Covid to be dealing with. For a start, they would all be returning not just after a six-week break but effectively after a six-month break, there having been no full school since March. However hard it had been returning after a month and a half off, I could only begin to imagine the sheer shock to the system of returning after half a year away from the place. Then there were all the new Covid restrictions to deal with: the social distancing, the staggered break times and lunch times in order to keep all the different year groups apart and firmly in their 'bubbles'. The requirement to teach wearing masks; the need for each room to be 'deep cleaned' before it could be used by another class; the lack of social contact between colleagues because no more than six members of staff were allowed to be in a room together at any one time. The list went on and on and I thanked God that I was not going to have to deal with any of it.

No. I would not be returning on the First of September this year because I had now retired.

However, this year, I had agreed with my ex-colleague Barry that we would both be away from home on the days that the schools returned. We didn't want to be sitting in our homes and dwelling on the fact that our services were no longer required; that we were now somehow surplus to the needs of the school which we had both served so loyally for years. We needed to be away and distracted and in a completely different environment.

In the end, Barry suggested that we go and stay in his sister's holiday home in North Yorkshire for a few days and distract ourselves from the fact that our old mates and friends were all returning to work with a packed timetable of vigorous daily walks, fresh air, inspiring scenery and plenty of wholesome food and drink. This sounded like a good idea to me. I also particularly appreciated the opportunity to share this important time of transition with someone who had only recently been through the same process.

Retirement is a big thing in anybody's life. You are leaving the role which you have taken for a lifetime; saying "Goodbye" to an institution which has sustained and nourished you; leaving a job which has provided you with a sense of purpose and a function and reason for being for years and years. Suddenly you are cast adrift and having to find a new role, new routines, new ways of organising your time in order to feel satisfied and fulfilled. There is also a strong sense of loss, not that much different to a bereavement and you have to acknowledge and process those complex feelings.

It was with some of this in mind that I woke on that first day of September and got myself ready for Barry to pick me up in his car for the long drive up the A1 to the North Yorkshire Coast. Being a Tuesday in September, the traffic was relatively light and we made it in fairly good time, with only one stop for coffee and the toilet. We arrived at the house in Sandsend at about three p.m. and I was pleasantly surprised at how spacious it was. It was certainly bigger than your average holiday home, It was a pebble-dashed 1930s semi-detached house, with three bedrooms and a couple of bathrooms and a good large living room, dining room and kitchen. Barry kindly allowed me the double bedroom with its handy en-suite and after we had unloaded the car, we set off for a stroll around the village so that I could orientate myself and get acquainted with the place.

Barry had spoken of our destination as being Whitby but in actual fact, the village of Sandsend was about three miles down the coast from there and had its own distinctive character. I learnt from Barry that this was a place in which he and his family had holidayed from a young age. They had had relatives there and on our wander round, he pointed out places that had been lived in by now long dead aunts, uncles and cousins. In fact, at one house an elderly auntie turned out to be still living there and as part of our little tour of the place, we stopped off to say "Hello". It was lovely for him that he was so connected to the village and I was immensely charmed by its chocolate-box character. I loved the warm, golden sandstone of the cottages and the ways in which they were ranked along the hillside in neat little rows, each house with its own view of the sea. It seemed like a delightful place and was totally un-spoilt. Apart from an ice cream stall, a pub and a village shop, there was very little there. There was one hotel, I think, but otherwise it was just a collection of ordinary houses. Not an amusement arcade or fast-food outlet in sight. I could now well understand its appeal.

For food that evening, we decided to try the local pub. We hadn't been able to book but they managed to squeeze us in at an outside table where we both ordered an excellent plate of steak and chips and a couple of pints of bitter. We didn't linger for very long because the evenings were now starting to get quite chilly and there was a fairly biting wind starting to blow. I was glad to get into the warmth when we returned to the house in the middle of the evening and sat down for a good bit of telly. We both very much enjoyed the homage to 'Are You Being Served?' which was being shown that night. Apart from being wickedly funny (and very non-PC) it also had great nostalgic appeal being so much a product of its time, the 1970s, when we had both been growing up.

The next morning, I decided to try out the promenade for my morning jog and managed to run as far as the outskirts of the town. This probably was a shorter distance than I would normally have run but it was enough to blow away a few of the cobwebs, especially in the bracing wind which was coming off the North Sea.

We made some sandwiches and then set off early for our day's walk. Barry was a great one for starting the walk first thing in the morning. I normally preferred to walk in the afternoon, so that I could use the morning for reading and writing but obviously I had to be flexible and adapt myself to someone else's routine on this occasion.

Packing waterproofs, our lunches and plenty of water into our knapsacks and then donning hiking boots and thick socks, Barry drove us the few miles up onto the Moors to find the starting point for our walk. Barry had been there many times before so I was naturally happy to be guided by him. I'd only a limited knowledge of the area, having been at York University when I was studying for my degree years before but then only occasionally venturing this far-east. Most of the time I had been wanting to explore the more cosmopolitan delights of Leeds,

Bradford and Huddersfield, all in the opposite direction.

The villages here were picturesque and quaint and it was good to be able to see them just out of the main tourist season when they weren't quite as overrun as I imagined they would normally have been. We stopped at Goathland, that had been made famous by the television series "Heartbeat" which was clearly making a feature of its 1950s signage and atmosphere. We parked the car just outside and set off for our morning's hike, following the course of a river for most of the first part and then climbing up onto the tops of the moors in order to get a bit more height. The river path was slippery and uneven and involved us in scrambling up a fair few rocks in order to keep the river in sight. It certainly wasn't particularly easy walking but the scrambling element added a touch of challenge and it felt good to exert and push oneself a bit, in spite of it being, as Barry kept reminding me, the first day of my retirement.

Momentarily, we thought of our colleagues back in school all sitting through the first of three school Inset Days planned for that week. This year, of course, they would be doing these all online but it was impossible not to remember all those "first day backs" of the autumn term in which we had all sat in ranks in the school hall listening to the Head talk about the latest set of exam results and outlining his or her aims for the following school year.

How lucky we were, we reminded ourselves, to not be having to sit through all of that today but to be out in the fresh air surrounded by the rugged scenic beauty and emptiness of the North York Moors. What a joy and pleasure that was!

About half-way through, we sat down by a dry-stone wall and took in the panoramic views of the moors as we ate our lunch. How good even the simplest food can taste when eaten outside! Although we'd kept up a fairly steady stream of chat till then, we were now both happy to eat our food in companionable silence, just drinking in the quiet majesty of the landscape. It felt great to be outside and to be free of the stresses and worries of work and to know that this was the future.

Eventually we got ourselves back to the car and the starting point of our day's trek. There was a tea shop nearby so we stopped off there for some coffee and cake before heading back towards Sandsend. On the way back, Barry asked that we might stop at a butcher's which did "legendary" pies and he bought a big one for our tea the following evening. We both thought that sometimes it would be quite nice to be in of an evening and not always have to go out to a pub to eat.

The time back at the holiday home seemed to pass quickly, with food preparation, washing up and tidying. I was mindful of the fact that the house did not belong to me and therefore wanted to try and keep it as spick and span as possible. I certainly wasn't going to allow myself to slob about and let things go in the way that I sometimes did at home. Instead, I was scrupulous about washing things up and putting them back and keeping the place as neat and tidy as possible.

We did have a couple of glasses of wine with our supper in the evening but after that, it was a few self-indulgent hours of slumping in front of the telly and gradually nodding off as the evening progressed. The shared domesticity and companionship were enough of a change from how I had passed my evenings since the middle of March to feel like a novelty and these added to the holiday feeling; this was a welcome break from my normal patterns of behaviour. It was actually quite enjoyable to share a house with another person, I realised to my surprise.

The next day was another walk but this time along the coastal path. This was a real revelation. We began in the sleepy fishing village of Staithes, with its winding narrow streets that descend down from the hilltop above. It seemed like the archetypal smuggler's cove, a bit like something out of "Moonfleet" or a Robert Louis Stevenson novel. Again, apart from people's homes there was very little there; perhaps a couple of village shops and then a pub by the harbour at which we stopped for morning coffee but not much else. I guess they found it nigh on impossible to get supplies down those tiny winding streets, especially in the colder weather. For now, though, all was tranquil and calm in the early autumn sunshine. I had always thought that this could be a blissful time of year, that peculiar mixture of summer and autumn as the year begins to turn. For now, it was all bright blue skies and balmy temperatures as we sat at a table outside overlooking the harbour to take photos to send to our poor beleaguered colleagues back at work.

The rest of the day was spent marching along the coastal path, every so often dropping down to explore a village or beach on the shore below. This had obviously once been an area of industrial activity at some time long ago and there were remnants of this past everywhere along the way: information boards with details of the population and buildings in days gone by; ancient sepia tinted photographs; surprising stories and tales from bygone eras.

The sea air along the way was very bracing but it was surprisingly warm for September and for most of the time it still felt as if we were on summer holidays.

So that was how the time passed: long, invigorating hikes starting first thing in the morning and then afternoon tea or coffee and a slice of cake afterwards and then back to base to unwind with a mug of tea and then start to prepare whatever we were going to eat that evening. A glass or two of wine and then a couple of hours of choice television and then bed. It was an extremely enjoyable, relaxing and happy week and as a good a way as any of transitioning from work into the new world of enforced leisure.

On our final day, there was a promised trip into nearby Whitby itself for fish and chips and a wander round the town. We'd not done any towns during the week, having seen only the moorland and fishing villages so it would make a bit of a change to wander round streets filled with shops and people. Being a Saturday, Whitby town centre seemed to be jam packed with day trippers. I suppose it was people wanting to make the most of the pleasant early September weather which was still remarkably mild. There were blokes wandering around in shorts and with their shirts off. Not sure it was quite hot enough for that but the atmosphere in the small, cobbled streets was certainly jolly and festive that day. I have to say that I did feel a bit concerned about social distancing, though, which did not seem to be very strictly observed. The streets of historic Whitby were narrow and extremely crowded and people were jostling each other to pass by. There was also a distinctly more urban crowd here than we had seen earlier in the week. The voices of the day trippers were loud and braying as they passed the gift shops and handled the trinkets on sale. Whitby Jet seemed to be a big draw here: a deeply black form of stone that had been particularly popular in Victorian times. It seemed to have a funereal charm about it that I could imagine appealing to our nineteenth century forefathers very strongly. It was severe and austere and somehow glamourised the 'colour' in a way that I had never been aware of before.

We climbed the steep steps leading up to the Abbey which dominated the headland and was visible for miles around. It did have a bleak and eerie quality and one could well imagine how it had been part of the inspiration for Bram Stoker's 'Dracula'. When we got to the top, we took a few minutes to explore the church that also sat on that headland. It felt like something out of 'Moby Dick' with its white, nineteenth century panels and its rows of Victorian pews. The Abbey itself we decided not to visit, mainly because there did not seem to be that much to see. The best of it was in the view of it from miles away. Up close, it wasn't much more than a pile of stones. Also, we wanted to get back down into the town for our lunch of fish and chips, which we'd been looking forward to for days.

Descending the large number of steps from the headland which overlooked the town, we crossed the bridge spanning the river and went back into the centre of the town. The plan was to have fish and chips for lunch as the climax of our stay and there was certainly no shortage of options to choose from. Almost the whole of the harbour front seemed awash with fish and chip restaurants of various kinds: some make-shift stalls serving it as the local equivalent of 'street food' and others occupying gaudy palaces clearly offering a 'dining experience'. Apparently, though, these were not the best and so Barry led me to a more traditional looking diner down a back street which didn't seem to be attracting the crowds in the way that some of the other more obvious places were doing and we settled down there for a delicious lunch of cod, chips, mushy peas, tea, bread and butter and ice cream. Fattening and calorific surely but absolutely delicious and the chunkiest, freshest piece of cod I had ever eaten. Well worth the wait!

Afterwards, we did a bit of wandering around the rest of the town, past the old fashioned-looking shops and the faded facades of once grand hotels before heading for the beach and a brusque stroll across the sands back to our accommodation. The early autumn weather was now starting to take hold and we had to battle a bit against the strong wind that was rolling in off the North Sea. The seasons were starting to turn.

After an evening in of Saturday night telly, we packed our bags and set off early the next morning on the road back to London. Barry played the radio station Magic of the Musicals in the car on the way back and we spent the time chatting about our favourite shows and the productions we hoped to see once the theatres were allowed to open up again. How soon would that be, we wondered?

While we were away, I had heard that the small half-house owned by another of my ex-colleagues was now available again. The vendors (my friend and her husband) had got fed up with waiting for their buyer to complete and so had pulled out of the sale. They had given their buyer the deadline of end of August to complete but now that this date had been and gone, they decided that they could not wait any longer and so were now offering me first refusal.

I told my friend that I wanted the chance to go and look at the house again before I made any definite commitment to buy and so on the first Monday after our Whitby trip, I found myself in the garden of the "half-house" in Bush Hill Park having a good look round with my friend's husband and telling him that I now definitely wanted to go ahead. In order to do this, I would need to get my flat on the market, so I promised to do that. This all felt very positive. It was going to be a new start. I was going to be a house owner and I was at long last going to have a garden. This was something I had dreamed of for ages and this garden was particularly spacious, with a lovely pergola and a paved area on which I could imagine serving drinks and nibbles of a summer evening for an unending stream of guests. I had a local estate agent come round to my own apartment to take pictures and measurements and to put the flat on their website and within a few days, I was starting to get viewings. It all seemed very promising.

In the meantime, I needed to prepare for my eye operation which was going to take place later on that week. I had been for various consultations and tests and two days before I needed to go for a Covid test to prove that I was not harbouring the virus before I went into the King Edward Hospital for my treatment. It was all costing what seemed like a small fortune but I really felt that I could not wait any longer and I was keen to get it over with.

I was due to take the Covid test in the afternoon a couple of days before the operation. This was performed at a small annex of the King Edward Hospital in Marylebone. The test was not particularly pleasant but I felt sorry for the poor woman who had to administer the test, shoving that cotton swabbed stick up people's nostrils. What a horrid job! Of course, I flinched and winced a bit while having it done but tried to seem cheerful and appreciative and didn't want to make a fuss. As I came out, all the students from the nearby Marylebone High School were coming out of school at the end of their day. This was the first time in my retired state that I had been out on the streets when the schools were being let out. It felt very strange, being surrounded by hordes of school students all in their uniforms, jabbering away to each other, full of gossip and complaints about how some teacher or other did not like them and had not marked their homework fairly or had told them off for some minor breach of the school rules. There seemed to be hundreds of them, which there were of course, and all coming out at the same time because I guessed there was no longer the busy programme of extra-curricular activities which would normally have helped to stagger the after-school exodus. For years, I had never been surrounded by school kids all dashing out of school at home-time, because I had been inside the school building and generally staying behind either to attend a meeting or run a rehearsal or activity or deal with some task or other that would prevent me from leaving at the same time as the children. Besides which it was always somewhat frowned upon to be seen dashing out of the building on the bell. There had always been this unspoken understanding that one would somehow be available for at least an hour or so after the students had left – should another colleague wish to speak to you or a parent need to ring in with some concern. It was certainly a new experience to be out on the streets at the same time as this swarm of exiting pupils.

Thursday was the operation day and I was told to report to the King Edward at four p.m. that afternoon. I would apparently need some assistance in getting back home after the operation, so I managed to persuade both my sister and my neighbour Mr Ali to be on hand afterwards: her to collect me from the hospital and him to drive me home in his taxi.

In spite of being the second week of September, the weather still continued to be balmy and quite humid. As I made my way up to the hospital that afternoon, it still felt like the summer. The hospital was more like a private hotel than a hospital and I was shown on arrival into a small private room which looked out on to a quiet London street, which appeared to be dozing sleepily in the September sunshine. Various staff came and introduced themselves, all wearing their masks and their rubber gloves. I was told to relax and make myself at home in the room, so I lay stretched out on the bed and almost forgot that I was in hospital about to undergo a procedure. It was as if I had booked myself into a central London hotel and was taking a few hours rest before dashing out to a theatre or for an evening of meeting friends to eat and drink in a restaurant.

The staff seemed incredibly polite and solicitous. A lovely nurse bustled about and made me feel very looked after and then a bright and self-confident young man came and administered a sedative. After that I didn't feel very much at all. I was wheeled into the operating theatre but any fear or trepidation had been medicated away. I must have dozed off as a result because the next thing I knew, I was being wheeled back to my room with the operation having been accomplished.

I rested for an hour or so and was then released. I took the lift down to the ground floor and was pleased to see my sister loyally waiting outside to take me to the place where I had arranged to meet Mr Ali and his taxi. I wore an eye shield plastered over the eye which had been operated on and did look a little alarming but I was delighted that my sister was there in order to steer me through the streets and across the busy main road to Madam Tussauds where we waited outside for Mr Ali and his cab.

It was such an unfamiliar luxury to be driven home from central London and the forty pounds I had offered to give Mr Ali for his services that evening seemed worth every penny. Through the eye guard (which I had to keep on overnight) I tried to see whether there was any noticeable improvement in my sight but it was hard to tell. I guess I would not know until the next morning. There was also a full course of eye drops which I would have to administer to myself over the next four weeks in order to avoid infection, so that was going to take a bit of discipline. I wouldn't be able to exercise either for at least a month for fear of jolting the implant I had had inserted, so that was also going to be another change of sorts.

The next day, I took things very slowly as I didn't want to jeopardise my recovery. Eventually, though, I decided that I did need to go to the supermarket so I ventured out to Waitrose but wearing my usual spectacles. As I was going round the store looking at things on the shelves, I realised that everything seemed distorted. Obviously, I soon ascertained that the old specs I had were not going to work with the "new" eye. I pushed the specs up on to my forehead and suddenly, miraculously, I realised that I could see and read labels without them. This seemed extraordinary. The operation really had worked. What a thrill that was to me at the time!

Gradually, things settled down into more of a routine after the interludes of the trip up to Yorkshire and the eye operation, both of which had made the start of September uncharacteristically eventful. My flat was now well and truly on the market and so every so often, I would have potential buyers of my flat wanting to come round and view and, of course, I still maintained my reading, writing and walking routine. Every Tuesday night, there would be an online play-reading with the theatre company and during the daytime, I would try to arrange walks and meetings for coffee with a variety of local friends and so the days quickly passed by. The patterns of the days were not dissimilar to the earlier part of lockdown, the slow sun-drenched days of April, May and June. I guess the main difference now, though, was that there were no work commitments and duties to fulfil. There were no online lessons to prepare and deliver; no meetings or training sessions to attend; there was not that once a week day in school supervising the children of key workers. There was just me, whatever book I was reading at the time, my half hour of exercise, a spot of creative writing (when I could summon up the energy and the discipline) and the reasonably frequent meetings with friends in the local park or nearby for coffees and chats and a bit of a walk. There was business to do for my amateur theatre company, particularly the online play-readings which all needed organising and casting with details of the Zoom codes required and how to access the scripts and other admin tasks. I tried to cook something to eat every day and that involved regular trips to the supermarket. While previously, I'd always have eaten at least one meal a day at work and then often eaten in a restaurant on a Friday or Saturday night, now I seemed to be having all three meals at home, seven days a week and that involved quite a bit of planning, preparation and shopping. Because I was there all the time, I needed to spend more time cleaning my flat and there always seemed to be piles of ironing to deal with, floors to scrub, surfaces to constantly dust and tidy. All of these things took time. Therefore, it was not as if I was ever exactly feeling at a loss for things to do. There was always some chore to deal with, an email to send or a walk to do and for much of the time, I did not feel that I was particularly missing not going out to work. On the other hand, spending the day doing little tasks was not especially satisfying and I found myself beginning to hanker for a bit more structure and just feeling that I had some talents which I needed someone to use.

For the most part, I was able to fill my days just pottering about but I knew that eventually I would need to be doing something a little more demanding. It was impossible not to wonder how things were going back at my place of work. The schools had all returned in September, for the first time since March and although I knew that they were under a whole raft of restrictions at least they were back, everyone was together again and schools were functioning after a fashion. It felt strange and sometimes saddening to no longer be a part of this. Of course, I messaged some of the friends I still had on the staff and received their reports from 'the front line' and I found myself extremely curious to know how it was all going.

With this in mind, I arranged to meet my friend Nicola who had, like everyone else, recently returned back to work in September. I knew that she would be able to give me the full 'lowdown' and some good chunks of gossip on how it was all going: who was coping and who wasn't; what directives had been issued by the folk in charge; how all the new rules were affecting behaviour and staff morale. She would be able to "tell it like it is". I was looking forward to our catch-up session and arranged an Uber to whisk me over to the pub in Walthamstow in which we had agreed to meet.

I must say that I wasn't that keen on getting into a taxi with a potential virus carrier but if I wore my mask and sat in the back, then surely it was safer than getting on a bus and then travelling on a crowded tube? The taxi driver was a particularly talkative chap and didn't shut up for the whole journey. So strange were those times, though, that all through his monologue, I kept wondering if he was going to turn out to be the person who later infected me with the dread virus. What if his cab had not been properly cleaned? Was I going to touch a handle or a seat belt or pick it up from an infected surface? Who would have thought that a twenty-minute cab ride could be so fraught with danger?

I leapt out of the cab on arrival and joined Nicola on a bench outside one of her favourite boozers. She had a pint of lager waiting for me, which I duly guzzled before we ran off down the street to an artisan pizza restaurant which we'd visited several times before. It was a jolly evening and great to be brought up to speed with all the gossip from school. She kept telling me that the new protocols were an utter "nightmare" and how she longed to be back teaching from home and on her laptop instead of having to wear a mask all day and walking between year-group bubbles with the constant fear about who was going to get infected with the virus and that she might well be next. It all sounded ghastly but at the same time I was secretly envious of the fact that she was back in harness and with all of the old gang. In spite of her protestations of grimness, I could tell that there was clearly a 'Blitz Spirit' that was keeping everyone going and I envied the camaraderie and the shared jokes and laughter that I imagined was getting everyone through. It made my own existence seem sadly solitary and not a little futile.

This sense of futility began to grow. I realised that eventually I would need to find something to do in order to fill my time. Originally, I had scoffed at this idea, believing that I was more than capable of creating my own schedule and packing it with creative and fulfilling activities but now I was beginning to feel that just a bit of reading, a jog in the park, an hour's or so writing on my laptop and yet another afternoon stroll, trekking through, by now, over familiar streets was not going to be enough to sustain me for the next however many years. Of course, if we hadn't been in that strange half-world of being semi-locked down, it might have been easier to find some more fulfilling distractions. There might have been opportunities to jet off to foreign shores or take in an afternoon play or movie or even sign up for some sort of course or training. However, with the current state of affairs, all of these activities were still off-limits.

I started to wonder about what I could do. I went on to various websites and started enquiring about volunteering opportunities in my local community. The libraries in particular, seemed to have a whole host of roles available. They advertised for people to 'meet and greet'; to read stories and help people with their English language skills; there were people with special needs who needed assistance, the elderly, the visually impaired, the disabled. Yes here, surely, there was a role for someone like me, especially with my love of literature and books and my recent lifetime's experience as a teacher? I downloaded an application form and spent an afternoon completing it. They seemed to want a huge amount of information just for a voluntary role. I had to upload photos of my passport and driving license and then had to ask two friends to act as my referees. What a palaver. Eventually, though, the application was completed and I press Send to submit it.

At last, I started to feel a little more optimistic about the future. I wasn't just going to fritter away my days with domestic chores and sending out email reminders to members of my Am Dram group. Instead, my talents were going to be tapped into and used as I reinvented myself as a valuable member of my local community.

Within a few minutes of sending off my application, however I got a reply: "Owing to Covid Restrictions, we are no longer accepting applications from new volunteers. Thank you for your interest"

So that was that. I could now no longer see myself as some great pillar of the community, forging ahead with a new life of altruism and service in the pleasant and unthreatening environment of Enfield Town Library.

Never mind. I had plenty of books to read, friends to meet for coffee and walks and TV shows to watch but I could not help wondering whether this would really be quite enough.

In terms of the virus, things seemed to be creeping back to normal now. I had another night out in a pub and restaurant in King's Cross with my friend Jonathan and apart from us having to download and register with the App on arrival and the fact that we had had to make sure to book our tables, things hardly seemed very different from how they would have been before the pandemic.

My friend Angela sent me some pictures of her and a friend enjoying a few days' break in Venice. Slowly, it seemed as if foreign travel was coming back. She was lucky enough to own an apartment in Venice and in her texts to me from while she was away, she kept telling me that now was a great time to visit that magical city. Normally over-run with tourists, now apparently, the streets of Venice were almost completely deserted and the few visitors who were there could have the place almost to themselves. I felt very tempted to give it a go myself. I could book her apartment and could easily pick up a cheap mid-week flight from British Airways.

Surely, this was the sort of thing I had dreamed of doing in my retirement? Flying off to European cities on mini-breaks just for three or four days. Wandering around the galleries and museums out of season, sitting in the parks and squares and watching the world go by.

It felt like an uncharacteristically bold and reckless thing to do but with Angela's encouragement, I made a booking for her apartment via Airbnb and printed off a ticket for a midweek flight from Heathrow via British Airways. Yes! The cosmopolitan, jet setting retirement I had always imagined for myself was now starting to happen.

And Italy, Angela assured me, had the virus completely under control. Because they had had such a terrible time of it way back in January, by the autumn they were taking no chances. Everyone was tested at the airport and there were strict regulations in force but once you had got through those, you could more or less forget about Corona and just concentrate on enjoying the delights of that most welcoming and stylish of European destinations. I could not wait to get on that plane. OK, the local library did not want to make use of my talents but so what? I was flying off to the city of canals and gondolas and the Rialto and the vaporetto. I'd be eating a bowl of pasta overlooking the lagoon, washed down with a glass of Rioja after a day of sunning at the Lido and looking at spectacular Renaissance canvases in the Academia. If the Enfield Library service didn't want to use me as a volunteer, then so what when these exotic delights were beckoning?

October

I was surprised how optimistic I felt at the start of this second month of what was now my "proper" retirement. I remembered that when I had been agonizing about my decision of whether or not to retire from work, way back in the early spring, and wondering whether I would ever cope with the forced inactivity, I never imagined that I would be able to survive the later mornings and the empty afternoons and the marking-free evenings and weekends but here I was and I felt that I had barely noticed the lack of work. In fact, this new life of a slightly later start to the day, the chance to read a chapter or two of whatever book I had on the go before the rest of the morning kicked in; the bracing jog around the park for a couple of laps, the succession of meetings with friends for a walk, coffee and a good catch up and then the luxury of just being able to sprawl out on the sofa in the evenings binging on trash TV and not having to worry about working through a set of students' essays or annotating some text for teaching the next day felt like a not inconsiderable luxury.

Of course, I didn't always feel completely guilt free. I realised that there would eventually have to be a bit more structure and that I probably needed the discipline of, if not work, then at least some sort of volunteering activity to get me back out into the real world and interacting with people again. At the moment, life just felt like a permanent extension of the summer holiday and I had the sense to recognise that this may not be a good thing forever.

I went on the various websites which seemed to offer opportunities for unpaid work to members of the local community in Enfield. Most of them sounded very worthy and quite a few of them sounded tediously mired in political correctness and clearly involved not actually really doing anything very much at all. Too many seemed to require people to 'support' outreach programs and 'diversity' initiatives. Quite a lot seemed to require people to take on some sort of 'caring' role or needed people to drive around in their cars ferrying about the elderly and infirm. I can't say that I felt exactly inspired or found any of these so-called 'opportunities' particularly alluring.

I discussed it with my friend Lee, who had already been retired himself for a number of years and had got "the retired life" down to a fine art. He was the friend who had advised me to make sure that I maintained a full social life and always had plenty of meetings for coffees and walks lined up around which to structure my week. "Try to see someone every day" he had told me. "Even if it's people who aren't necessarily your closest friends". He then reeled off people he saw on a regular basis: ex-work colleagues, old-neighbours or friends of his parents; people he'd met from evening classes; parents of students he had taught. "You might start meeting up with people you wouldn't have dreamed of spending time with before" he said. "They don't have to have been your bosom buddies but it's someone to see, someone to spend time with. You don't have to meet up with them for long. An hour or so for coffee and a chat......really helps you to get through the day and stops you getting lonely." I knew exactly what he meant and I certainly started to agree to seeing friends I might not normally have met up with and as I got into that second month or so of 'official retirement' I'd got a good little circle of pals who were happy to meet up for a couple of hours on a fairly regular basis. Funnily enough, even though life was constricted and uneventful as a result of the pandemic, there were always things to talk about. Apart from everything else, there was always the government's handling of the health crisis to discuss. Their woeful record of incompetence and mismanagement; there were the alarming prognoses for the future; the latest revelations and near scandals to chew over like the hypocrisy of Dominic Cummings and his infamous trip to Barnard Castle or the failure of the 'world beating' track and trace system to deliver or the inability of the prime minister to be decisive when it came to ordering a "circuit break" in the early autumn in order to avoid another lockdown and a worse resurgence of the pandemic later in the year. These issues could always be chewed over ad-infinitum. Then there was the TV and whatever nightly crime drama was showing or some eye-opening documentary; there were books to be talked about and titles swapped; there was family news ("how's your dad?"; how were siblings, partners, sons and daughters; mutual acquaintances coping); who was doing what on Zoom and how successful or fulfilling was the virtual choir or the virtual play-reading or the virtual Pilates or yoga class that one or other of us had been attending. There was never a shortage of things to talk about. Following Lee's advice about making sure that days were booked up (sometimes several weeks in advance) with meetings for coffee and that a good range of different pals were seen, became a bit of a lifeline in those weeks.

Going back to the volunteering issue, however, he seemed less than enthusiastic when I mentioned it to him.

"Hmmm..." he mumbled, definitely not sounding convinced. "You see, I tried all that. I did loads when I first retired. I did Story Time at the library, Bereavement Counselling at the Hospice, helping Primary school kids with their reading..."

I nodded enthusiastically. All of these activities sounded worthwhile and fulfilling and were definitely the sorts of things I could imagine myself doing.

"Don't do any of them now," he said.

I asked him why that was.

"They all sound good on paper but the fact is the reality of them is that they are all run by these really bossy people and most of them just treat you worse than they would do if you were in a paid job. Right little jobs-worths they are, most of them. I just got fed up with giving up my time and turning up each week and then being bossed about. Also, they become a terrible tie after a while. You sign up to do a couple of mornings a week and it may not sound like much but it's amazing how quickly these things come round again. Another morning when you can't meet up with a friend or do something you really want to do because you've got to go to your volunteering activity. One by one, I've just dropped them all. Don't miss it – at all."

It was shortly after this that I'd sent off the library volunteering application and then been told that they were no longer recruiting more volunteers. After that, I felt somewhat deflated and let down. All that time filling in the form; all that debating with myself about whether or not I wanted to make the commitment just to have my hopes dashed at the first hurdle. I guessed that this was how it was going to be with a load of other volunteering opportunities, as well. We weren't in normal times and so all those areas in which local people might have mucked in and given of their time in a voluntary capacity just weren't going to be happening. This felt unfair and was annoying when here I was willing and able and wanting to make some sort of constructive contribution, only to be told "Not at the moment, thank you".

I was determined not to give up, though. In all the 'self-help' literature I had read about how to have a happy retirement, they had all stressed the importance of volunteering as a way of maintaining good mental health. The social contact, the structure and sense of purpose it provided was obviously bound to be beneficial, so I looked at other avenues for securing myself some sort of volunteering role.

The local council had a website which listed a whole range of opportunities. My own little routines of reading, exercising, going for walks and meeting friends for coffees was sustaining up to a point but it wasn't quite enough. I certainly needed to do something a bit different and get out and meet a few new people and make something of the skills or talents I'd developed during my years in the workplace.

Eventually, I settled on a couple. One of my local parks required some volunteers to join them for gardening duties one morning a week (no experience or knowledge required, just "enthusiasm") and the RVS were looking for people to join the Home Library Service, which delivered library books to the house bound in the local area. These seemed like the least bad options. I went to the pub with my friend Deborah who had been back at work as a teacher for about four weeks and was already wrung dry from the overwhelming demands of the new term, with all the Covid restrictions on top of the normal pressures of a teaching day. She was very encouraging and thought that the volunteering opportunities sounded very rewarding. She encouraged me to imagine the delight of a house bound pensioner when I turned up at their door with a stack of library books to help them through their long hours at home. She thought that working at the local park and being outside in the fresh air for a few hours doing some honest, practical work would be a great way to break up the week. Not too onerous and a nice change from the normal routine. I might even get to know some new people.

All this time, I was making my preparations to escape to Venice for a few days but as the day for my departure approached, I started to develop some misgivings. It was impossible to ignore the fact that we were still in the middle of a global pandemic. Italy had been one of the worst affected countries at the start of this and, try as one might to disregard it, we were now only a few months down the line. Could travelling there really be without hazards and dangers? Yes, Italy claimed to have it all under control but there seemed to be a mind-boggling set of restrictions, rules and regulations when I went on to the government website to check the latest travel requirements. At the same time, I started to get some rather grim images in my head of me wandering forlornly around Venice on my own for three days. Initially, the thought of it had been exciting and exhilarating but as the day for my departure approached, the whole prospect just made me feel extremely sad and lonely. I had images of long, solitary mornings spent sitting alone in pavement cafes trying to eke out a coffee before setting off for some church or gallery. I imagined myself trawling around looking at all those ecclesiastical interiors, trying to take a serious interest in the art work but probably just longing for a bit of company and chatter. I thought of those long, slow afternoons when I would have gone to wherever I had planned to go to that day and would then be wandering back to my apartment for a snooze, drained and exhausted by the tedium of it all. And then worst of all, the evenings: that sad, nerve wracking wandering around looking for somewhere to eat where I would not feel too conspicuous or out of place; that dragging myself past restaurant after restaurant and observing all the tables crowded with couples and families and groups of friends all laughing raucously or staring dreamily into each other's eyes or enjoying their companionable silences while I trekked past wondering whether that was a place at which I dared ask for a table for one at which I would hurriedly eat a Margarita or a bowl of pasta with a small carafe of house red.

No! Suddenly, the thought of three days on my own in Venice became complete anathema to me. All that money: the flight, the accommodation, the food and drink, the gallery entrance fees – just in order to be wishing the three days away and longing to get back home. No, it could not possibly be worth it. And that was not to mention the danger of it all. I'd be cooped up on a plane for three hours with God knows what risks attached. And then what if I was unlucky enough to contract the wretched virus while I was out there? I'd been out in London, travelling around on the tube, seeing friends, going to pubs and restaurants. What if I suddenly became ill while I was out there? There was no knowing was there? Worst of all, what if I got it while I was out there and then was not allowed back on the plane to get home?

Just that very morning, I'd seen a news story on Breakfast TV about a young bloke who had been quarantined in Italy because he had tested positive at the airport on the day when he was supposed to be coming back. He had since been kept in Italy on his own in a hotel room for the last twelve weeks, unable to leave until he was able to present three consecutive positive tests. On the tv news, his family and friends were all interviewed and talked about what a nightmare the whole thing had been. The guy was trapped there, unable to return. Could I be certain that the same thing would not happen to me?

For days, I dithered: to go or not to go? It was only three days. Surely, this was what 'retirement' was supposed to be: jetting off somewhere exotic and glamorous and paying next to nothing for the privilege because now you were free to travel outside the school holidays? Yes, of course, it was a bit of a risk but surely, I was supposed to be stretching myself and moving out of that comfort zone that had so constrained me for the last thirty-six years? Besides, I'd told all my friends that I was going. Wouldn't it look incredibly wimpy to suddenly back out now? All of my most recent phone calls and emails had ended with "Enjoy Venice!" "I do envy you just being able to take off whenever you fancy it now" "Hope you have a fabulous time…" How humiliating to have to turn round now and tell people that I'd bottled it; I'd chickened out at the last moment; I'd lost my nerve.

Actually, I realised that I didn't care. I wasn't going and that was that. The image of some great scary and hirsute Italian law enforcement agent standing at the entrance to Departures at Venice airport and barring my way was just too strong. I would only have to have developed a slight cough or a temperature from a poor night's sleep or a bit of a hangover and there I would be: effectively incarcerated in an alien hotel room in a foreign country, unable to speak the language or to go out; locked in the room day after day with nobody else around; in total isolation.

Therefore, I decided to cancel everything: the flight, the

accommodation and even took the guide books back to the library. I was slightly anxious about telling my friend that I had cancelled the Airbnb booking on her flat and I imagined she'd think I was completely mad but to me it seemed at the time absolutely the right thing to do.

Anyway, there were things to be doing here. There were the volunteering opportunities to explore; there was my flat to be sold and the new little house to be moved into round the corner...Talking of which, I seemed to be getting very little interest from potential purchasers of my flat. There had been the predictable flurry of interest when it first went on the market but that seemed to have dried up very quickly and for weeks afterwards there was nothing. Not that that stopped me fantasizing about living in the new place. I thought about it most of the time. What would it be like to have a garden? Would that be a huge amount of work? Would I knuckle down and do it? If I didn't, then how much would it cost to pay a gardener to do it for me? What about the inside of the house? It needed some built-in cupboards or wardrobes in both of the bedrooms. Where would they come from? How much would they cost and how long would they take to install? Then, was the house secure? It was a small house, made out of a much larger one but half hidden by a fence and some shrubs? Would it get burgled? Would I feel safe there at night? What would it be like walking home from the station late at night if I'd been up to the West End to watch a play or meet friends for drinks? Was the new station that I would need to start using as good as the one that I used now? Was it more or less of a walk? Was the train-line as good as the one that I had used for years in my current place? Was I really sure that this house was what I wanted? After all, I had the choice now to live wherever I wished, was this really going to be my forever home?

Of course, once I started to think like this, I began to plague my mind with doubts. I didn't worry that it seemed to be taking ages to sell my flat because, honestly, I was no longer sure that the little house was quite what I wanted. It all seemed a bit suburban, a bit safe, a bit dull. I began to fantasize about a swish apartment somewhere and seriously wondered if I couldn't upgrade to a "sexier" pad in a more "happening" part of London.

There seemed to be blocks of apartments going up all over London. In spite of the pandemic and the way in which it had decimated most people's work, the construction industry just seemed to keep on going. Of course, most of these more centrally located flats were way beyond anything I could afford but my Inbox was regularly contacted by housing associations offering various "Shared Ownership" schemes which seemed to make buying a modern apartment instantly more affordable.

I contacted one such scheme and got told to ring a number for a "financial assessment" and got through to a very warm and friendly sounding gentleman who said that he would "assess my housing needs" and make a recommendation as to where I might go.

A few days later, I found myself getting off the train at Canary Wharf and walking across a bridge which spanned one of the waterways there in the direction of a large high rise apartment block run by Notting Hill Genesis. I had made an appointment to meet a lady there who kindly showed me what was on offer. We went up in a lift to the twenty sixth floor and she ushered me into a one-bedroom apartment. Instantly, I loved the newness and smartness of it. I adored its heavy duty black front door; the solidity of the spaces; the impregnable concrete floor; the floor to ceiling windows. Most of all, I loved the view. The whole of London seemed to spread out before me: the Thames, with all its riverboat traffic; the shard, the London Eye, St Paul's; Tower Bridge..........It was breath-taking and so full of energy and life. Forget reading a book, if I was living there, I would just sit and stare out of the window at the view all day long.

The sales lady asked me if I wanted to go out on to the balcony. I agreed before remembering that I'm not good with heights. As she pulled open the floor to ceiling sliding door and we went out on to the wooden decking of the balcony, I realised that I was almost completely paralyzed by vertigo. My heart started to palpitate and it dawned on me that I would never be able to live here because the outside space would be a complete no-go area for me.

Afterwards, I made various excuses to myself, saying things like I didn't think I could live without a spare bedroom (I'd only have been able to afford a One Bed) or that I wasn't too keen about the fact that there were only a couple of lifts for the whole building. I stood outside and observed that some of the residents didn't use proper curtains and this had made their apartments look shabby and make-shift. I wanted to live somewhere in which people took pride in their homes. Gradually, I weened myself off it but truth to say, the apartment was a stunner and the sales lady had not exaggerated when she claimed that it boasted what had to be one of the best views in London.

Afterwards, I walked around the streets and headed for the river. It would be wonderful to be so close to the Thames, to the beating heart of the great city. There was something particularly beautiful about London that afternoon as I wandered around in the mid-autumn sunshine, loving the fact that now I had the freedom to do so, while my old colleagues and students were all stuck in the classroom. I was free, free, free and I still could barely get over that. Free to have all these adventures and to explore the different alleys and byways of the city in the middle of the day in a way that I had never been able to do before.

Seeing the Canary Wharf flat with its fabulous views and distinctly urban feel had given me a taste for city centre living. After all, the fact was, now that I was no longer tied to my job, I was free to live wherever I liked. For the last twenty-five years, I had got used to being only about ten minutes away from my work. This had been particularly handy for all those after-hours commitments like parents' evenings and late rehearsals and coach trips into the West End for theatre performances, when we wouldn't normally get back to the school until after 11.30 p.m. and then need to be back in the following day for the usual 8.30 in the morning start. For those reasons, it had always been extremely desirable to live so close to where I worked. There were some weeks in the middle of a busy term when you'd be doing a three-hour parents' evening from five till eight p.m. at the end of which all you ever wanted to do was to get home and collapse in front of the TV. You didn't want to be waiting on some draughty station platform for a late-running train to transport you back to some more trendy part of London, knowing that you wouldn't be home for another hour or so and wondering whether the endless commute could ever really be worth it.

I started looking at all the property pages in the free newspapers and finding out about all the latest new developments. There seemed to be so many up-and-coming parts of London and the gleaming and hugely glamorous tower blocks seemed to be springing up in every conceivable location. I booked some more viewings.

The following Friday afternoon, I was standing in a swanky new apartment in Tottenham Hale overlooking the marshes and the River Lea and with panoramic views of the vast London skyline again. As with the Canary Wharf apartment, I loved the newness of it; the sparkling new appliances and the solid concrete floors. Again, the floor to ceiling windows filled the place with light and I started to feel that it was in such a place as this that my new 'rebirth' would take place. From here (or somewhere like it) I would launch myself into my new life of adventures and freedom from the restrictions of work. Up here, I would start to write that novel that had been burning inside of me for the best part of thirty years. Here I would host those frequent dinner parties at which the wine and conversation would flow well into the early hours. From here I would set out on travels to cities all over the globe. Here I would bring lovers and new friends and companions who would re-energise this next phase of my life.

Brazenly giving the sales lady the impression that I was once again on the verge of signing on the dotted line (but, in actual fact, with no idea at all of how on earth I was ever going to fund these property purchases), I thanked her for her time and promised that I would be in touch within the next couple of days. (With an asking price offer, I imagined she thought).

Once again, enjoying the fact that I was my own master and did not have anything that I needed to rush back home for, I decided to take myself off for a walk down the nearby River Lea, which I had seen from the apartment up above. It was a sunny Friday afternoon and I thought it would be fun to explore for a while: I could walk along the river for a bit and then catch a train home when I'd walked as far as I could.

The river-bank was pretty empty at that time, with only the odd cyclist or dog walker. Barges lined the banks of the river and a few grungy looking characters sat on the decks of their houseboats, mending equipment or sipping from cans of beer. It was a peaceful and fascinating scene and it was also refreshing to be walking alongside water. On the river-banks there were more blocks of older style flats and every so often a park or green space. Although not high rises like the apartments I had recently seen, these smaller three or four storey blocks, although less chic, were also attractive and I wondered what it might be like to live in one of those (considerably cheaper I imagined).

After a couple of miles, I started to look for a café or somewhere to pick up a drink. The walking in the warm autumn sunshine had made me thirsty and I also quite fancied a bit of a sit down. Once again, I was enjoying the fact that I was free to wander and explore and had no timetable that I was working to, unlike in the days of my working life. At the same time, there was a slight nagging feeling of something I couldn't quite put my finger on. As I walked along the towpath by the side of the river, not really sure where I was going or how long I was going to walk for, I began to feel a little lost and disorientated, aimless almost. Yes, it was interesting to go and look at apartment buildings in unfamiliar parts of London but was this really enough to sustain me, intellectually and emotionally? I realised that I was starting to feel slightly depressed and sad. It was all very well being free and feeling that I had been 'let-out' but I could not also help but feel "Well, what now?"

The more I walked and without a real destination in mind, the sadder and more rudderless I started to feel. I walked past a couple of blokes on bikes who had stopped to have a conversation with each other. They must have just finished work because I overheard one of them say to the other "Have a good weekend then, mate and see you Monday!"

"Have a good weekend". It was the start of the weekend for them but for me it was just another day. For a few moments I felt envious of those who could enjoy that Friday afternoon feeling; that feeling that they had earned their two days of rest after five days of toil. I was no longer entitled to feel that. My days were all the same.

Was I really envious of the fact that these people were working and I was not? I certainly, for a few moments, envied them the structure of their lives, the fact that they didn't have to work at inventing a routine for themselves and thinking up activities to keep themselves occupied and sociable and to stop themselves going insane.

Yes, I had to acknowledge that retirement needed to be worked at. You couldn't just stop and then expect things to happen. You had to be disciplined and have routines and achieve things and make yourself go out and do things. Maybe I did envy the fact that in the working world lots of stuff was done for you. You got told what to do; you had goals set and that gave a sense of purpose; you had people around to chat to and laugh with and gossip about. In this retirement business you were pretty much by yourself and left to your own devices. That was supposed to be great and a release from the burden and obligations of paid employment but it was hard to keep at it sometimes.

In taking my first steps into this new life of what, it seemed, would be unpaid work, I decided that it was best to start small and then see how I got on. I could take on more as time went by. In the list of volunteering opportunities on offer, one of the least threatening looked to be working in one of my local parks for one morning a week. "No experience necessary, just a willingness to muck in". They also didn't seem to require anything like DBS checks, which most of the other volunteer roles did. Not that I minded being checked and I assumed that my record was as clean as it could possibly be but I thought that this would slow things down. I knew how those things worked, however. It would require identity checks and cross referencing and various bureaucratic hoops to jump through, which in the current "locked down" climate would presumably take weeks to complete. Now that I had decided to apply for something, I really wanted to get going with it as soon as possible.

I sent off an email to the woman who seemed to be in charge of organizing the local band of volunteer gardeners saying that I'd like to apply to join the gardening group and she replied fairly promptly. It all seemed to be quite simple: I just needed to turn up on a Wednesday morning in the park at 9.30 a.m. and make myself known to a lady called Lynda, who would be running the group. I had emailed her a couple of days before and she wrote a charming reply back, inviting me to come along and to bring gardening gloves and a bottle of water.

I must say that I felt strangely apprehensive as I made my way down to the park on that Wednesday morning. I guess it was a bit like starting a new job and I had all the associated fears that a similar situation might have aroused. I wondered what the people would be like; would I get on with them; what would I have to do; would I pick it all up easily enough?

The set-up seemed fairly casual when I got there. There was a group of about half a dozen elderly ladies and gentlemen all standing around a rose bed with hoes, forks and wheelbarrows. I located the lady in charge, Lynda, who had a pleasant and welcoming manner and she pointed me in the direction of three white haired but robust-looking blokes and suggested that I go and work with them on tidying up one of the more overgrown flower beds. I introduced myself and did my best to muck in. I can't say that the others took a great deal of notice of me. I tried to ask questions and seem interested but they clearly had a long-standing and well-established relationship and didn't pay me much attention. They kept up a fairly constant stream of banter and jokes that I didn't really feel I knew them well enough to join in with. The chatter was incessant, full of catch phrases from long dead TV situation comedies and ancient movies. There was much reminiscence about old celebrities: Norman Wisdom, Tommy Cooper, Larry Grayson, Sid James. There was casual talk about the pandemic, with frequent reference to "Boris" but not coloured by any of the scathing contempt with which my own friends and associates savagely criticised his appalling mishandling of things.

These were "salt of the earth" types: "little Englanders" and all married with children and grandchildren and dogs and nice, comfortable houses. Suddenly I felt very out of place and slightly miserable. I was never going to fit in here. This had been a dreadful mistake. Having started reasonably enthusiastically and having made a bit of an effort to keep asking things about what we were doing along the lines of "Is this a weed?" "Where do I empty this barrow?" "Should I dead head these?" I started to become more and more silent and withdrawn. I felt strangely nerdy and awkward. I didn't want to give the impression that I thought I was slumming it but that's how I realised I must have been coming across. The only thing for it was to throw myself into the tasks on hand. While the others seemed to work fairly haphazardly, stopping for minutes at a time to finish an anecdote or to exchange some opinions, I worked non-stop. The lady in charge, Lynda, had warned me not to overdo it and I hadn't really known what she was talking about. Overdo it at gardening? Surely not! But as the three and a half hours slowly ticked by, I could feel that the endless bending down was starting to take its toll. She was right, it was completely knackering.

It had felt like a long, long morning. All of the others had stopped for twenty minutes or so to take a drink or to sip from flasks of coffee, sitting with each other on some of the benches scattered around the park but I didn't feel entitled to do that. This was partly because I felt that I had to prove my worth by working all of the time non-stop but, also, I didn't feel that I yet knew anyone well enough to sit with them at the break time. I felt like the new kid at school who nobody wanted to sit with.

Eventually, it got to 12.30 and it was time to leave. I was thankful. It had been a long, uncomfortable morning. The work had been far harder than I had envisaged and relentless, too. Three and a half hours of solid physical graft. Also, socially I had just felt like a fish out of water. I had absolutely nothing in common with any of this lot and although I am sure they never intended to make me feel this way, I could not help but feel rather awkward and uncomfortable. I really could not envisage myself going back. So much for the Gardening Group.

Would the Home Library be any better, I wondered? I had an email from the person in charge of this inviting me to report to my local branch, where I would need to undergo a process of "induction". This would require a DBS check and I was asked to bring my passport and other documents to verify my identity.

The lady in charge of this was a very forceful American woman with that particularly American 'Can Do' positivity and energy that could not have made her more different in manner from the rather reserved leader of the gardening group. She warned me that in order to be taken on as a volunteer by the Home Library service there was a formidable amount of paperwork that would need to be completed. At first, I thought she was exaggerating but I must have been there for a good couple of hours, sat in front of her while she waded through form after form in order to complete my application.

Once again, I felt strangely gauche and shy with this woman. It was as if I had never had a job, let alone worked in a demanding profession for more than thirty-five years. My replies were halting and diffident; my attempts at humour feeble and half-hearted. How would this woman ever imagine that I had held the position of a Head of Department in a top North London school when I seemed so quiet and unsure of myself?

Again, I found the experience completely draining. This was partly to do with the fact that I had felt as if I had been talked at for nearly two hours and I found all the endless form filling and listening to all the fairly obvious rules and regulations to be just frankly tedious. On top of that, of course, were all the references to Covid and the various precautions that needed to be endlessly adhered to. I could just imagine the relish of the Health and Safety brigade as they had devised all these new codes of practice, loving every last pedantic little rule and regulation. As I emerged after my two-hour grilling, I felt exhausted and all my enthusiasm for being part of the Home Library Team held completely evaporated. I was, apparently, to be put on a 'Reserve' list and would effectively be used for cover if any member of the team was ill or unable to report for duty. Part of me imagined that it was then fairly unlikely that I would be called upon because I surmised that the people who had these roles clung on to them possessively. I could just imagine the types: bearded and sandalled Guardian readers, who would be ferociously territorial and never ever want to give up their particular pitches.

Imagining that I would probably not be called upon to serve, I was somewhat surprised to receive a text a few days later, while I was in the queue at Sainsbury's, asking whether I was free to do a library delivery the following day. Unable to think of a reason not to, I agreed and duly reported for duty the following day.

The American lady was, of course, hyper organised. She had laminated cards with all the details of the library users whom I was to visit and neatly arranged carrier bags, each containing a selection of library books for the people whose homes I would be visiting. Each bag had a label with the name of the person on it, hand-written in a bold beautifully confident hand.

She sat me down and went through each of the "readers", giving me a brief description of where they lived and what I would need to do when I got there. Something along the lines of:

"Right, now reader number 2 is Mrs Brownlee. She lives in a small cul-de-sac of sheltered housing flats and she's deaf, so she won't hear when you ring the bell. However, if you go round the back and bang on the window, she'll be able to see you and then she'll let you in".

I was handed a lanyard with my photo on it and a Royal Voluntary Service logo which would identify me as a bona fide type.

"Reader number 4 is bed bound but her daughter arranges to be there on a Thursday morning so that she can open the door to you and collect the books. Just make sure that she sees your lanyard…"

"Reader number 6 lives in the Oakwood care home so you won't get to see him individually but you can hand the books over to the reception desk. They should have his old bag of books ready for you to collect and bring back here."

"Now when you take the books from them, make sure that you give everything a good wipe down with hand sanitiser and put them in the boot of your car. At the end of your delivery, we'll take all of the books out of your boot and then we put them all on a shelf over there to quarantine for forty- eight hours. After that, one of the other volunteers will reshelve the books and we'll select for the next delivery…"

"So, off you go. You've got twelve deliveries to make. If you can try and get them done by mid-day, then I'll be here to take all of the returned books out of your car. Try not to be any longer than that because I'm due at another branch by one o'clock…"

The pressure was on, it would seem. After we had loaded my small car with the book bags, I set off but I was conscious of the fact that I was working to a strict time limit and that I would need to get all of the deliveries completed within the next couple of hours. Couldn't be that difficult, could it? They all seemed to be within the local area and most of the roads were familiar to me. Or so I thought.

As I set out on my first delivery, I realised that I only had a vague idea of where I was supposed to be going. I had got into my car and headed off in the right general direction but I quickly cottoned on to the fact that the roads I thought I knew weren't exactly the same as the ones on the directions I had been given. There were subtle differences. For example, I thought I was heading towards Oakwood Road but it turned out to be Oakwood Avenue that I needed, which I soon realised when I started ringing on the wrong door bell. Where the hell was Oakwood Avenue, then? There was a kind of map supplied with the addresses I had been given but I couldn't make head or tail of it. The print was minute and I had always been hopeless at reading maps anyway. Why not try Google Maps, I thought? So, I got it up on my phone and started to trying to drive according to the directions I was being given. Even though I thought I knew the area quite well, the Google directions seemed to take me along all sorts of strange and unfamiliar routes. Eventually and quite by luck, I managed to stumble across the first of the addresses I was supposed to visit but even that wasn't straight forward. For a start, there was nowhere to park and then when I did manage to park, it appeared that the address I needed was on the other side of an extremely busy road and was at the opposite end of the street. There seemed to be some strange numbering system that did not follow at all the pattern one would have imagined. When I eventually found the number I wanted, I seemed to have to wait an age for the door to finally get opened. An ancient and extremely fearful looking pensioner pulled the door open a few inches.

"Yes?" she said, oozing extreme suspicion.

"Good morning!" I beamed in my friendliest, helping-the-old-folk-but-not-on-any-account-patronizing-them sort of way. "I'm from the Home Library Service" I continued, lifting up my lanyard with its rather grim photo and waving it about cheerily. "I've brought you your library books!"

There was a distinctly unimpressed pause.

"Where's Pat...?" the pensioner mumbled. "It's Pat usually brings me my books. Why isn't it her?"

"I don't think she can come today," I said breezily, making a huge effort to show my teeth and to give some sort of impression of being smiley and super friendly.

"They never told me that there'd be someone else today..."

The two bags of Mills and Boon and big doorstop trashy romances were now starting to get quite heavy and I really needed to be able to just dump them and go. The cheery persona obviously hadn't worked so I lapsed into officious ex-teacher mode:

"Anyway, these are your books" I said, thrusting the two bags in her direction. "Can I collect the ones you want to return and then I'll be on my way..."

The old lady bent down and handed me a Morrison's carrier bag with a pile of more trashy romances and passed them over reluctantly.

"Will it be Pat next time?" she asked timidly.

"I expect so," I replied, resuming the jolly persona I had affected at the start of our interaction. "Thanks for these," I shouted, clutching the Returns as I stepped away. "Have a lovely day!"

After that encounter I was feeling less than good about myself but also worried about the time. That had been my first delivery and I had eleven more to go. Just doing that first one had already taken more than half an hour. If I worked at this rate, I wasn't going to get back to the library for another five hours.

I tried to work out a plan of campaign. Perhaps better to try and devise a route for all of the deliveries rather than trying to do them one at a time. That way I could do more than one drop-off if the addresses were close by to each other.

The Google Maps thing was starting to drive me mad. I'd keep losing my internet connection and then the images on the maps always seemed to be extremely confusing and never the right way round. Eventually, I managed to deposit a few more bags and to collect some returns, although I realised that I needed to be more scrupulous about hygiene. I was so relieved to have got the bags of returned books that I just grabbed hold of them and forgot entirely about wiping them down with antibacterial wipes and smearing my hands in sanitizer. With one old lady, I even forgot to hitch up my face mask. Really, I must not be so haphazard, I told myself, especially on my first tour of duty.

In spite of Google Maps, I seemed to be driving up and down the same streets for ages, taking right and left turns all over the place, often in spite of the road signs which forbade these at some particular junctions. Honestly, though, by that point in the morning, I was beyond caring. I just needed to get through my list of deliveries and get back. I am sure that my 'boss' would already be fretting about why I had taken so long.

The other thing which also worried me somewhat was that about half way through the drop-offs, I began to develop an urgent need to go to the toilet. As always, I had drunk two large mugs of tea and then a coffee first thing before setting out and by about eleven o'clock I was absolutely bursting for the loo. Where was I supposed to go? There were no public toilets around as far as I knew and I couldn't exactly ask one of the old biddies whether they would mind if had a wee at theirs. Not when we weren't even supposed to go further than their front doorsteps.

Realising that I would absolutely explode if I didn't get to a lavatory, I decided that the only thing for it was to drive back to my flat and have a wee there. This could not be avoided and I thanked God for the release of it as I stood in front of my toilet bowl and let it all out. Of course, it was going to make me late getting back but as far as I was concerned, I just did not have any choice in the matter.

Eventually, I got back to the library, with all of my deliveries accomplished and a boot full of bags of returned books.

"Sorry I was so long." I said apologetically as I stumbled in through the library doors, huffing and puffing and looking distinctly frazzled.

"Yes, I was about to send out a search party," the library lady quipped.

"Just quite hard finding all those places, especially when you've got to find somewhere to park and some of them are blocks of flats or roads with strange numbering systems."

"You need to do the same set of deliveries a few times and then you'd work out a system. I'm sure that it will be easier next time..." she said beaming a bright and encouraging transatlantic smile and nodding at me supportively.

Already I was doubting that there would ever be a next time. The whole escapade had involved two of the things I disliked most in life: driving and following directions. I am not a confident driver and hate going to unfamiliar places and I have never ever been any good at following directions and can always guarantee to get hopelessly lost if I am looking for a place I do not know.

I deposited the returned bags for 'quarantining' and made for the car park. I could not say that I had found my first delivery for the Home Library Service to have been a particularly fulfilling experience. It had been stressful and anxiety inducing in the extreme.

Five days later I received a Penalty Notice for making a prohibited right turn at some point during that morning. I would need to pay a fine of £65 for my morning's volunteering. £130 if I did not pay it immediately.

I think that was the end of me and the Home Library.

In the meantime, I was having intermittent viewings of my flat which had been on the market since the start of August and which I was still attempting to sell in order to move to the small house round the corner. I didn't seem to be having much success with finding a buyer and in spite of the flurry of viewings at the start of the autumn, these were now starting to dry up. I wondered if I needed to do something to make it more attractive to buyers. Certainly, my spare room could do with a bit of a tidy-up, if nothing else. When I looked at it objectively, I could see that it was something of a mess. I used the room as my study and it was filled with floor to ceiling bookshelves. These, of themselves, were not a problem but it wasn't just books that were occupying the shelves. I had far too many things like old shoe boxes piled on top of the books and loads of ancient box files which contained all of my old bills and paperwork, stretching back more than twenty years. There were also ancient bits of tech equipment such as leads and plugs, none of which I ever seemed to use; there were old mugs full of dried-up biros and felt tipped pens; there were cheap photo albums containing holiday snaps from the late nineties; funny little tokens of appreciation from old students such as toy cars or miniature cuddly toys and mementoes from various Am Dram productions all littering the shelves and obscuring the very book titles that I was otherwise keen to show off.

(Impressive looking bookshelves had certainly been a big feature of lockdown. Every Zoom conversation with anybody of note featured a "library" backdrop: rows and rows of well-thumbed novels and reference works, testifying to the serious intellectual credentials of the speaker. This had quickly become a massive fad and every single person interviewed on TV at the time appeared to be backgrounded by a mighty-looking personal library.)

I wanted anybody Zooming with me to behold a similar background, testifying to my great passion for books. For me this was a genuine love and wasn't just something I wanted to display 'for show'. I read a huge amount and have an enormous number of books. However, any display would be completely obscured by all the other rubbish on my shelves.

I decided to do something about it. The twenty-five or so box files (one for every year I had lived in that flat) of ancient bills and paperwork certainly did not need to be there. Most companies had gone "paperless" now anyway and I definitely did not need to keep paper evidence of my utilities and other purchases stretching back into the previous century. I started to take down each of the files and began discarding all the pieces of paper I no longer needed. Yes, there were one or two essential items that I probably should keep like the lease details for my flat but it was clear to me that most of the stuff was now completely redundant.

As I began sifting through, I started to accumulate great piles of paper. I wondered what on earth I would do with it all. While effectively "rubbish" I noted that some of these items did include sensitive personal information like bank account details and sort codes. Maybe it wasn't wise just to shove them all in the communal rubbish bins outside? I decided that it would be a good idea to invest in a shredder. I had bought my sister one for Christmas a few years before so took myself off to Ryman's to purchase one. There was a very helpful young man in the shop, who showed me the latest models and with his help I made my selection. That Friday evening, I amused myself feeding page after page of ancient pieces of personal information into my brand-new shredding machine. A bit like clearing out all those years' worth of stuff at my place of work, this was a strangely therapeutic experience. It gave me great joy to see the piles of paper transformed into shavings and to empty the shredder's bucket into a white plastic bin bag, knowing that this could all be safely deposited in the re-cycling bin outside. I particularly enjoyed destroying each box file as their contents were slowly emptied and they were no longer needed. One by one, the files disappeared and I could start to see order and clarity on my bookshelves. As the shredder whirred round, making its deafening sound, I felt a sense of almost industrial purging and letting go. This was the detritus of my old life that was being eaten up by the machine and churned into little slivers of paper and I resolved forever more to be "travelling light". The shelves of my spare room were no longer overhung with ancient, bulging box files of completely redundant paper work. They were now streamlined, neat and clear. Much more appealing for a potential buyer of my home!

As October began to run its course, I was conscious of the fact that I could now start to exercise again following my eye operation. I had been told not to exercise for four weeks – something to do with pressure behind the eye – but as we got to about half-way through the month, I gathered that this was something I could now start to do again. For the most part, during lockdown, I had alternated between jogs round the park and Joe Wicks on YouTube. In particular, Joe's positive and chirpy manner had kept me and many thousands of others going during all those months when we had been confined at home. I remembered his promise that we would feel 'miles better' if we joined him for twenty minutes or so of workout at the start of each day and I certainly agreed that his workouts were great for lifting the spirits and for helping to start the day in a more positive frame of mind. On the days when I hadn't "done Joe", I'd generally managed to stagger round a couple of laps of the park and that, plus the usual lengthy daily walk, had managed to "keep the beast from the door" fitness wise.

Of course, all of this had had to stop in the wake of the eye operation and for four weeks I did not do any exercise at all. At the end of that month, though, I was certainly desperate to get back to it. Unfortunately, the weather had now changed. For months we had been blessed with what seemed like unending summer weather: beautiful, bright sunny mornings in which a jog around the park first thing seemed a most enticing and attractive prospect. It was a great and uplifting way to start the day, guaranteed to get the endorphins pumping. Not so much so by the time we got to last few days of October, though. The mornings were now wet and a bit cheerless and that cloudless golden summer was now well and truly behind us. I wondered, therefore, about resuming my gym membership. I had let this lapse since March when the gyms had closed but decided to go along and see whether I could get it re-activated.

I'm afraid to say that there was a rather unhelpful girl on the desk there, who did not seem that interested when I enquired about re-joining. She said she would take my number and that someone would call me back but nobody ever did. Also, there was something distinctly unappealing about resuming there again. Over six months had gone by since I had last visited the gym. So much had happened, to both the country and to me personally. Somehow going back there and picking up again from where I had left off seemed as if to discount the momentous events of the last half year. Better perhaps to find another gym as part of my "fresh start" in my new retired person's life? There were loads of other gyms in my local area and most of them a good deal cheaper than that one. Yes, it had the freshly laundered towels and the artificial smiles and obligatory cheery greetings from the reception desk staff but apart from that it was really nothing special. Also, as a newly retired person and now on a more limited income, I started to resent the eighty quid or so a month that this could cost me, so I began to explore other possibilities.

One morning, I tried out one of the local council-run gyms at the Southgate Leisure centre, which was about a ten-minute drive away. I had always quite fancied the look of this. It had a massive gym floor, visible from the roadside with rows and rows of machines. It looked enticing and so I decided to give it a try. I paid about £6 for a one-off visit, which seemed quite pricey but I quickly discovered that I could get a monthly membership for just over thirty pounds a month, which seemed to me to be incredibly reasonable. Yes, there was a bit of a palaver attached with Apps and websites to be signed up to and joined but with a bit of help from the warm and friendly girl on the desk, I managed to do all that and was soon surprising myself at my ability to book gym sessions on the App on my phone.

Of course, everything had to be booked online in these Covid conscious days. They weren't allowed to have more than eight people training in the gym at any one time and you had to make sure that you got online early to book your place. Even so, somewhat miraculously, I managed to get the hang of all this and was soon visiting my new gym almost every morning of the week. Yes, the car journey there and back was something of a drag, especially as I had barely driven my car at all for the last seven months and the stress of having to negotiate the busy traffic before I could get on to the treadmill did feel like something of a drawback. On the other hand, it was good to be getting out and to be practising my driving skills again after all this time and, certainly, after the first few journeys, the drive there just became absorbed into my routine.

I must admit that I had forgotten what it was like to get that real sweaty high that you can only ever get from a gym workout. After forty-five minutes on the treadmill and a few weights, my t-shirt was dripping in a way that it never did after a Joe Wicks session or even after my short jogs round the park. This all made me feel that it had been well worth signing up for a gym membership again and I certainly loved the post-session highs, that I had not enjoyed for many a month.

As things started to open up more and return to some sort of normality, I had begun to get into the habit of travelling around London a bit more as well. In one of the Sunday paper travel supplements, I had seen an advertisement for a book that sought to Help You to Explore London. It was attractively presented in bright green colours and took you on guided walks along the banks of the Thames from Hampton Court to Greenwich and around three of the royal parks: Hyde Park, Richmond and Greenwich. Now while it was impossible to get away or to travel and as I had a fair amount of time on my hands, I thought that this would be a really good book to have. I could be a tourist in my own city and explore some of its lesser-known nooks and crannies.

It arrived in the post a few days later and I immediately took it out with me, determined to follow one of its suggested routes. Picking up on my experience of the Docklands apartment with the fantastic views, I decided to follow the Thames path all along Limehouse and out to Canary Wharf. There was something especially bracing and appealing about walking by the river Thames in the middle of the day on a weekday afternoon. It was practically deserted and, of course, there were no tourists or office workers around. I seemed to be able to walk for miles along its banks and barely saw another soul. I loved looking at the apartments which lined the riverside and then following the route inland down the narrow streets with their tucked away pubs and restaurants. I was particularly struck by the signs pointing to the Museum of Docklands and realised that this was a place to which I had never been. This was in spite of always having been fascinated by the history of the area.

On one of the last Fridays in October, therefore, I decided to take myself off for a visit to the Museum. Again, I had to book a ticket and secure a place online (limited numbers allowed, even here of course) and when I got there was met with a very friendly welcome by one of the museum's volunteer staff. They suggested a good route through the museum and so, starting on the top floor, I then worked my way down through the building, amazed that I seemed to be practically the only person there. Of course, children were still at school and there weren't any school trips being organised. Foreign travel was banned so I guess, apart from strange solo visitors like me (also retirees or the recently furloughed?) there was almost nobody else visiting the museum that day. Hence, perhaps, the reason for the excited welcome I'd received from the volunteer standing by the desk when I arrived?

Taking the lift up to the top floor, I started my wander through the museum's exhibits. Straight away my imagination and interest were captivated. All the displays were attractively and strikingly presented and I learnt a huge amount within the first few minutes. Most of the top floor was devoted to the seventeenth and eighteenth centuries and told the story of our shameful colonial past. It was horribly clear that much of the trade and wealth which had gone into the founding of the original Docklands had come from slavery. It's probably obvious to most but certainly had not occurred to me before that the very names of the places which we associate with the area derived from trading posts, such as Canary Wharf which is a reference to the Canary Islands and was the last place from which ships were loaded before they set sail across the Atlantic. East India Dock, Tobacco Road and Limehouse were all similarly associated, to name but a few...

The displays were fascinating and I marvelled at the cruelty and also the bravery of the lives they depicted. I felt quite moved standing in that old warehouse building and contemplating all of the history and enterprise which had gone into creating that area. There was a true sense of being in touch with the past and I was enthralled by everything that I was able to learn on that day. I had a real sense of the richness of the history of the city in which I lived and, once again, thanked God for the opportunity I now had to explore and enjoy it in all of its infinite variety.

Of course, there was far too much to see and take in just in one visit and I promised myself that I would come back again very soon. I wanted to get down to the last floor – which I had not managed – in order to sample everything that it had to tell, about the Thatcher years and the development of the financial centre which now proliferates. I found it fascinating that an area could take on such a radically different personality in the course of a couple of centuries. That it could have gone from this area of trading and warehouses and drunken sailors and shipping to a desecrated, bombed out waste land, to its present incarnation as a zappy, high rise dominated financial powerhouse populated by slick young men and women in dapper office gear all wheeling and dealing between the tower blocks and the designer waterways. It was something to do with the power of history to obliterate and then to resurrect a whole landscape that was so compelling. It was completely fascinating and I longed to re-visit the museum in order to study the final floor, in particular, in more detail.

November

I managed to just about squeeze in that second visit to the Docklands Museum before the next lockdown was announced in the second week of November. We had all known it was coming sooner or later. Since the schools had returned at the start of the autumn, the numbers had been rising again. Somehow, during the summer it had seemed that life was starting to return to normal but as the autumn progressed, the figures for hospitalisations and deaths were gradually increasing. The Labour party was calling for a "circuit break" to coincide with the October half-term holiday but this was ignored only for the inevitable lockdown with all of its restrictions to be brought back in again at the start of November.

This was dispiriting because for a few weeks a kind of normality had returned. We'd been able to go to the pub on a Saturday night and people had begun to eat out in restaurants again. Yes, there had been restrictions such as only being able to go to the pub if you also ordered some sort of a meal but it had felt that we were reverting back to something more like the life we had known before.

I had been able to visit my father on a more or less weekly basis and had met friends up in the West End fairly regularly again. No, we still did not have the theatres, cinemas and concerts back but there was tube travel and drinking in bars and walks in the big parks and access to all of the large Oxford Street stores. Suddenly it was now announced that this was all to be banned once more and it was back to the long, solitary evenings with little or no social contact with anyone else during the day, apart from on those endless walks in the park.

The first few days of November were dominated by preparing for the second lockdown when things like fitting in a final haircut became a priority because this might be the last opportunity for weeks to get one. I got mine cut as short as I dared, guessing that this would probably have to last me now until Christmas.

I met up with my friend Jonathan for a coffee and a walk along the Thames, starting at the Tower of London. We grabbed our coffees from a nearby Pret, both making the most of the fact that we could still sit on seats at tables outside and could still take advantage of their toilets. In a few days, we realised, even these simple pleasures would be banned again. We walked along the banks of the river, enjoying the November morning and the bright sunshine, the only cause for optimism being the trouncing of Donald Trump by Joe Biden in the recent American presidential election. That alone engendered a slightly positive feeling in the midst of the otherwise gloomy predictions of further restrictions and months more of lockdown, rising numbers of infections and hospitalisations and ever-increasing deaths. At least, the election of Biden appeared to signal that occasionally some things can go right and this news provided a little beacon of hope on the horizon. Of course, even that wasn't straight forward, as Trump had now decided to query the validity of the election and was refusing to give up his office. It did seem that he was seriously intending to contest the result in what was clearly, to the rest of the world, a perfectly proper election. We British, with our instinctive love of 'fair play' were appalled that Trump wouldn't do the decent thing and step down. But no, he was clearly not going to go without a fight and we imagined then that it would be messy and brutal (which, of course, it was). It was this issue which dominated our chat that morning plus a sense of foreboding that this might be the last time for a while that we'd be able to meet up. It was the sheer inability to plan things that made the situation so intolerable. Normally, we'd have been fixing dates to do concerts, plays and go out for dinner or to meet up on Saturday nights at his house. Now, none of that was possible again, although thinking ahead as much as we dared, Jonathan did broach the subject of New Year's Eve which we always traditionally spent together and which was now less than eight weeks away. Was I free? Did I want us to spend it together? Dared we plan that far ahead? I thought so, yes. Let's have it as something to work towards; let's hope to goodness that by then – the very end of the year and after this second dreaded lockdown – we would have the thing under control and life would be allowed to return to something more like normal.

We said our goodbyes after a pot of tea in a Canary Wharf café, both secretly wondering how we'd get through the coming weeks. It had been so much easier in the spring, when the weather had been so un-characteristically warm and the sun had seemed to be shining constantly. Now the days were short and cold; the evenings seemed long and it was getting dark by about half past four in the afternoon. The novelty of lockdown had worn off; the 'joke' was now wearing very thin. I no longer felt the urge to bake any banana bread and even Joe Wicks had started to pall. I'd worked my way through all of the TV box sets and had now done all of 'Killing Eve' and 'Line of Duty' and all those dramas with Katherine Kelly, Suranne Jones and

Nicola Walker.

Yes, I loved reading but however much I loved it, I couldn't read all day. I loved walking but before, when I'd set out in the afternoon for my walk, some time after two, I knew that I could stay out until around the time of the six o'clock news. Now, it was getting dark almost two hours before that so any walking I did would have to be very much curtailed.

I did, however, enjoy finding a couple of new places to walk to. At the end of October, my pal Barry had arranged for a group of ex-teachers from my old school to meet at Trent Park on the Friday of their half-term. I had never been there before. I have to say that it was almightily crowded and when I tried to find them in the car park there were no spaces at all. Because it was half-term, it was overrun with Mums and small children so we had to seek out the alternative car park in the other less busy section of the park. However, once we had relocated and all pulled on our walking boots and set off for a walk round the place, I have to say that I liked it very much. It was amazing that after all these years of living so close by to it, I had never once visited the park before. That day, however, I discovered many of its delights. There were some colourful woodlands, particularly beautiful at this time of the year with their golden autumn foliage, as well as rolling parkland, a couple of lakes, a grand drive and an obelisk with views stretching down over the whole vista of the place. I adored the park's variety and sense of space and its remarkable contours. I'd always thought of our local area as being more or less flat but this had little hills and "up and down bits" as one of my pals described it that morning.

I promised myself that this would be a frequent destination for walks over the coming weeks and during that month of November I must have arranged to meet at least four of my friends there for walks through its woods and for a delicious hot chocolate in the snack bar afterwards. What a find!

Seeing as walking had become such a lifeline and as, somehow, it still remained one of the activities we were permitted to do, I decided to try and go a little further afield one Sunday. Rather than just sit in with the paper, after a quick jog round the park (because gym visits were no longer allowed) and wait for the Sunday evening tv to kick in, I decided to get in my car and drive over to a place I'd been to a few years before and had always wanted to revisit. I knew that I could get to the famous Ashridge Estate in the Chilterns in probably little more than a half an hour drive, if I left fairly early and providing the M25 was clear. I imagined that few people were going anywhere so banked on it being a fairly straightforward journey. Luckily, there was little traffic on the road that morning and I got to the junction I needed for Ashridge in about twenty-five minutes. The remainder of the journey through Berkhamstead wasn't quite so easy, mainly because of speed restrictions and shoppers all pouring into its supermarkets (the Waitrose here seemed to be especially popular). Eventually, I managed to get through the town and found the turning off to Ashridge, feeling convinced that I would be able to park quickly and could then start a nice bracing walk.

If I had thought Berkhamstead was busy, then Ashridge was like Piccadilly Circus that morning. There was absolutely nowhere to park. Every parking space was occupied, every lay-by was full. Cars were crawling along the road through the estate at the speed of a cortege, all of their owners as desperate as I was to find somewhere where they could just pull over and get out. I drove along the whole length of the place which must have been at least three or four miles. Not a parking space in sight. How come so many other people had had the same idea as me? All of us desperate to get out, I suppose. And true to form, it was another uncharacteristically warm and sunny day; the sort of day likely to attract visitors to an alluring spot such as this.

Thinking that I could not possibly turn round and go back home when I had made such an effort to get myself here (well, a half-hour drive round the M25 certainly constituted an effort for me!) I retraced my steps and managed to find one space in the car park right at the entrance to the estate. I suppose most people drove past this, hoping that they would be able to get somewhere nearer to the estate's Bridgewater Monument with its tearoom, toilets and ice cream van and which was generally perceived to be the place's main "draw". Personally, I wasn't too bothered about that. I just wanted to be outside and to be somewhere different and to be in the 'countryside' as opposed to a park on the outskirts of Greater London. No, I was quite happy with the parking space I'd eventually located, even if it was somewhat, away from the main throng. After pulling on my thick woollen socks and walking boots, I then set off through a woodland path, not really having any idea where I was going at all. I knew that I was heading in a generally northerly direction and hoped that, eventually, I would get to a lovely open bit of heathland that I vaguely remembered from a previous visit. This stretch of greenery was particularly attractive in my mind's eye. It reminded me of one of those great stretches of heathland that feature in Thomas Hardy novels. It also contrasted attractively with the woodlands which surrounded it. Eventually, I emerged from the woods and stumbled out on to this very plain which, just as I remembered, had a magical and particularly distinctive quality. Even though there were many other people trekking across it, it seemed strangely silent and was bewitchingly beautiful in the autumn sunshine. I felt exhilarated at the fact that I had managed to get myself there and thrilled at the change of scene. It was like suddenly being on holiday in that I felt as if I had escaped to somewhere completely different and barely familiar.

This sense of euphoria carried me along for the next couple of hours. I had no idea where I was going as I left the common and plunged back into the woods but, for the moment, that was all part of the fun. I must have walked for a couple of hours and, as I was there, I thought I probably ought to see if I could at least glimpse the famous Bridgewater monument that would have drawn most of the crowds. After that I would turn back and try and find my car to take me home. As things turned out, I must have missed the monument somehow because I ended up having to ask a couple of very posh ladies how to find it. They pointed me in the opposite direction to the one in which I had been walking and eventually I found it but I disliked the crowds and huge number of cars it had seemed to attract, so I swiftly set off back in the direction of what I thought was the car.

This seemed to be easier said than done and I ended up getting very confused and definitely lost. I walked for ages and then realised, when I emerged through a hedge and into a field of brightly waving grass that I had been there, in exactly the same spot, about an hour before. I must have just walked in a gigantic circle and now had no idea at all where I was. I was reminded of the fact that I have a poor sense of direction at the best of times and can easily get very lost in unfamiliar environments. It was then that I began to panic a little. I certainly needed to get back to the car park before it got dark and the light was already starting to fade. I realised that I would probably be OK if I could find the road that ran through the estate. Then all I would need to do would be to follow that. This also turned out to be easier said than done because, of course, there is more than one road through the estate.

After a couple more false-starts and not a little bit of panicking on my part, I eventually managed to find my way back to the car which I was then extremely relieved to see.

It had been a good adventure, though, and wonderful to get out to somewhere different. Even the fact of getting lost had somehow added to the enjoyment and the sense of breaking some of the now rather deadening routines with which I was starting to bolster my life.

One of the other things I had participated in all through the lockdown was a series of online play-readings with members of my amateur theatre group. Once a week, we had got together online in order to read a play. These were plays that we had thought about doing for a full production or plays that we had always wanted to read and never had. Plays are hard to read on one's own. They are much harder work than reading a novel because all you have is the dialogue and a few stage directions to go on. You don't have the narrative voice of the author filling in the gaps; commenting on the action and making connections between different episodes; you don't have their wry and amusing observations (as you do, say, with Jane Austen or PG Wodehouse); there are few of those lavish descriptions to help you to visualise a scene or which paint a character's traits and idiosyncrasies. When everything is done through the dialogue, the reader has to do so much more. That is why it is always much easier to read a play in a group. You have different voices to characterise the individual roles and because you are all in it together, you can all sit down for an evening and read the thing straight through from beginning to end, so it has the sort of impact that it would have in a live performance. A solitary reader of a playscript would probably want to read it in short chunks to make it more manageable but that would certainly lessen its overall effect.

We had been reading these plays for many months now. We did comedies, thrillers, courtroom dramas, torrid slices of Tennessee Williams and outrageous bits of Joe Orton, all with varying degrees of success. The readings had become a staple of Tuesday evenings and certainly counted as one of the things which had helped some of us to get through those fallow lockdown months.

However, I for one was beginning to think that the readings were starting to become a little routine – or, if not routine, then at least a bit repetitive and that we needed something more.

All of the time, we were all starting to think about what we might do once the theatres were opened up again and we were able to relaunch ourselves. What would the play be? Who would be in it? Where would be put it on? Would we get an audience? How could we even begin to rehearse when things were so precarious? How could you get people to learn lines when they might be forced to "isolate" at the drop of a hat with the production shut down and then weeks of work would have been for nothing?

I trawled through theatre websites, trying to get a few tips about what other theatres were doing. Sadly, it seemed than most theatres were not doing very much. They had either closed down completely and were asking their audiences to just "watch this space" or they were doing rather dull sounding things just involving one or two actors. The theatres that were active seemed awash with dreary monologues or "solo performances" and rather uninspiring two-handers. 'Educating Rita' and the 'Talking Heads' series seemed to be everywhere. Or there were strange, specially commissioned works involving lots of video and audiences having to watch shows in car parks or shopping centres – none of which I could ever imagine would go down well with our patrons at the local amateur theatre.

However, I did come across one theatre that was doing something I rather liked the sound of. The Windsor Theatre Royal had launched a series of what they were calling "On Air" productions in which a cast of actors would read a play in front of a paying audience, who would be asked to watch the performance as if eavesdropping on a vintage radio studio recording. The audience's imagination would be helped by sound effects and a bit of narration but basically the cast was just reading the script out loud and the audience was buying into this.

I thought this seemed like a very promising idea and I suggested it to my group. They all seemed very up for it and, so, a few weeks later we started rehearsing the one act play by Noel Coward, 'Still Life' on which the famous romantic movie 'Brief Encounter' is based. I sent out a notice to the Company inviting people to take part and was somewhat taken aback to find that the whole enterprise was proving to be extremely popular to the extent that we had enough actors to be able to cast the play twice. Not wanting to turn anybody away, I decided that the best thing would be to double-cast the piece and so we started rehearsing the play with two sets of actors, each of whom would eventually do one performance.

At last, I felt that I had a project or something to get my teeth into. Directing plays was what I had spent most of my professional life doing as a drama teacher: directing the huge annual productions every November of Broadway musicals, Shakespeare, Brecht and other 'epic' plays but also directing students in their exam scenes for GCSE Drama, as well as helping them to make some very elaborate and often quite experimental devised work. Directing shows of one sort or another had been 'meat and drink' to me for the last thirty-six years or so and it was certainly one of the things I missed most about giving up work. Here, it seemed, there was an opportunity to revisit these skills, albeit in a very different context. Over the years, because of my work as a drama teacher working in schools, I had often been asked by my amateur theatre colleagues whether I would consider directing a show for them. However, I had always resisted this, imagining that directing adults would be very different from directing teenagers. I imagined that this was so for a whole host of reasons. For a start, as a teacher working with students, you are automatically in a position of authority. It is easy enough to tell people what you want them to do. Less easy when working with your peers. Hard to insist on things like punctuality and getting lines learnt when everyone is participating in the production as a 'hobby', something they are doing voluntarily and "for fun" in their spare time. In school, it was somehow easier to crack the whip and lay down the law. Also, in what is perhaps an unkind observation, teenage actors are generally quicker at picking things up, at taking direction and they certainly find it easier to learn their lines. When I'd been at school, I'd generally rehearse quite intensively, over a relatively short space of time and, therefore, would often end up working on a show almost every day of the week, at lunchtimes and again after school. That intensity paid off. Doing the work almost every day, albeit for not much more than an hour and a half, meant that things started to take shape very quickly. With adult actors rehearsing in their own time, often after a gruelling day at work and never starting much before eight p.m. and not doing more than a couple of evenings a week, progress was far slower. The rehearsal periods in which I had participated as an actor often seemed to drag on for months. The process became irksome and tedious after a while and there was almost always the feeling of "one step forward, two steps back".

For all of these reasons, I had hitherto resisted the temptation to direct my fellow amateurs in a play but now that I had retired, the opportunity presented itself and I decided to seize it. I had the concept that we would perform "Still Life" not as a full production but as a radio play and that it would therefore be more akin to a rehearsed reading than a fully staged production. This was a good move and it eliminated that factor which so often dooms amateur theatricals: the need to learn the lines! Everyone would be reading from the script and there would be minimal movement around the stage. We would all appear to be speaking into microphones, as we held our scripts and so the only rehearsal work to be done was on delivery of the lines: making them make sense; communicating the characters and their relationships; bringing out the comedy; conveying the poignancy of Noel Coward's tea room romance.

There would be none of that tedious and time-consuming business whereby we worked out how to handle the props (when to pour the tea; how much of it; when to drink it; how to hold the cup and saucer without impeding the flow of the dialogue). There wouldn't be the need for all those endless retakes while somebody dried on a line or paraphrased the words of the author or fumbled about for a cue. The work was purely to do with bringing the script to life in a way that would entertain an audience and be true to the spirit of the piece.

I cannot pretend that it felt anything other than very strange trying to rehearse the play on Zoom. This alone created its own set of hazards and problems. It seemed that however many reminders of the Zoom code and password had been sent out beforehand, somebody in the cast claimed not to have received it and delayed us all by failing to log on in time or, in some cases, even to turn up at all. Inevitably, at least one cast member would fail to turn their sound on and so would be on mute for the first part of the rehearsal. Another would have a dodgy Wi-fi connection or their picture would be blurred and pixelated. Others had microphones that reverberated and distorted everything and made it impossible to understand what the actor was trying to say. Yes, there were challenges to rehearsing in this new format but people seemed to be resilient and determined and, somehow, we managed to power on through and after about four weeks of rehearsing twice a week, we had a pretty serviceable and well-rehearsed reading of the script that I thought an audience would appreciate and enjoy.

There were even a few moments during those rehearsals when I found myself completely absorbed in the process of creating a performance again. I loved the discussions with the actors about individual lines and how they should be interpreted; how we all read little nuances of meaning into the most apparently banal chatter; how the lines reflected a character's inner life or their status or self-delusion or inner turmoil. That close analysis of the text was almost like being back in the classroom again and I was surprised how much I enjoyed this and how delightful it was to get back to doing something which I had done so well for so many years of my professional life. In the end, I started to really look forward to these rehearsals and I began to get a kind of joy in seeing the actors starting to develop their characterisations and to commit themselves to the style and mood of the play. It felt like we were together creating something very worthwhile and that was extremely fulfilling. After all those arid months of lockdown, at last here was an opportunity to be creative and to make something that was funny and touching and had energy and might eventually entertain an audience.

We were aiming for a public performance at the end of January but the project certainly sustained many of us through some grim weeks in November and in the run up to Christmas.

December

Somewhat surprisingly, Christmas had come round again and suddenly it was upon us. When life had fallen into such a circumscribed routine of morning exercise, a stint of creative writing, the lunchtime news on the television, an afternoon's walk, a bit of cleaning, ironing or cooking; washing up and then slumping in front of the TV for the rest of the evening – the thought of this little life being suddenly disrupted with all of the hullabaloo of Christmas seemed somehow difficult to imagine. Were we really all going to be allowed to slip out of our straitjackets and into such a sudden semblance of normality for those five or so days of the festive season?

This was what the government had promised. Providing we were all 'good' now and stayed at home and wore our masks and didn't invite people into our houses, then we would be rewarded with a brief amnesty around the twenty-fifth of December. This was certainly what we were being promised and what we all were promising ourselves.

This year more than ever, people were feeling a need to celebrate and to cheer themselves up with a more than usually festive holiday, a break from the dreadful, life draining austerity of the last nine months.

It was in this spirit, that I decided to treat myself to a better than average Christmas tree to be purchased in this particular year from Waitrose, rather than Sainsbury's. Feeling more than a tad self-conscious, on the first morning of December, I whipped into my local branch and shoved one of their cheaper trees into a Waitrose shopping trolley and wheeled it into their car park. I hoped that I would not be seen. The tiny tree was so obviously a 'tree for one' that I really did not wish to be observed in public with it and identified as one of those sad souls who might possibly be spending Christmas alone.

When I got the tree home, I felt pleased with my purchase. Although it had cost a bit more than one of the Sainsbury's 'mini trees' you could tell straight away that this one was better quality. Its branches were thicker and more robust and it just looked hardier and more flourishing once I had unwrapped the cellophane which had been wound around it. I watered it and then retrieved from the loft my meagre selection of Christmas decorations: my cheap string of lights (bought from the now defunct Woolworths many years before, I seem to recall), some still sprightly looking lengths of tinsel and a few old baubles for the tree. I'd decorated it in about half an hour and then had a ceremonious turning on of the tree lights. Though I say it myself, I thought it looked pretty good. This was a Christmas which I for one would celebrate, in spite of it having been such a rubbish and fallow year.

I was also looking forward to the fact that in a few weeks' time, I'd be going to stay at my sister's house for three or four days, as I always did at Christmas. The thought of just being in a family group for a while was a holiday in itself; a welcome relief from the solitude of the rest of the year. Yes, I was sure that they would infuriate and annoy me at some points during my stay (as I would them, too, of course) but basically, we would all rub along together pretty well, as we always did. It would be lovely to just 'hang out' together, making cups of tea, reading the papers, chatting, watching TV, going out for walks, laughing and joking and occasionally arguing. For a few days, it was as if I would be admitted into a normal family life, the sort of life that most people had, rather than the more ascetic single person's existence that was mine for the vast majority of the year.

Just three weeks to go, I thought, and then I could pack up my car and drive over for four glorious days of companionable and warm togetherness with all the usual festive accompaniments: turkey, carols from Kings, presents and wrapping paper strewn all over the floor; Morecambe and Wise, frosty walks by the Thames, stifling central heating and constant noise, chatter and laughter.

In the meantime, though, there was normal life to be getting on with. I still continued to attend the gardening group every Wednesday morning and, somehow, I had begun to enjoy it as the weeks had gone by. I realised that I quite liked having a reason to be out in the open air for a whole morning, once a week. I also enjoyed having a physical activity to perform like digging or shovelling as I bent over to clear the weeds from a flower bed or helped to distribute a truck full of manure around the rose beds. There was something particularly satisfying about working your way through a flower bed that appeared to be completely over-run with weeds and then after a couple of hours or so transforming it so that it looked neat and cared for, the plants suddenly visible and now surrounded by neat little patches of freshly dug, brown earth. That I found particularly gratifying and it no longer mattered that I had not engaged in meaningful conversation or joined in with any group banter. The work itself was its own reward. I even managed to get a few words of praise from the otherwise rather taciturn and gruff head gardener: "You done a good job there, son," he mumbled as I wheeled my barrow, fork and hoe back into his store at the end of a morning's session. As the weather got colder and the ground got harder, the lady who ran the group said that she needed to remember to bring a fleece for me to wear. I had noticed that nearly all of the other members of the group wore blue jackets with the name of the group embroidered on the front. I wondered how many weeks I would have to put in before I was deemed to be worthy of receiving this "uniform" item. Sure enough, in about that first week of December, I was presented with a blue fleece to wear and felt that I was now well and truly a part of the group.

Like many other voluntary groups across the land, the gardeners were also preparing for Christmas and in the last session before the break, we were all asked to pose for a group photo and invited to partake of a cup of mulled wine and a mince pie. I found the mulled wine went straight to my head at eleven o'clock in the morning and I suddenly became more voluble and forthcoming with the other gardeners. I wondered if they noticed this sudden transformation in my personality?

As well as this, I also had the online play rehearsals for the radio version of 'Still Life' taking place two evenings a week. It was starting to feel like quite a full existence. The play rehearsals had begun to get a little "stickier" than they had been at first. I could tell that people were starting to get a little tired of the regular commitment, in a way that I don't believe they would have done if we had not been rehearsing on computers. If we'd been meeting face-to-face, there would have been a different dynamic, but just watching each other's shadowy images on the computer with some often very distorted sound, was not conducive to much of a feeling of company camaraderie. Then there were all those moments when people had to be chased up because they weren't there and thought they had told someone that they wouldn't be but had either forgotten to do so or I had forgotten that they had done so And then those moments when people were there but were clearly pre-occupied or weren't in the mood to rehearse or had something else going on and so seemed prickly or unfriendly or sulky And for which I, of course, blamed myself thinking: "They hate my direction. I'm not being clear about what I want. I'm confusing them. I'm making heavy weather of this. I'm expecting too much. Too little."

In the end, I was starting to slightly dread the rehearsals. There was something about having everyone beamed into my home that I found particularly disconcerting. At least in a rehearsal room, you could close the door afterwards and walk away but somehow having everyone's faces there on the screen at my desk in my spare bedroom was strangely intrusive. In the end, I just had to tell myself not be so hard on myself and to stop beating myself up. At least we were attempting to 'do' something; trying to salvage what we could out of this dreadful situation in which nobody could any longer perform live on a stage or go and sit in an auditorium. At least, I had devised a project and a way of bringing a group of actors together to rehearse something that might eventually be put on stage at a theatre. OK, maybe it wouldn't be perfect but at least it was something. We were having a go and I was doing my best. Why not just settle for that?

All the while, the routines which had sustained me through the last nine months continued. I had got into the habit of reading at least a book a week and every morning after breakfast I would devote at least an hour to making my way through my latest "good read". I could have spent longer at this but there were always chores to do or social arrangements to make or emails to send, as well as my exercise routine and the various creative writing projects I had on the go. Nevertheless, that early morning reading session remained extremely precious to me. The process of just sitting quietly and immobile and immersing myself in the pages of a well-written book had become intensely important. It seemed like a way of nourishing my imagination. Even though the outward circumstances of my life did not change, that daily escape into a fictional world for an hour or so each morning did provide me with the opportunity to submerge myself in a completely different landscape; to have imaginary relationships with fictional characters; to enter into new and unknown terrain. I got the pleasure and sustenance from reading fiction that I had previously only ever experienced during the long summer holiday from school when I had been able to bury myself in a book and just completely "live it" without distraction. So often, when working, a book could only ever be experienced in bite-size chunks: a few paragraphs before falling asleep at night; a few pages read on a tube or bus journey at the weekend; the odd half hour on a Sunday afternoon. Always, there was the interruption of work which prevented that total immersion. Now it was different. Now reading had become a daily staple. My imagination needed it. My soul needed it. Making sure that I had something decent, something fulfilling and stretching, to read had become an absolute necessity. The titles consumed over that late autumn included 'Real Life' by Brandon Taylor; 'The Island' by Victoria Hislop; 'Mr Wilder and Me' by Jonathan Coe; 'Winterkill' by Ragmar Jonasson and a re-read of 'Persuasion'. High quality contemporary fiction; thrillers and the odd classic.

That was my reading diet and, oh, how necessary it had become to me!

The other important pillar of my life at this time continued to be the daily walk. As we entered the second lockdown, these became more and more geographically constrained. We were discouraged from using public transport, so once again I had to content myself with whatever was available in my immediate vicinity. Somehow, I didn't mind this too much. There was something particularly appealing about not getting into a car. The idea that one could walk from one's own front door to a whole variety of different destinations conferred a strange kind of power and feeling of independence. As always, I felt particularly fortunate that I lived in an area of London which was particularly well served with parks and green spaces. Out here in Enfield, we were within walking distance of the green belt and it didn't take more than a brisk stroll of thirty minutes or so to be out in fields and what could almost be described as "rolling countryside" – notwithstanding the distant roar of the M25, which marked the boundary between our Greater London borough and the surrounding Hertfordshire countryside.

I imagined that I would get bored with continually walking to the same places but there were always the changes in the weather and the seasons to vary the experience. Watching the leaves turn and seeing the ground get muddier and the sun setting earlier as dusk started to descend all added a different flavour and character to my walks. Then there was the company I was walking with. Quite often I was on my own but at least a couple of times a week, I'd be walking with a companion. This could be a long-standing friend or an ex-work colleague or someone from my Amateur Dramatic Society or even someone I hadn't known particularly well before the pandemic but with whom I had set up a meeting for a walk and this had then developed into a regular engagement. In fact, I realised that having imagined that retirement would be a very solitary and lonely affair, I was probably more sociable now than at any other time in my life. Quite often, when I had been working, I would have had almost no social interaction with other adults during the day apart from during the coffee break and occasionally at lunchtimes. The rest of the time, I'd be in the classroom teaching students and firmly in my professional 'teacher persona' with little or no personal interaction between them and me outside the classroom discourse of a typical lesson. Evenings, I would be at my desk marking and preparing and then afterwards sprawled out on the sofa in preparation for another day. Apart from those few minutes of daily break-time chat, as a school teacher there'd be very little social engagement with other adults.

Nowadays, though, I would regularly be with another person for at least a couple of hours and this would often be several times a week. We would chat, laugh, discuss, share, exclaim, bemoan, berate, complain and generally off-load in a way that I had almost never done before, except at weekends when out on a weekly social evening with a close friend or family member.

There was also something extremely liberating about the process of walking and talking. The physical act of striding along while speaking or listening was strangely un-inhibiting. I found myself so much more able to talk freely and even to listen more attentively while walking along, side by side with my companion. It seemed somehow easier to engage and interact than if we had been sat face to face across a table in a bar or café. Those natural lulls or pauses in the conversation seemed easier to negotiate when walking through the park or a by the side of a field or up a hill than over a half-drunk cup of coffee or peering across a pint glass of lager. For this reason, walking with a friend had now most definitely become my preferred way of socializing.

As the months had gone by, I found myself acquiring more and more new acquaintances. People I really had not known very well before gradually became regular walking companions and I began to relish the new social contacts which walking was providing. I guess it was slightly risky, arranging to meet someone one hardly knew for a two-hour walk. There was always the fear: will we be able to keep it going for one hundred and twenty minutes or more? Will there be enough to talk about? Will the new companion be willing to walk at the same pace? Will they want to walk as far as I always do? Will they want to keep stopping for refreshments or to check their phone or for the toilet? Do we share an understanding of the same walking etiquette? I was always particularly delighted when someone who I'd barely known before put themselves forward as a new walking companion. For example, over the space of a couple of weeks, I had kept bumping into one of the music teachers from school who was out strolling with his partner and who I seemed to keep repeatedly coming across. I joked that we must have the same walking routes, as we seemed to keep bumping into each other. Eventually, we exchanged phone numbers and then, after a few weeks, made an arrangement to meet each other for our first walk together. True to form, I was slightly anxious about this and wondered whether I had enough to say to this person I hardly knew. Would we be able to keep it going over the four or five miles which would normally constitute a half-day's walking session?

I need not have worried. It turned out that we had loads to say to each other. Apart from anything else there was all the gossip about the school at which we had both worked: our colleagues, the senior management, the parents, the more recalcitrant students. We never stopped for the couple of hours that we were together and I am only sorry that we didn't arrange more trips out together before things returned to something more like normal.

Then there were the walks with the older ladies from my amateur dramatics group. With them, I found myself talking for most of the time about the politics of the society, mostly along the lines of who had got which role, who deserved it and who did not; who was in the group just for their own glorification and who needed more recognition and who should get less. We talked about our mutual love of the theatre and the plays that had made the greatest impact on us; our favourite actors (nearly always Dames Judi and Mags, of course; McKellen, Jacobi, Simon R-B) and plays that we longed to be able to do and plays that we knew we would never be able to do and plays that we should not ever have dreamed of doing. Again, the chat just kept on coming and there was never a dull moment.

There was a huge fashion around this time for dogs. Nearly everyone seemed to be acquiring one. I guess this was as a result mainly of lockdown. People were confined to their homes and they needed something to provide distraction and variety and what better than a new little canine friend? They also created a reason to get out of the house and forced people to do some exercise.

I was however, slightly taken aback when one of my 'least doggy' friends announced his intention of getting a dog. When he told me that he and his partner had applied to offer a home to a rescue dog from Greece (where apparently hundreds of poor animals had been abandoned, partly as a result of the economic hardships endured there in recent times) I must say that I was, to say the least, sceptical. They were always so house proud and their home was absolutely immaculate at all times. How would they cope with a dog marauding all over the place? Dropping its dog hairs everywhere, climbing up on the furniture, running in from the garden and leaving grubby paw marks everywhere? I could not see it myself.

Nevertheless, they insisted that this was something they were determined to do. They had been subjected to a lengthy vetting process and were now on a waiting list. They would be informed as soon as a suitable dog became available and would be asked to collect it from the airport after it had been flown over from Greece.

I secretly wondered how they would ever cope. They were both such creatures of habit that I could not imagine for a moment how they would survive their long established and much-loved routines being interrupted. They weren't the most athletic couple and the thought of them having to take the dog out for walks morning, noon and night was not something I could ever imagine them doing either. Least of all, how would they cope with the toilet arrangements? Dogs were not allowed to leave their mess in parks or on the pavement and owners had to scoop it up into plastic bags and dispose of it. They were both so fastidious, I could never imagine them ever coping with that.

Thankfully, I ended up being very pleasantly surprised. Around early December, the new dog arrived (by air) and a few days later, we were introduced while out on a walk up at Forty Hall. The dog herself was a sweet and beautifully docile mongrel, with quite a strong streak of griffin. My friends had been clear that they didn't want a young puppy, cavorting around all over the place, yapping and jumping up at them. Therefore, the dog which they had been sent was not like that at all. Instead, they had been asked to give a home to a somewhat elderly creature who waddled around the park on our first meeting with a distinct aura of faded gentility that was immensely endearing. My friends were clearly completely smitten with her and their decision to get themselves a pet had clearly been the right one. It was wonderful to see the love, care and affection which they lavished on this poor little animal. The dog itself must have thought that she had ended up in the lap of absolute luxury when she found herself transported from the backstreets of Athens to the comforts of their home in rural Hertfordshire. She certainly exuded an air of satisfaction that was a joy to behold. The first time I met the new dog, she seemed to walk quite slowly and was clearly enjoying sniffing the many distractions offered by the woodland paths of Forty Hall. Our progress was quite stately and it was evident that the dog was not a great walker but this suited my friends and after twenty minutes or so we turned round and headed for the tea room. The new pet was clearly going to be treasured and enormously loved and it was great to see the effect of their new arrival on my friends and knowing the joy and pleasure she would bring to their lives for the foreseeable future.

As well as seeing my friends, I was keen to keep up with my sister and her family and we thought about ways in which we could manage to see each other without breaking too many of the rules. With both of my nieces still school age and with my sister having to continue to visit my elderly father several times a week, we needed to be careful about the sort of contact we would be able to have. It would probably have to continue to be outdoors and at some meeting point that was mutually convenient. Earlier in the summer, when we'd first been allowed to meet up again, we had converged on Chorleywood Common which was half way round the M25 in an anti-clockwise direction and about midway between both of our homes. In the summer months, it had been a lovely place at which to meet: green, hilly, wooded and always sunny. There was a free car park there just by the church and it was only five minutes or so off junction 18. It seemed like the perfect spot in which to meet up and in June and July we had enjoyed some lovely walks around there, taking in the River Chess and then climbing the hills as far as Sarratt churchyard. Those had been almost blissful meetings in which life had begun to feel like it was returning to normal.

Now, though, in early December I wondered whether this location would have quite the same appeal. We arranged to meet one Sunday afternoon. My sister is never that great at getting out of the house promptly (understandable when she has two teenage children who definitely don't want to get out of bed before midday on a weekend) so when we met up it was probably already gone half-past two in the afternoon. Being a winter's afternoon, the light was already starting to fade. Normally, we would have set off along part of the Chiltern Way and forged our way through fields and beside streams but that afternoon it seemed safer to stick to the streets of nearby Chorleywood village. We walked by the station and commented on how remarkable it was that you could catch a tube from Baker Street that would take you all the way out here on the Metropolitan line. There were a few shops, most of them quite smart because it was clearly an affluent area. As we walked past the Costa Coffee and considered getting a hot chocolate or a pastry, we glanced in the windows of an estate agent and remarked on the high prices of the properties around there. As we wandered away from the main high street and into the more residential parts of the village, we were struck by the elaborate displays of Christmas decorations outside most of the houses. It seemed that there was some sort of competition for the best decorated home and this had certainly spurred on the residents of Chorleywood to pull all the stops out. The numbers of Christmas lanterns, reindeers, Santa Clauses, sleighs, robins, baby Jesuses, Mary and Josephs, three wise men, snowmen, Ebenezer Scrooges were legion. These Christmas displays had clearly become a labour of love for most of the locals and appeared to be almost a defiant gesture of resilience against Covid: "We won't be beaten; we WILL celebrate; this dreadful pandemic will not destroy Christmas!"

We felt "good for them" as we walked the streets of Chorleywood on that December evening while dusk descended, marvelling at the creativity of the people of that village and their determination not to give in to gloom and negativity. They seemed determined that this was going to be their best Christmas ever!

Later that week, I found myself in my local department store (Pearsons of Enfield) looking for some Christmas gifts to present to two of my friends who I'd arranged to meet the following Saturday. It was traditional that we would always meet to celebrate the festive season at a bar and restaurant in Soho and we were determined that this year would not be any different. Of course, it was different this year because of Covid. For a start, the bar that we would normally have gone to was closed. Pubs could only serve alcohol if they also did a "substantial meal" but the bar we all liked had never done food. Its whole point was to be a drinking venue. We always met there to get reasonably well-oiled before hitting the restaurant. It was a pints-of-lager-only sort of place and we loved it for that. There was no way it was going to start serving food and we certainly didn't want to eat anything there when we had booked to eat lunch at the restaurant. So that part of the day's programme would be different. There would be no meeting in a bar for a good hour's soaking beforehand. Instead, we would just spend longer in the restaurant.

I got there before the others. I think I had booked it and it had been quite hard to secure a table so I needed to get there well in advance in order to make sure that we got in. When I arrived, it was already extremely crowded. This was somewhat alarming in the current climate because there really did not seem to be much social distancing going on at all. All of the tables were full and there was even a tent with heaters outside on Compton Street but all of the tables there seemed to have been taken as well. I stood in line to give my name wondering where on earth we were going to be sat – as there didn't look to be any spare places. On the other hand, the turn over between tables seemed to be fairly quick: I'd had to book us a two-hour slot so could only suppose that we would take our places as soon as one of the earlier bookings came to an end and we could then take over. I looked slightly enviously at the tables in the 'tent' outside, hoping that we might get one of those. However, they seemed to be highly prized and I guessed that we probably weren't regular enough customers to be rewarded with one of them. On the other hand, I really didn't fancy being cooped up inside for two hours. It just did not seem very safe, given the current situation. The restaurant was narrow and deep and some of the tables stretched way back into the cavernous recesses and, of course, it was one of these to which we were shown. However, as soon as the first drinks were quaffed, any misgivings or concerns about safety quickly fell away. After a few minutes, the fact that we were at a table jammed into a corner in the furthest reaches of the place and miles away from any sniff of fresh air was quickly forgotten. In fact, there wasn't even a window nearby. Looking back on it now, I wonder how on earth they ever got away with it or what we could have been thinking to have risked our health in that way. I suppose we were just so glad to be out and so conscious of the fact that this could well be it for months to come. It was unlikely that there would be another opportunity for a boozy lunch with close pals until well into the New Year, so we just closed our minds to the potential dangers and concentrated on having the best time that we could.

Sure enough, a huge amount of booze was consumed: beers on arrival to quench the thirst, then cocktails, then glasses of wine, then brandies, then more beers. Although only booked in for a couple of hours, for some reason we managed to avoid getting turfed out. Maybe it was something to do with the fact that we kept ordering more drinks and were obviously going to clock up an enormous bill but nevertheless, we managed to stay way beyond our allotted time. Because this had been such a forbidden pleasure for so many months and was likely to become so again (if rumours about a second full lockdown were to be believed) we just went all out to drink and eat as much as we possibly could and hang both the expense and the damage to our livers.

Part of the ritual of this pre-Christmas get together was the exchange of presents and cards and that was done at a fairly early stage in the proceedings. Normally, we'd just buy each other funny little token gifts from the pound shop, accompanied by cheap cards but this year it was clear that each of us had put a bit more time, effort and money into things. I'd certainly chosen my cards carefully, selecting a couple of quite classy affairs with witty messages and graphics. This year more than ever, I felt a particular sense of gratitude to my two pals and I wanted a way of expressing this to them. This meant no longer proffering a 99p card from Asda or its equivalent but instead something much more upmarket through which I could demonstrate my feelings of gratitude and appreciation. Similarly with the gifts. Proper presents this year, from Next or Waterstones and costing a fair amount rather than a chocolate willy or joke book from Poundland because this particular year, I wanted to show that I cared. Funnily enough, they had done the same, both of them giving me something I actually wanted and would use when I got home: a luxury bath oil and the new biography of Victoria Wood, which I had coveted from afar when I'd read a review in a Sunday paper a few weeks before.

Eventually, bloated and extremely intoxicated, we emerged back out onto the street. It was strange to be walking down a Compton Street on which only the restaurants were open but no pubs or bars. Normally we would have headed off to one for more drinks but that night it was not an option. Anyway, we'd drunk more than enough in the restaurant. Time to make for the tube home.

As Christmas approached, there were the usual tasks to perform: Christmas cards to be bought and presents to be purchased. Although, I cannot pretend to be a lavish bestower of Christmas gifts, there were a small number of people that I needed to buy for: mainly relatives and token items for a handful of pals. Because my brother and his family lived so far away in Devon and we would be unlikely to see each other over the Christmas period, they usually just got something I could post easily like John Lewis Vouchers or book tokens. As always, I'd left it very late so scrambled around trying to get these items all into the post before the last posting date. This, I knew, would involve a trip to the post office and a queue and that started to take on the proportions of an epic operation. Everybody else, of course, was doing the same, sending gifts to relatives by post instead of planning to hand them over face to face. Therefore, the queues outside the post offices were gargantuan and had been since the middle of November. The thought of joining one of these queues for at least an hour or so was not appealing. The weather had turned cold and wet, so being forced to wait outside for ages was a definite deterrent. Also, once inside, the thought of standing in line in a poorly ventilated post office with a load of strangers who could all be possible carriers of the virus was not at all enticing.

In the end, I did it but full of resentment, I'm afraid, and cursing the wretched pandemic for making what was usually a not unpleasant pre-Christmas chore into something extremely wearisome and anxiety inducing.

Then there were the cards. Where would they come from this year? Generally, every December, I prided myself on my choice of cards, which were always quite classy and more expensive than most. I liked to buy mine from places like the National Gallery or the National Theatre foyer, which always had a selection of tasteful cards all being sold in aid of suitably right-on charities. There was no hope of getting to either of these regular sources this year. The National Theatre was closed and you had to book to get a place at the National Gallery. Plus getting to either of these places would involve a potentially dangerous tube journey, which I felt that I couldn't justify. So, it looked like my Christmas cards this year would have to come from somewhere like W H Smiths or Next, which was not a very inspiring thought. I went to the local shopping centre and rummaged through the selection offered by both of these stores and reluctantly chose a couple of packs from each. I was worried that sending them would signal some sort of decline in standards. "Ooh look, you can tell he's retired now. Can't be bothered to choose decent cards any more. It's the slippery slope"

Convincing myself that it was the thought that counted and that most people probably barely glanced at the outside of the card or where it came from, I took my purchases home and began the lengthy task of penning my Xmas greetings. Because I only send cards to close friends, most of mine had to contain a few sentences of news. Not that there was that much to report from this particular year. "Have watched loads of Netflix and do a walk every day," was about the sum total of it. Even so, each card took a while because I felt that I had to write something personal and considered in each one. How different the messages were to what I had imagined writing a year ago. With retirement looming then, I had envisaged that my messages this year would be full of news of foreign travels undertaken and projects started; new hobbies taken up and new friends made. Nothing like that, of course, because for almost nine months we had been 'locked down'. There really wasn't much to say.

Having spent a couple of afternoons writing my cards, I then deposited them in the post box at the end of the road and wondered how many cards I would receive in return? Of course, this year I would be in receipt of far fewer cards than normal because I was no longer working. A good number of my cards were usually from work colleagues or, occasionally, even students and their parents. This year, of course, that would not be happening except in the case of the one or two special friends with whom I had maintained contact since leaving work.

Even so, still determined that this Christmas was going to be as normal as possible, I had a reasonable number of cards on display in my living room from friends, relatives and other sources which I hung up and placed around my space in order to give it a semblance of festive cheer. While the number of cards was considerably diminished, as if to remind me that as a retired person I no longer had the network of acquaintances afforded to working people, the offerings I did have still managed to create a suggestion of yuletide celebration.

I suppose like most people at this time, I was determined to make this Christmas coming as normal as possible. In spite of having been locked down again at the start of the month, the government kept promising the country that we would be allowed to celebrate Christmas come what may. We'd be able to go to each other's homes and even to stay over-night. We would be permitted to eat a meal together and to spend time with each other in the ways that we always had done at Christmas. Those long hours slumped in front of the telly together, watching repeat after repeat of Morecambe and Wise and those re-runs of 'White Christmas' and 'The Sound of Music' and trying to follow the twists and turns of big Christmas storylines in 'Coronation Street' or 'Eastenders' – and all of it in baking hot rooms with the windows firmly shut and the central heating on full blast, with a stomach stuffed full of food and a head foggy from too much cheap booze. All of us were working towards this as a kind of reward for having been so "good" all through the year. We'd done what Johnson and the government had asked us to do. We'd stayed at home. We'd not gone to each other's houses. We'd avoided pubs and restaurants. We'd done without theatres and cinemas and live music. Surely, things could be relaxed just for a day or two? It was Christmas, after all.

As December 25th approached, we were all aware that things did not seem to be going in the right direction. The number of infections was increasing and the death rates were soaring in certain parts of the country, particularly in the north west (Bolton, Manchester, Liverpool). The government seemed unable to deal with the looming crisis. There were attempts to impose the restrictions more strongly in some areas than others but that never seemed to work. People just crossed the border from one county to another, where restrictions were less severe, if they wanted to go to a pub or a restaurant. The government was floundering with the usual mix of fudge and indecision and bluster. Even so, we were all still convincing ourselves that Christmas would still be on. A couple of days let up, surely, as a reward for doing well? After which we would all obediently go back to being locked down…

I still kept in touch with my old school colleagues and heard with a hugely sympathetic ear about how hard it was to continue teaching in the current climate. They particularly hated having to teach in masks and having to work with students similarly encumbered. Teaching is all about communication and they regularly bemoaned the difficulties of trying to teach without the benefit of facial expression, which masks completely obliterated. They equally disliked the constant interruptions to teaching as one group of students after another was 'told to isolate'; they loathed the new 'one way' system around the building; the staggered lunch breaks which decimated all lunchtime and extra-curricular activities; the constant need to test and to prove a clean bill of health. It was a wearing and extremely stressful time but somehow, in spite of all these huge challenges, my ex-colleague Joanne had still been able to put together an end-of-term school show. This was no mean feat, given all the many factors which were working against her at this time. As a way of responding to the current crisis, she had decided not to do a conventional school musical. The logistics of doing something like 'West Side Story' or a big Shakespeare would have just been impossible in these circumstances. So, instead, she chose to do a compilation show, a sort of "songs from the shows" – with each item performed by a 'bubble' from a different year group. This meant something along the lines of the Year 10s performing a medley from 'Rent'; the Years 11 doing some numbers from 'Evan Hansen'; Year 12 doing songs from 'Les Mis' and Year 13 performing items from 'Hamilton', for example.

Each 'bubble' would have their own twenty-minute slot and, of course, it was a way of getting a cast of thousands involved at a time when few schools were doing anything at all by way of public performances. I thought it seemed like an ingenious and extremely enterprising idea and I was very much looking forward to returning to the school for the first time in nearly six months in order to watch it.

As the day of the performance approached, I started to think about how it would feel to return to the workplace in which I had spent over half my life but which I had not revisited since my last day there in July. I had now had a whole term of 'retirement'. Had it been what I imagined? I suppose my worst fears about it had not been realised. I had not withered and died on the vine, as I imagined I might do a few months before. I had made relatively constructive use of my time: I read frequently and hungrily; I had made a good effort with my creative writing and had more or less completed the draft of a short autobiographical novel; I continued to maintain my exercise regime; I had established and deepened a good range of social contacts; I'd kept my theatre company work going; I cooked for myself, always from scratch and cleaned my flat on a fairly regular basis; I went out walking every day and made the most of my local amenities; I had contacted and worked with a couple of local volunteering groups.

Actually, put like that, I could see that it wasn't a bad record for four months. I certainly hadn't "gone under" as I feared that I might do, without the structure and routine of work. Other routines and structures had evolved and established themselves. I'd enjoyed the freedom of not being tied to a gruelling daily timetable; I'd liked being able to get up a bit later and not having to spend hours doing school work in the evenings and at the weekend.

On the other hand, I'm not sure that it was the joyous or blissful existence that people sometimes dreamt of when they thought of retirement. There had been no luxury cruises or adventures in foreign parts; no extremely well remunerated 'consultancies' or opportunities to work just a little but for a huge fee; new and exciting friendships or love affairs had not come my way and swept me off my feet; I had not delighted myself with the discovery of a hitherto undetected talent and passion for surfing or ballroom dancing or cordon bleu cooking.

Solid, uneventful, a bit pedestrian perhaps. I certainly would not be whizzing into my old school awash with anecdotes of adventures from the last work-free four months. On the other hand, we were all still struggling with a global pandemic and life continued to be extremely constrained, in spite of the let up during a few weeks of the summer. Foreign travel continued to be more or less banned (and nobody wanted to get on an airplane at the moment); the vast majority of people were still not back at the office and were continuing to work from home. Pubs and restaurants were still only partially open. The scope and opportunity for adventure had been severely limited.

Therefore, I would be returning to the school as an audience member for the end-of-term production somewhat subdued; not crowing about how brilliant it had all been but modest and dignified; gently supportive and appreciative of the performance to come, I had no doubt, but otherwise unflamboyant and probably not a little reserved.

Unfortunately, the opportunity to return was then scuppered by the news of rising figures, infections and deaths. A few days before opening night, the school decided that it could not possibly allow a public performance of the kind that had been planned. This was hugely disappointing, of course, but not unexpected and so all those who were interested were sent a video link and were able to watch the show online.

I signed up to do this, of course, but had many uneasy feelings to contend with as I watched the various images on screen. It was especially strange looking at the school hall and stage, which had been the platform for so much of my own work over the years. I could imagine all the bustle and excitement backstage, and in the wings, as one group after another took to the stage to perform. I could feel all that anticipation and adrenaline; that energy and focus; that sheer love that the students exuded about all being a part of something and that magical sense of collective responsibility which being in a school show always generated. It was this almost more than anything else that so moved me. In this year so unlike any other which had been so much about isolation and keeping oneself apart, here was an event which depended upon and celebrated togetherness. I could not but feel deeply moved.

Less enjoyable was an online Christmas get-together organised by my theatre company: an opportunity to "see each other for some festive cheer, have a good catch up and maybe sing a few songs, tell a few jokes and anybody wanting to perform please let our Social Secretary know." The very thought filled me with dread and horror. I loathed Zoom meetings anyway and the idea that we would just be sitting there having some sort of free-wheeling chat was just beyond the pale. It certainly wasn't something I wanted to do at all. Nevertheless, as always, I felt that I had an obligation to take part and would be considered a 'misery' if I didn't. We'd already had a rehearsal for our radio production on the same evening and by the time the wretched event was due to start, I was feeling tired, jaded and cross. However, as I logged on and various cheery faces, all in Christmas jumpers and some wearing tiaras of tinsel, raised well-filled glasses of cheap plonk to the camera, I tried to plaster on a smile and attempted to look like I was ready to party. The trouble was, it was quite hard to hear everyone and it was never clear where the focus was supposed to be. Someone would launch into an anecdote about, say, queuing at M and S to get their turkey, then someone else would launch into a similar experience at Morrisons, while another would want to talk about her preparations for assembling a vegetarian alternative. It seemed almost impossible to get a word in and as I, for one, felt that I had very little of interest to offer, I just sat there dumb while all the loudest and most assertive Zoomers took over. I'm afraid it seemed all too typical of my habitual experience of any group gathering and was just dispiriting. The minutes ticked by and I kept glancing over at my face on the screen and noting how depressed, disengaged and bored I was looking. I certainly wasn't doing myself any favours by attempting to participate in this ghastly online shindig. Could anybody be enjoying it? Did everybody else really want to be doing this on the Friday night before Christmas? Had nobody else really nothing better to do?

Thankfully, one of them started to launch into a medley of Christmas musical numbers, which at least relieved the rest of us from the need to keep some sort of conversation going. We nodded along and sipped from our glasses. I think I had a can of cocktail left over from some sort of gathering at my flat pre-lockdown. As always with those beverages, though, the amount of alcohol included was minimal and try as hard as I could, it seemed to have absolutely no intoxicating effects whatsoever. I suppose I do have to admit that as the lovely Sharon (our chanteuse at that moment) launched into her rendition of "Have Yourself a Merry Little Christmas" there was a moment or two of that tingling Christmas feeling that we all crave at that particular time of the year and she did well, in the circumstances, to evoke the nostalgia and warmth of the season. However, the effects of her turn were soon enough obliterated with more trivial anecdotes and gossip as the Zoom gathering started to grind to a natural close and one by one people made their excuses and left.

I often wonder at things like that whether I am simply incapable of relating to other human beings at all? I had nothing to say and spent the entire hour and a half just thinking about when I could leave and get away without incurring comment. The whole event had left me feeling socially inadequate and angry and bitter at my inability to participate or derive any kind of pleasure from such a gathering.

It didn't put me in a very good mood for the next day, when we were all expecting the government announcement about Christmas to be made. Rumours were circulating that in spite of Johnson's repeated assurances that the Christmas holiday itself would be safe, he was now about to do another of his notorious U-turns and tell the country that Christmas was off.

While nobody could believe that after such a year of sacrifices (no foreign holidays; families not able to meet up; nobody able to go to work; pubs and restaurants shut for months; no theatre, no sport, no music) we were now going to be told that there was to be no Christmas either!...

On the other hand, the pandemic was now starting to take hold again in a way that it had not done since the start of the first wave. It was raging through the country and the thought that people were, in a few days, going to start travelling all over the land and share food together for hours in stuffy, overheated, unventilated rooms was beginning to beggar belief. How could teenage children who had been in schools for weeks, mixing with dozens of others from a whole range of different backgrounds and travelling backwards and forwards on public transport every day, how could they suddenly be allowed to go and see grandparents and older relatives from whom they had been banned for months? Had the pandemic suddenly disappeared? No! It was more virulent than ever, it would seem. Wasn't it crazy to allow this, to encourage mixing and travelling. That afternoon, I had been out for my usual Saturday afternoon walk with my friend Deborah and we'd finished with a coffee in our favourite local café on Winchmore Hill Green. Normally, these were happy and chatty affairs in which we were each able to offload the detritus of the week and to have a good moan and a declutter before returning to our separate worlds. Today, though, we were both somewhat subdued and not a little tense as we awaited the news about whether the Christmas holiday as we knew it would be able to go ahead.

I got back to my place afterwards and tried to distract myself with a book and then some ironing. It got dark early at that time of year and by about 4.30 p.m. it was already evening. Everyone had their tellies on awaiting the broadcast to the nation but it kept being delayed. Reeta Chakrabarti was hosting the news that evening and she kept cutting to pictures of 10 Downing Street waiting for signs of the forthcoming pronouncement. Eventually, some hours later than billed, it came.

Christmas was not going to be happening. As before, we were all urged to stay in our homes and to not mix with other households. People were told not to travel and not to risk taking the disease from one part of the country to another I, like everyone else, felt stunned and dismayed by the announcement. Even though we had guessed that it was coming, to hear the directives being so starkly and unambiguously given was a great blow. There had been a sliver of hope before. Maybe, we could travel to each other for the day, we'd hoped but no, even that small concession had been expressly forbidden.

Suddenly the grim reality of the situation started to sink in. I, like all the other single people in the country, would now be facing Christmas alone. For the first time in over sixty years, I would be spending it on my own. Just me, a bottle, the television and whatever food I could manage to procure and prepare.

Part of me saw it as a kind of challenge: "OK, you can do this. You won't be the only one. Get some food and some drink in and make it as good as you can......"

Another part of me just wanted to curl up and withdraw, bury my head in the sand and pretend that it wasn't happening. After such a year of privation and of having to try and be resourceful and make the most of things, this just felt like a demand too far. How much more could we all take? Did I really have the energy and inner resources to endure the three days of Christmas completely on my own, stuck in a dismal kind of solitary confinement?

This was a time of year I had always loved because it was a time when I was guaranteed to be with the people I was devoted to. For three days, from Christmas Eve through to the day after Boxing Day, I would always have been ensconced in the bosom of my sister's family, surrounded by their warmth and chatter and laughter; sharing their food and their entertainment; sleeping in the spare room and getting up as part of a family again. It was all those little things like stroking the cat and dozing off in front of the tv and listening to the clatter of washing up and all getting our outdoor coats on to go out for a walk or to go round the shopping centre on the first day of the sales and shouting up the stairs and piling into the car and clearing plates from the dinner table.........all that bustle and life and noise and that being with other people. Such a change, such a relief, such a holiday from the silence and solitude of the other three hundred and sixty-one days of the year. It was an oasis of companionship and social inclusion but now, for the first time ever, was not to be.

I felt dazed and in a state of shock for the rest of the evening. It was the night of the 'Strictly' final, an event usually shared with friends over a bottle or two of prosecco, but tonight I watched it, like so much television that year, alone.

I quickly realised that I wasn't in the mood for all that grinning and showing off and all those false smiles and that relentless energy. It did not chime at all with my mood of feeling intensely sorry for myself, cut off, abandoned and alone. I turned it off. How could they put something on that was so out of kilter with the national mood?

The next day, I went for a long walk along the banks of the New River and as far as Alexandra Palace. I needed to somehow walk off the restlessness and the churning anxiety I was starting to feel. I bought my copy of the Sunday Times and started reading all the details about what was and was not to be permitted over the Christmas period. The paper was full of annoying tips about how to get through this forthcoming period of enforced incarceration but these were all rubbish. Stuff very much along the lines of "Now's the time to tidy your sock drawer" or "Why not send an individual email out to all the friends you won't be seeing this Christmas?" Useless, desperate, gratingly cheerful and upbeat – when all I really wanted to do was wallow.

I talked to my sister on the phone and we "formally" agreed between us that Christmas was cancelled; that I would not be coming to her for a few days or even just for the afternoon. I would stay in my flat on my own and she would be at her house, with her family. She would break the rule for my father, both of us thinking along the lines of "Well at the age of ninety-one, what's he got to lose?" So, he was going to be collected from his house before lunch on the day and then driven back again later on that afternoon. Why not? But I would not be joining them. I would be spending Christmas cooped up in my flat, alone.

It wasn't just Christmas Eve, Christmas Day and Boxing Day arrangements which were now thrown into disarray. Over the years, I'd acquired a whole raft of Christmas rituals with various different friends centred around the days leading up to the main festivities and in the days immediately afterwards. For example, with my pal Deborah, we would always spend the whole weekend before December 25th together. We'd meet at London Bridge station on the Saturday morning and then do a mooch around Borough Market, looking at the array of gorgeous Xmas treats on display. We'd then make our way to a favourite "greasy spoon" for a fry up lunch (the liver and bacon with chips was a particular hit with me) and then wander down to the Menier Chocolate Factory to go and watch their annual winter musical. In previous years we had watched their sparkling productions of 'Sunday in the Park with George'or 'Fiddler on the Roof' or 'Merrily We Roll Along' or 'La Cage aux Folles' or 'Sweet Charity'… to name but a few and we had been going to those Menier Christmas shows for years. Sitting on those benches in that cramped little theatre on a late December afternoon had come to mean the run-up to Christmas to both of us and we sorely missed it this year. After the show, we'd get the train back up to Winchmore Hill and pile into one of the local pubs for a good amount to drink before going back to her place and crashing on the sofa in front of a recording of that night's 'Strictly' final. However, this year, like so much else, this was not to be. We'd also normally have spent the best part of the following Sunday together as well, going along to the Enfield Baptist Church to watch our friend Mandy, who is the Minister there, presiding over one of the biggest services of her year. This was always a jolly and uplifting occasion. There was a full orchestra to accompany the congregation's singing of the carols (all of the usual big hitters like 'Hark the Herald' 'Oh Come all Ye Faithful' and the rest); there were readings from various members of the church community; a choir and an absolutely packed congregation. (So much so, it was sometimes difficult to get a seat if you arrived less than fifteen minutes before the start). After the service we'd go back to Deborah's place for what she dubbed "the Christmas meal" – a feast of turkey, pigs in blankets, cranberry sauce and all the trappings washed down with as much booze as we could drink. This weekend over the years had become sacrosanct and was ring-fenced by both of us. We had an agreement that no other invitations could be accepted by either of us for any rival event planned to take place on the same weekend. It certainly marked the gateway to Christmas – but, like everything else this year, we'd had to cancel it. No Menier Musical, no going to the pub; no carol service and no Christmas feast.

Another ritual was seeing in the New Year with my friend Jonathan. Every December 31st for years we had spent it together, neither of us wanting to be out partying or in a restaurant, pub or, heaven forbid, a club! We wanted to spend it quietly together, ruminating on the year just gone and tentatively making plans and expressing aspirations for the year ahead.

This particular year, we had 'booked' each other for New Year's Eve weeks or even months beforehand. Because the year itself had been so constrained and, in many ways, dull and socially uneventful, it felt more important than ever to have this date earmarked as a beacon towards which we could both work.

We'd predicted that Christmas itself would either be cancelled or at least very pared down but, as Jonathan himself had said about our plan to meet for NYE "At least, if I know I have that, then I'll have something to look forward to".

I was assuming that the whole sale cancellation of Christmas by the government would now mean that our arrangement to get together on the 31st December to eat, drink and for me to stay over afterwards would also have to be abandoned. However, in some short text exchanges after the Saturday announcement, I realised that he was still hoping it might yet go ahead. He'd say things like "We've both been in isolation. We haven't been mixing with other people, so I'm sure it will be OK"… I wasn't convinced, I had to confess. While it was true that we'd both been keeping ourselves apart as per the rules, the fact was I'd still need to travel over there by public transport; we'd both have been in shops and in environments where there had been other people, all possibly contagious. It was beginning to seem like an un-necessary risk.

I thought that I had better ring him up to sort this out rather than attempt to convey my misgivings by text. Our phone conversation was a little strained, both of us perhaps hoping that we could convince the other that it would be OK to meet up and spend the evening together. Nevertheless, the rules that we were attempting to circumvent were unambiguous: there was supposed to be no mixing of households; there were to be no overnight stays; unnecessary travel should be avoided.

It was impossible to pretend that we would not be breaking the rules and, both of us being exceptionally law-abiding people, we reluctantly agreed to do as we were told and decided to abandon the plan for our usual NYE celebration. We told ourselves that by making this sacrifice, we were each "doing our bit" and playing our part in the national effort. Many other single people across the country would be spending Christmas and New Year alone this year. We weren't going to be the only ones.

I did feel slightly mean, at being the one to initiate the cancellation, especially when he seemed to be willing to risk it. I guess a kind of martyr syndrome had set in. If we were going to have to forego Christmas, let's abandon New Year's Eve as well and go for all out, full on, ascetic misery! Let's not allow even a sliver of festive joy or camaraderie to lighten the gloom. Let's go the whole hog and shut down and shut off completely. There was also a niggling part of me that felt as if I wanted to be tested and challenged by the complete abandonment of all the normal routines, rituals and meetings of the Christmas season. What inner demons would I confront and wrestle with if all the usual props and distractions were taken away? Had I the mental resources to deal with this?

There was also a nagging sense that it might even be quite restful and simpler to not have to deal with that relentless round of Christmas socializing, 'performing', drinking and eating that the two weeks around the 25th December normally involved. I did recognise that I, like many others after so many months of isolation and having to be largely self-sufficient, had become somewhat de-socialised. Being with other people inevitably involved a degree of compromise, a requirement to make an effort, to engage, to listen, to tolerate, to contribute, to participate. For months and months, for those of us who lived alone there had been no requirement to accommodate other people or to get out and do things. It was rather sobering to recognise that the prospect of spending a first ever Christmas and New Year completely alone was now not without its appeal.

Of course, I wasn't the only one. According to programmes like 'Woman's Hour' 'You and Yours' and 'The One Show' practically the whole nation would be spending Christmas alone this year and these shows were full of advice and tips about how to survive it.

"Treat Yourself" seemed to be the gist of the advice offered to singletons, incarcerated in their flats by Covid for the whole of the Christmas period. Pour yourself a bottle of bubbly, cook yourself a proper Christmas lunch and settle down for the rest of the day with the telly and a box of chocs. That was exactly what I intended to do.

I got up early on the morning of Tuesday 22nd December and managed to get to my local Sainsbury's for 7.30 a.m. Even at that hour, I was only just about able to find a parking space. I grabbed one of the last remaining trolleys and set about piling it as high as I could with all the items I thought I might need in order to have the Christmas I wanted. Yes, I even managed to get myself a small turkey. Then I got sprouts and cranberry sauce to go with it plus all the other bits and pieces. I got myself a small Christmas cake; a huge bag of nuts; loads of snacks like cheese balls and twiglets and Pringles; a good bottle of red wine and lots of stuff for sandwiches and teas to be eaten when not working my way through the turkey left-overs. I couldn't believe that I had got so much stuff and it came to well over a hundred pounds. Something about that was rather guilt inducing but another part of me was defiant: "If they want us to spend it on our own then I'm damn sure that I'm going to be miserable in comfort!" I reasoned.

That evening was our final online play-reading of the year,

appropriately enough Alan Ayckbourn's "Season's Greetings". I read the role of a disgruntled middle-aged doctor which I had been asked to do, slightly resenting the fact that the character showed traits not a million miles from my own: diffidence, indecisiveness, social ineptitude. As always, Ayckbourn is disconcertingly accurate in his portrayal of middle-class angst and, far from lifting the spirits as this seasonal reading was intended to do, I could feel it pushing me into an unwelcome mood of disconsolate melancholy. The play had made me laugh out loud when I'd seen it in the theatre done by gifted professionals at the National a few years before but in our reading I'm afraid it just seemed tired, cliched, over-long and not a little embarrassing in places.

The next day, I felt restless and in need of a good walk so I took myself down to Ally Pally and walked up the hill to see the wonderful views of the London skyline and then into Highgate Woods, where it started to pour with rain. Along the way, I'd walked along Muswell Hill Broadway, smiling inwardly at the orderly queues of the incredibly smug, 'arty types' all waiting obediently in line outside the organic butcher's shop for their free-range turkeys. Afterwards, I walked back along the Greenway to pick up a train at Finsbury Park station, enjoying the winter's afternoon and the sensation of mild exertion from the exercise.

I then went round to a couple of local friends to drop off some rather meagre Christmas gifts. Both of them had presented me with offerings a few days before and I had had nothing for them, which had been embarrassing. Therefore, I needed to pay my dues and take them each a small offering. I knocked on their doors and handed over the token gifts in a rushed and awkward way. Even so, it felt good to have people living close by who I knew well enough to want to exchange Christmas presents with, however modest the items themselves might have been.

That evening, I turned on the TV and watched an interview with Dame Diana Rigg, a double episode of 'Coronation Street' and then 'White Christmas', which I must have seen a thousand times before. I was watching it with fresh eyes that evening, however, and wondered why I had never noticed before how immaculate the costumes and make-up were, everything absolutely perfect. And those wonderful songs!

The next day was Christmas Eve and after a quick jog round the park to freshen up and get a few helpful endorphins going, I settled down to read a creepy Icelandic thriller all set in a snow-covered small coastal town well north of Rekjavic. The wintery atmosphere of this novel and its frequent descriptions of falling snow felt like an appropriate read for Christmas. Later on, I'd arranged to meet a friend down at Palmer's Green. Knowing that we would both be on our own, she had kindly invited me to come and "walk through" her church with her, which had been decorated for Christmas. The church choir (or a handful of them) would be singing carols and the building would be candle-lit. Because of Covid, we would not be allowed to linger and it had literally to be a walk-through of just a few minutes but in that cold, candlelit Church building with its crib and choir, there was just a hint for a moment or two of authentic Christmas atmosphere. This was enhanced as we emerged from the church building into the encroaching dusk. That was probably as much of a taste of real Christmas as we were likely to get this year.

I went back home to 'Carols from Kings' on the television and a very simple supper of beans on toast, in anticipation of the feast which I would be giving myself the following day.

The following day was Christmas Day. My first ever Christmas spent completely alone and not one I would ever wish to repeat. If there could be any good to be said to have come out of this, I guess it was to make me see that however self-sufficient I might tell myself that I am on occasion, the fact is that I need other human beings to enhance my life. There is little pleasure and enjoyment to be had in things that are not shared.

I felt that the day needed to be different in some way so I thought that I would start it with a walk in a place I did not normally frequent. I had a notion that I would go up to Hampstead Heath. I hadn't been there since the summer and at least on a day like Christmas Day, I reasoned, the roads would be fairly empty and it ought to be possible to park.

As it turned out, I could not have been more wrong. Even arriving at just after ten a.m., the roads were already congested and most of the parking spaces on Bishop's Avenue had been taken. The Heath itself was swarming with people and more crowded that I had ever seen it. Obviously, everyone in the whole of North London seemed to have had the same idea of deciding that a Christmas morning stroll on Hampstead Heath would be a great way in which to start the day. On the other hand, there were almost no single people around. In spite of the government's injunction against mixing households and plea for us to keep ourselves apart, the place seemed overrun with large family groups and gangs of friends all crowing and chattering away in that self-congratulatory and braying manner that you only ever encounter within the vicinity of NW1. There was no evidence of any social distancing in place, as the crowds passed, nearly all of them arm-in-arm or pushing and shoving each other in a playful and joshing way. I suddenly felt extremely conspicuous at being by myself. How is it that everybody here had managed to find people to hook up with for Christmas and yet I had not?

In the end, I did a brisk circuit of the heath, walking as quickly as I could and keen to "get the hell out". I felt like an alien intruding on these scenes of camaraderie and shared hilarity. If I'd felt disaffected and depressed at waking up alone on Christmas morning, the experience of traipsing around the Heath on my own in the midst of all this togetherness, only served to deepen my self-pity and sadness.

I rushed home to get lunch. This was a simple affair of humous and toast. I was then intending to put the turkey in to roast for about three hours and to start my Christmas feast at about four o'clock. Still feeling raw after the Hampstead experience, I opened the bottle of champagne that I'd had cooling in the fridge. This had been a gift for my sixtieth birthday a few years before, which I had kept thinking that I would save for a special occasion. Today felt like a good enough excuse to finally pop it open. Also, I was already beginning to find Christmas alone to be something of a strain, even though I'd barely got past the morning. I couldn't help but think that normally at this time, I'd have woken up in my sister's house in Staines, after a cosy night in her guest bed. Sister would have been up before me and we'd have had a good half hour or so to gossip and swap memories of Christmases past before other members of the family came downstairs and she had to start on the mammoth task of getting the lunch preparations going. I'd have had a spot of breakfast in front of some suitably inane Xmas morning tv and would then have got myself smartened up to go to her local church for the Christmas morning service. After that, she and I would have driven over to collect my dad, who would be coming for the day. He'd then be deposited in front of the television in the best and most comfortable chair in the lounge, while I assisted her and her husband with the remainder of the lunch preparations. (In my case, this generally meant locating the corkscrew and opening and sampling the first bottle).

None of that would be happening today, of course: none of that conversation or familial chat; none of that laughter and gossip; none of those opinions; none of that point scoring and scolding and exasperation; none of that chivying and sending up and mockery; none of that warmth and closeness and love. Today, there was just silence, apart from the perpetual sound of the television which would need to be on all day in order to fill the emptiness.

I shoved the turkey in the oven and started to prepare the vegetables: sprouts, carrots, parsnips. I gave them a good wash and set them to one side. No point in putting them on for another hour or so.

Luckily, the champagne started to kick in fairly quickly. That was always the wonderful thing about alcohol. Those first few sips. They worked a kind of magic. Suddenly, it didn't seem so bad to be stuck holed up alone in my flat for the next seventy-two hours.

My goodness, it was pleasurable having an excuse to open a bottle on my own at the beginning of the afternoon. In fact, I don't think that I had ever done that in my life before. I knew for certain that I had not opened a bottle on my own for at least twenty years. The thought of drinking alone never ever appealed to me. With me, drink always makes me more talkative and more outgoing. An essential accompaniment was at least one other person to talk to. No point at all in solo drinking if there was nobody else about to chat with, moan to, amuse, infuriate, provoke, console, counsel, confide in.

The drinking swiftly made everything seem OK. Suddenly, reality was pushed to one remove. It was almost like I had gone outside of myself and was now observing this "character" (me) as if I was a person in a movie. There was an uplift and an exhilaration, to the point where I wondered why on earth I didn't drink on my own more often.

Not having anyone there to talk to in the flesh made me seek out my contacts on my phone. I started texting liberally, wishing everyone I knew a "Happy Christmas" and wanting to know what they were doing to survive this very different 25th of December. Replies came back pretty rapidly. Maybe others were all doing the same, sitting round slightly inebriated and jabbing at their phones until they got some replies. I managed to keep a number of text exchanges going at the same time and was going backwards and forwards between various friends and acquaintances, while my turkey was roasting in the oven. Somehow the time up until four o'clock when the bird was due to be taken out and "rested" passed very quickly in this way, although I was beginning to realise that some of my texts were becoming more and more incoherent as I guzzled glass after glass of bubbly. Eventually, I became aware that I was starting to force the champagne down my throat so that I could get the bottle finished and move on to the red wine I had bought to accompany my food. Surely, I reasoned, I didn't have to finish the entire bottle on my own? Some of it could either be saved for another occasion or (sacrilege) poured down the sink if it hadn't been drunk. There was certainly no requirement to empty the bottle. Anyway, it was so gassy that it was now starting to make me feel bloated and I knew from past experience that if this happened, I would not be able to enjoy my food.

I watched the Queen's speech which was the cue for more frantic texting with various friends (not the known anti-royalists, of course) and I then put on a recording of 'It's a Wonderful Life' that I had saved to watch with my dinner.

After that came the epic operation of retrieving the bird from the oven and piling on the accompanying roast potatoes, veg, stuffing, cranberry sauce and lashings of gravy (specially bought in a pot). The turkey, although one of the smallest on offer, seemed to be enormous. After it had rested for ten minutes or so, I carved off some slices of prime breast and then took my heavily laden plate to my dining table. (This was certainly not a day to eat scruffily on the sofa, balancing a plate in front of some back episodes of 'Corrie' and spilling some of it down whatever top I happened to be wearing at the time as was my usual habit).

The bottle of red was opened and I poured myself a glass. The contrast with the bubbly was refreshing. Great to taste something a bit more substantial and serious, although I was now feeling quite drunk. Also, because I'd been nibbling on crisps, twiglets and other snacks while quaffing the champers, the edge had been taken off my appetite. The enormous plate of food suddenly looked rather daunting. Was I really going to be capable of getting through all of that?

I supposed that in the normal course of things, when eating Christmas dinner at my sister's, there would be all the conversation before, during and after the meal to break things up a bit, between mouthfuls so to speak. The social inter-action would force one to slow down and take breaks between each bite. Not so today, when it was just me eating on my own.

If anything, the plate seemed to grow with each mouthful. Halfway through, I wondered if I was ever going to get through it. I glanced over at my kitchen where the remains of the rest of the turkey were cooling down. It seemed that I had hardly made any inroads into the bird itself and that I would be eating turkey by myself for days to come.

Eventually, I cleared my plate but I cannot say that it had been a pleasurable experience. It had been laborious and dutiful but, I am sorry to admit, utterly without enjoyment. Above all else, I was mystified that the bird itself did not seem to taste of anything very much. Bland, stodgy white meat it had seemed to be, in spite of any seasoning or sauces I had spooned over it.

It had been disappointing. And 'It's a Wonderful Life' hadn't helped. Having previously adored that movie, now it just seemed hackneyed and horribly old fashioned and, apart from anything else, just plain boring. This must have been partly owing to my fuzzy mental state after having consumed nearly a whole bottle of champagne and then half a bottle of red wine on top of that. Also, the dialogue was hard to hear from my table when it had to compete with my chomping and guzzling. I turned it off and watched a Victoria Wood compilation instead.

This worked for a while but there seemed to be hours and hours of it and after a while I became bored with watching the same old sketches and listening to the fulsome and not a little pompous celebrity tributes in between. Some were making the most enormous claims for Victoria. Yes, she made us laugh in her day, but the sketches hardly stood up to the forensic analysis and deconstruction which some felt duty bound to indulge in.

Finding, true to form, that there was almost nothing of any worth to watch on television that night, I resorted to Netflix and thought that I could do a lot worse than tune in to another episode of "The Crown". I watched the one about Prince Charles going to Gordonstun, which I enjoyed and which held my attention even though I was by now bloated and jaded with too much afternoon drinking and over-eating. Afterwards, I read a bit more of the Icelandic thriller before bed and then turned in, congratulating myself that I had got through the day. I hadn't enjoyed it and had felt pretty dismal at times but I'd got through it. It was done.

The next day, I woke up feeling desperate to be out of my flat. I needed fresh air and some wholesome physical activity. A long walk was the solution.

I set off in the direction of the outskirts of Enfield and got myself on to the green belt in about twenty minutes. Thank God for some fields and some sunshine and just to be outdoors. It was wonderfully therapeutic and uplifting.

I walked for miles, right up into Trent Park and then back through Oakwood and Highlands Village, hardly passing another soul but rather enjoying walking through streets I had never come across before. After that it was a ham sandwich for lunch (not turkey, which I was saving for my dinner) and then I settled down to watch 'Coco', the Pixar film which had received a rave review on the Christmas telly page.

The film was somewhat tedious, I found. Being a kids' movie, the soundtrack was absolutely relentless. Could children really not watch films without a deafening accompaniment the whole way through? Also, every scene had quirky little bits of business in which it seemed as if nothing was allowed to happen without someone slipping on a banana skin or getting the equivalent of a custard pie in the face or their pants falling down. I felt like I always used to feel when watching Disney as a child: "Just blooming get on with it and stop all this arsing about!" Anyway, I made myself watch it through to the end but I must say that I was counting the minutes. Maybe it was different if you were watching it in the cinema but certainly on that lonely Boxing Day afternoon, it seemed like a very long ninety minutes. Even so, I guess it dealt with the theme of death in quite an imaginative way. Surely not an easy concept to tackle in a children's film? It seemed to be saying that you need to do things in your life which will keep the memory of you alive in the hearts and minds of those who come after you. This was a sobering message to be receiving during a pandemic Christmas, I felt.

The evening TV schedules seemed full of the usual vacuous post-Christmas fare: game shows and celebrity competitions and special hour-long episodes of all the soaps. However, I did manage to find something rather good to watch: because she had only recently died and was such a national institution, there were a number of tributes to Dame Diana Rigg, who had featured as the Mother Superior in the lavish remake of 'Black Narcissus' which had just played over three evenings. This was complemented by an extensive and quite probing interview with her conducted by Mark Lawson on BBC4 and a repeat of 'Motherlove' – a two-part drama in which she had starred twenty years or so before. The interview with the Dame was fascinating. I loved her "up for it" attitude and the way in which her very theatrical manner contrasted so sharply with her attempt to seem chummy and down-to-earth. She certainly came over as quite a tough cookie but she was also such a "lovey"! That in itself made for a compelling watch. Even better, though, was her performance in 'Motherlove', a drama which had first been aired at some point in the 1990s.

This was completely engrossing and the first of the two parts was especially compelling. Also fascinating was the style in which it had been shot. It seemed quite leisurely and very much of its time. It had a stagey, rather old-fashioned quality and was more like watching a play in the theatre than a television piece. There were no special effects or quirky camera tricks. The focus throughout was on the acting and telling the story. I loved it.

At last, the three days of complete solitude were over and the next day, I was pleased to be able to walk up to Forty Hall to meet my pal Lee and his dog for a post-Christmas walk. We were to meet at two p.m. and I was especially glad that I had decided to go on foot and had not brought my car. I had never seen the place so crowded. Obviously, everyone in the local area had had the same idea. All the parking spaces in the car park had been taken and the paths were so muddy as to be almost impassable. Lee had his dog with him but almost every other person seemed to be similarly accompanied. There were some rather rough and not very well-mannered people around, some of them clutching plastic pint glasses of lager from the nearby 'Rose and Crown' pub. "Keep socially distant, mate" one of them barked aggressively at Lee as he barged into him and his dog. Lee did not react well to this and for one awful moment I thought we were going to have a punch up on our hands. Lee was still adjusting to the responsibilities of being a dog owner and seemed a little preoccupied, with all his attention focused on his new pet. So, I chatted mainly to his partner, who is a Deputy Head in a small private school. I listened sympathetically as he told me all about how hard it had been to be in school over the last few weeks and how disruptive the pandemic had been for staff and students alike. It all sounded very draining.

We didn't stay out for very long. With the crowds, the mud and the typical December weather, we were all quite glad to call it a day after a couple of hours or so. Anyway, by four p.m. it was already starting to get dark so I walked back home and made myself a lasagne with some of the turkey leftovers.

That evening on television, there was the most absorbing biography of Maria Callas. It trawled through the usual tragic events of her life: her doomed love affairs, the temperament that had made her so unpopular with managements, her sad attempt at a comeback and then her lonely and untimely death. These were all things with which we were by now horribly familiar but the real treat was in watching filmed extracts from some of her performances. These were all thrilling and engrossing. What was so evident in every one of them was her deep love of performing and her total identification with the emotions she was projecting. She had such passion and such delicacy and total artistry; she was completely enveloped in the music with what seemed to be absolutely no show or artifice; the music just seemed to sing through her. It was quite extraordinary and breath-taking to behold.

The following day, I drove up to Welwyn to see my friend Stephanie for a walk in the woods near her flat. It was very cold and quite wet so we weren't out for very long. Afterwards, I came back and tackled a pile of ironing, thinking that I was just about managing to hold it together, The small amounts of social contact I had managed to organise for myself had been just about enough to get me through this fallow and mostly solitary Christmas period and I wondered what on earth I would have done without even these meagre crumbs of comfort.

Throughout, I had spoken to my sister on a daily basis and that regular contact also helped to support me through it. I heard about how their Christmas had been: apparently, they had missed having me there for the three days. Her youngest daughter had been kind enough to say that without me there, it had seemed just like an ordinary weekend. My presence would have made it seem different, special even. I appreciated that.

We had an interesting conversation about a controversy around the broadcasting of "Carols for Kings" which I myself had commented on at the time. Why was it such an exclusively white affair? Having taught in a school with a hugely diverse student population for more than thirty years, I was well used to seeing a range of different ethnicities represented at the annual school carol service. The choir from King's College had looked particularly exclusive this year and that had become a subject for national debate – albeit, a bit of welcome distraction from the impact of the pandemic on this year's festivities which had dominated the airwaves for days now.

Finding little to watch on the TV that evening, I abandoned the jaded schedules and listened instead to a fascinating play about Rodgers and Hart and their relationship with Oscar Hammerstein. What a story that was! Full of backstage intrigue but also so tragic: the alcoholic Hart rejected in favour of the more conservative and more commercially successful Hammerstein. Even ironing seemed less of a chore than usual with that on in the background.

The next day's walk was again up at Forty Hall, this time with my friend Val. With all of the visitors who had been tramping through the grounds over Christmas, though, the paths through the woods at the back were now completely impassable. We waded through as much of the mud as we could but in the end, we had to admit defeat and abandoned our original plan to hike over to Whitewebbs golf course. Instead, we got a couple of hot chocolates and had a nice, friendly chat on one of the benches over-looking the pond outside the Hall. Val is going to be eighty next year (which seems extraordinary) and we discussed her plans for her eightieth birthday party. She is thinking about holding it on a boat on the Thames – but realises that might be over-ambitious, given the dire state of things at the moment. It may have to be a more modest celebration next year and then hope that by the time we get to the year after that, we have at last got this thing under control and then the boat idea might be a bit more feasible. I hope so, for her sake. She is such a spirited person and has such a love of and interest in people. She deserves a big, noisy, fun-filled celebration and sailing along beside the banks of the Thames in the company of all her best mates would be just what she deserves!

After that I came home and watched an episode of "Worzel Gummidge" on Catch-up because I wanted to see Vanessa Redgrave, who was doing a guest appearance in it. She did not disappoint.

On the following day (by now the 30th December) I drove over to Chorleywood to meet up with my sister and her family so that we could exchange our Christmas gifts. It was a very cold, grey December afternoon. I got there early and did a circuit of the Common while I waited for them to arrive. As soon as they did, we swapped our packages and put them into the boots of our cars. Then we walked down by the Chess as we had done in the summer and then up the hill to Sarratt again. It was lovely to get some fresh air and to feel that we were out in the country, liberated from the tyranny of the television and the internet and the supermarket. Up there on the Chilterns, it felt as if you could breathe almost for the first time in months. Yes, it was muddy and crowded again but here at least there was a bit more space and, apart from the rumble of the M25 in the distance, a real sense of being in the countryside and away from it all.

Unfortunately, again because of the mud and owing to the fact that it got dark so early, we didn't have as much time together as I would have liked but it was so good to all be together again after our 'estranged' Christmas. Just the freewheeling chat and the jokes and the teasing and mild bickering was so refreshing after all those hours and hours of being holed up in my flat alone. It was enough to give me a bit of a buzz by the time I got in the car to come back. Unfortunately, my good mood was somewhat dissipated when I arrived home to find a WhatsApp invitation to a New Year's Day 'virtual party' which had been proposed by one of my well-meaning if somewhat misguided friends. How on earth could she think that this would appeal to me? Just the thought of having to sit there for an hour in front of the laptop wracking my brains trying to think of stuff to say was intolerable. The day would be depressing enough without having that hideous imposition to contend with as well. Of course, I then spent the rest of the evening torturing myself trying to think what reasons I could give in order to decline the invitation. What rival attractions or invites could I invent that would prevent me attending? It didn't help when the revelation came to me that all I needed to do, in fact, was just say "No". Why was that something I found so impossible to do?

In the end, I just think I made some feeble excuse about having another online event that I was expected at which was supposedly being held around the same time. I then beat myself up for not having the guts to tell people that these sorts of events were not my idea of fun and that friends should not impose them on each other, under any circumstances.

As New Year's Eve dawned that morning, it struck me that a bit like Christmas Day, this would be my first ever 31st December alone. Bad enough to have had to endure a solo Christmas Eve, Christmas Day and Boxing Day and for a while there had been a bit of an understanding that my friend Jonathan and I would momentarily break the rules in order to keep each other company as the midnight hour chimed. However, we'd since decided that it was sensible to do as we had been told and that it really was not worth the risk. To have endured so much isolation and privation over the last few weeks only to go and throw it all away at the last minute seemed misguided and foolish. After all, this was the month in which the vaccine had begun to be rolled out. We'd all seen the pictures on the news of that brave old lady offering her shoulder to be jabbed and thereafter imagined that it was only a matter of time before the rest of us would be summoned to be similarly inoculated. If the government was able to deliver on its promise, then we would certainly all be vaccinated by the spring and then life would be able to return to something more like normal.

With this in mind, our annual NYE celebration was cancelled and we both resigned ourselves to sitting at home on our own with a plate of food and the television on, passing the time in the way that we had all got so used to doing for the last nine months or so.

I wanted to get out early that morning, to start to walk off some of that oppressive sense of confinement and also the ennui of the last few days. It felt important to be out in the fresh air and to be active. Again, as it had done so often during the last few months, the physical act of walking made me feel invigorated. However low and sluggish my mental state might be at the start of the day, it always seemed possible to somehow walk it off. I headed off to the north of Enfield, walking up to the Ridgeway and then branching off on a lane to the right following the footpath to Forty Hall, by way of Hillyfields Park. I must have been out for a good three hours but felt a bit fresher and more positive on my return.

The afternoon seemed to slowly fade away, following a phone call to my sister and a few playful text exchanges with various friends. As always, it began to get dark shortly after 3.30 but today the dusk seemed to be more heavily weighted with significance than usual. This was the dying of the old year, for one thing. 2020 was slipping away – and good riddance to it! Would there ever be another year like it? Could any of us ever have imagined what the year was holding in store as we'd greeted in the New Year twelve months before? Could we ever have conceived of the months and months of isolation and solitude; the frustration at having your movements and freedom curtailed; the fear of where and when the disease might strike next; the dismay at the thought that it was never going to go away and that things did not seem to be getting any better. The month after month of not being able to have people round to your flat, of not being able to go the pub or to the movies or to the theatre. No travel no restaurants, no shops. And then for me, the now not having any work. Not having that place to go to every day; those people to see and greet and gossip with and laugh with and get frustrated by and score points off and long to escape from but also feel deeply connected to and comfortable with.

Would things ever go back to how they were? I could hardly imagine having visitors round to my flat again and cooking for them; or getting on a plane to jet off to some foreign resort; or driving up to the Lake District in a car to spend a few days walking the fells and then getting a bit tipsy over the hotel dinner in the evening......

None of these things had happened this year and yet how easy it had been to forego these pleasures. How quickly one had been able to drift into a completely self-sufficient routine of waiting it out, alone. That was probably the most frightening thing of all about this whole episode: it was as if it had killed my ability to connect with others. Had I now become too fond of the drawbridge being pulled up? Would I have to relearn how to be sociable, all over again, once this thing was over?

Slumped in front of the New Year's Eve TV and not being able to find anything on worth watching (I probably just opted for another couple of episodes of "The Crown" as I had done on Christmas night), I debated with myself as to whether or not to stay up for the chimes at midnight. What was the point, as it was just me there that night on my own? Surely this was something to be shared with a crowd or a close companion, when one was half sloshed on champagne after an ill-advised mixture of other drinks?

Part of me felt that I needed to mark the occasion of the year's passing, however. If for no other reason, I needed to check that the last wretched twelve months had well and truly been dispatched. Therefore, I decided to wait up and see them go. Anyway, the fireworks had started and it would have been impossible to sleep until they'd finished.

I went into my study, turned off the lights and pulled back the curtains so that I could get as good a view of the fireworks as possible. There was certainly quite a display. Somehow, in spite of the austere nature of the year, someone was managing to put on a pretty amazing show. I tried to work out where all the fireworks were coming from. My flat faces south and it seemed that they must have been coming from somewhere near the banks of the Thames. I'd thought that the usual public funded display on the Embankment had been cancelled this year, along with everything else? Certainly, somebody somewhere was making a pretty lavish show of it. As the fireworks shot up into the sky and boomed and crackled and sprayed their glittering stars into the clear New Year's Eve night, I marvelled again at the spectacle of what was on offer. How strange it felt to be watching these and yet to be so completely alone. Once again, I had a strong pang of nostalgia for my work and realised how sharply I missed it. I also missed being with my family, being with my friends. I was aware of the fact that the fireworks were expressions of celebration and hope; a positive accompaniment to the arrival of the next twelve months. However, watching them then I'm afraid I felt very little optimism or joy. To be observing this display of fireworks in the sky over head from my silent study room, I just felt bleak, sad, lonely, empty, frightened.

The Covid year was over but would the next one be any better?

At the same time, I detected a very slight stirring of optimism. Of course, I felt low attempting to celebrate the New Year on my own but at the same time, I did have the sense that perhaps the worst was now behind us. If all the talk of the vaccine was true, maybe it really would be rolled out and some sort of way of living with the virus would be achieved? Perhaps the year ahead would be better? Perhaps we'd be able to start travelling again and going to watch plays and meeting in pubs? Even if not, at least there was some comfort to be taken in the fact that I, along with so many of the people I loved and cared about, had at least got through it. We had survived. And eventually, life would open up again and the world would be there for the taking. The Covid year had ended but we had to believe that the next one would be better.